TRANS-
METRO-
POLITAN:

DIRGE

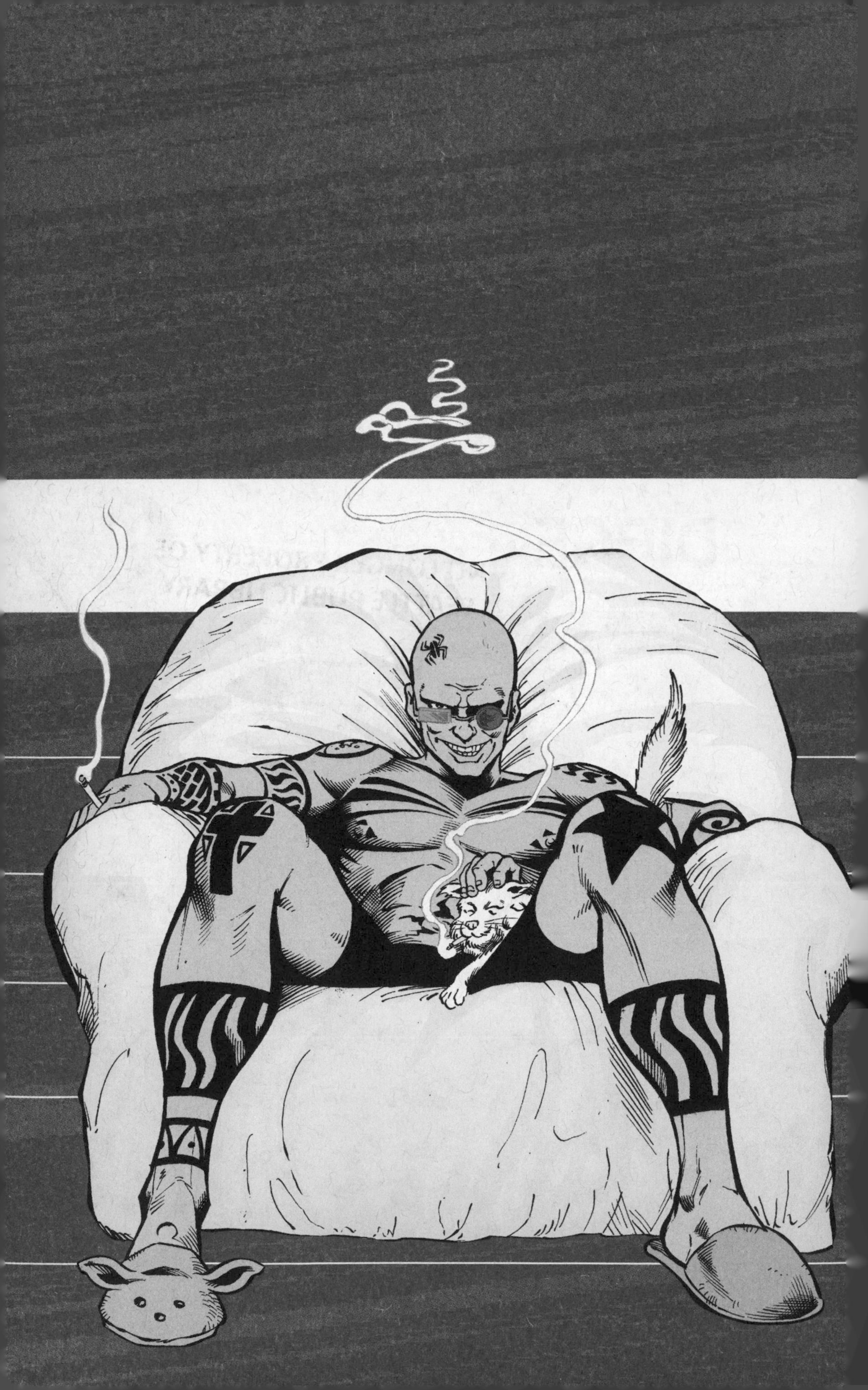

TRANS-METRO-POLITAN:

DIRGE

Warren_Ellis
Writer

Darick_Robertson
Penciller

Rodney_Ramos
Inker

Nathan_Eyring
Colorist

Clem_Robins
Letterer

John Cassaday
Cover Art
John Cassaday (#43-45)   J.G. Jones (#46-48)
Original Series Covers

TRANSMETROPOLITAN created by
Warren_Ellis and Darick_ Robertson

Tony Bedard Editor – Original Series Jamie Rich Group Editor – Vertigo Comics Jeb Woodard Group Editor – Collected Editions
Scott Nybakken Editor – Collected Edition Steve Cook Design Director – Books

Diane Nelson President Dan DiDio Publisher Jim Lee Publisher Geoff Johns President & Chief Creative Officer
Amit Desai Executive VP – Business & Marketing Strategy, Direct to Consumer & Global Franchise Management Sam Ades Senior VP – Direct to Consumer
Bobbie Chase VP – Talent Development Mark Chiarello Senior VP – Art, Design & Collected Editions
John Cunningham Senior VP – Sales & Trade Marketing Anne DePies Senior VP – Business Strategy, Finance & Administration
Don Falletti VP – Manufacturing Operations Lawrence Ganem VP – Editorial Administration & Talent Relations
Alison Gill Senior VP – Manufacturing & Operations Hank Kanalz Senior VP – Editorial Strategy & Administration Jay Kogan VP – Legal Affairs
Thomas Loftus VP – Business Affairs Jack Mahan VP – Business Affairs Nick J. Napolitano VP – Manufacturing Administration
Eddie Scannell VP – Consumer Marketing Courtney Simmons Senior VP – Publicity & Communications
Jim (Ski) Sokolowski VP – Comic Book Specialty & Trade Marketing Nancy Spears VP – Mass, Book, Digital Sales & Trade Marketing

TRANSMETROPOLITAN: DIRGE

Published by DC Comics. Cover and compilation Copyright © 2010 Warren Ellis and Darick Robertson. All Rights Reserved.

DC Comics, 2900 W. Alameda Avenue, Burbank, CA 91505. Printed by Transcontinental Interglobe, Beauceville, QC, Canada. Fifth Printing.
ISBN: 978-1-4012-2936-8

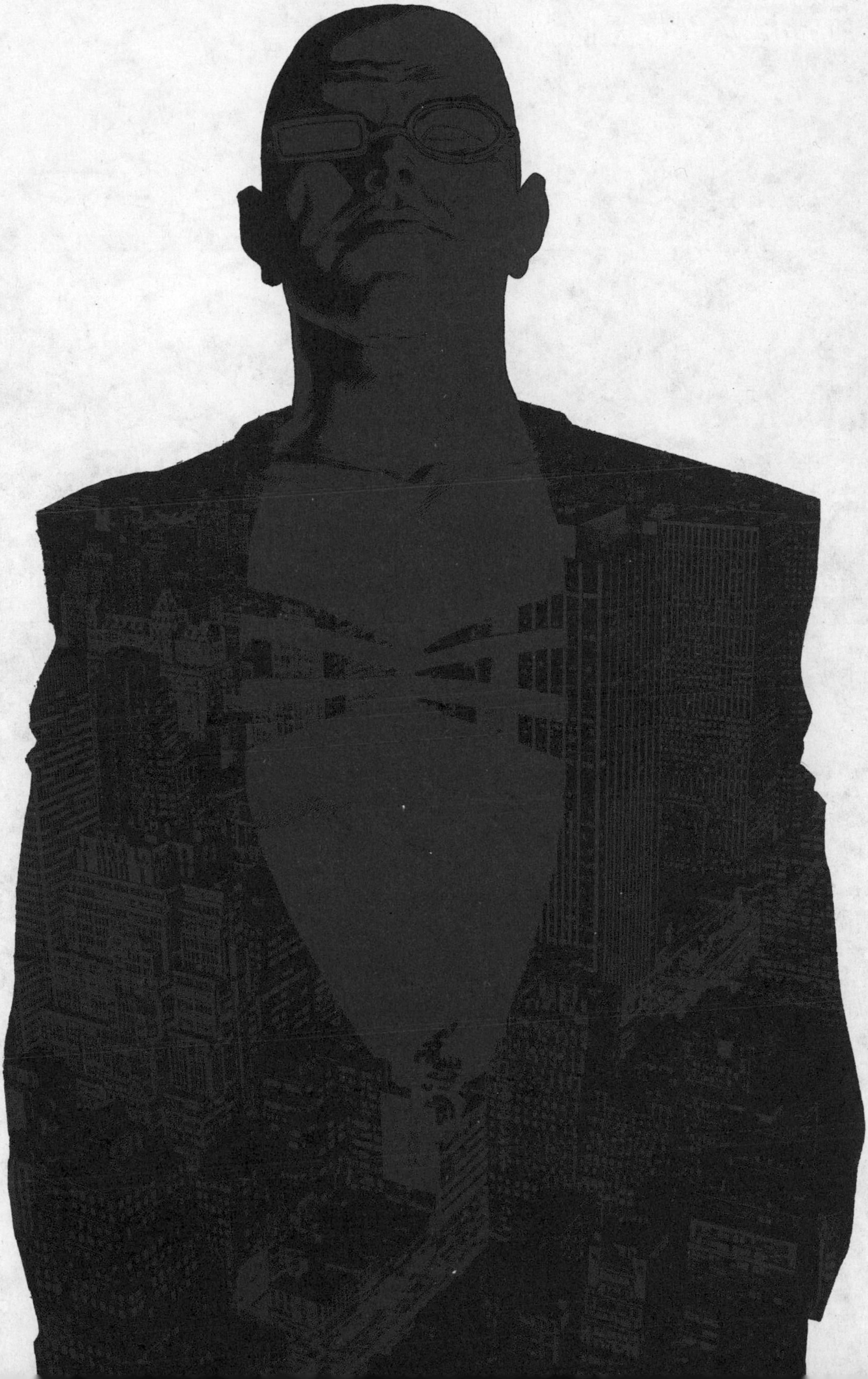

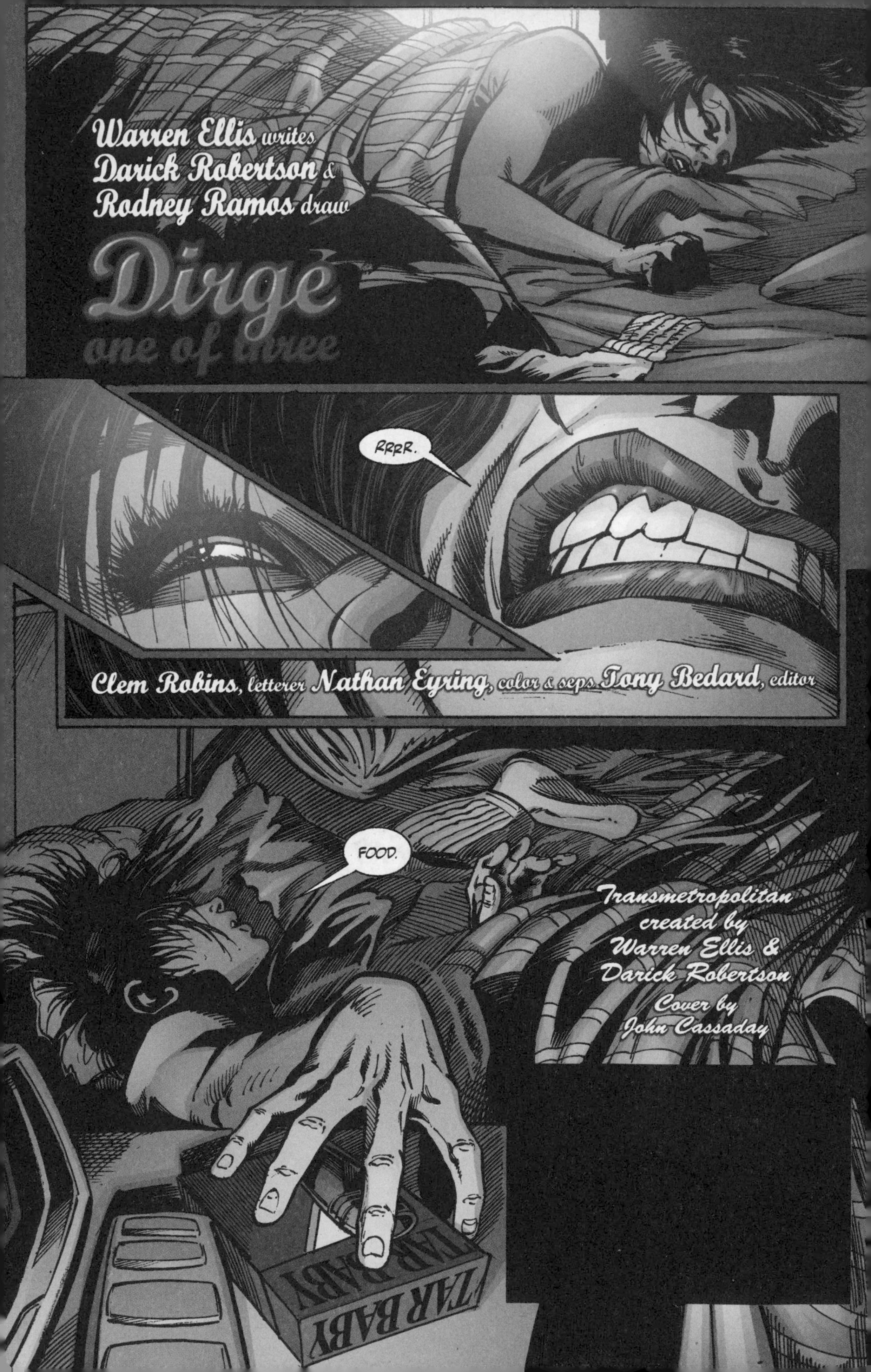
Warren Ellis writes
Darick Robertson & Rodney Ramos draw
Dirge
one of three
RRRR.
Clem Robins, letterer Nathan Eyring, color & seps Tony Bedard, editor
FOOD.
Transmetropolitan created by Warren Ellis & Darick Robertson
Cover by John Cassaday
TAR BABY
TAR BABY

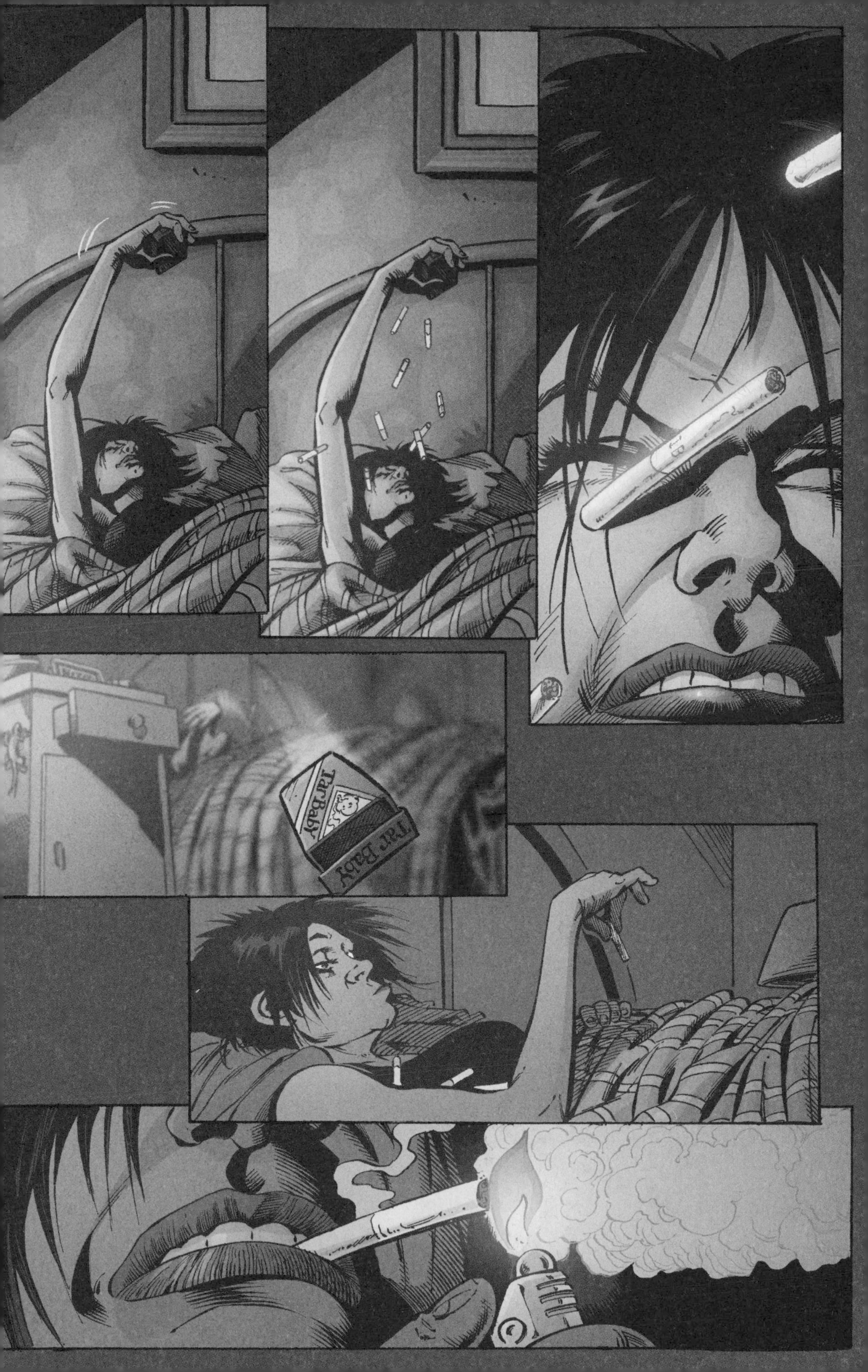
Tar Baby
Tar Baby

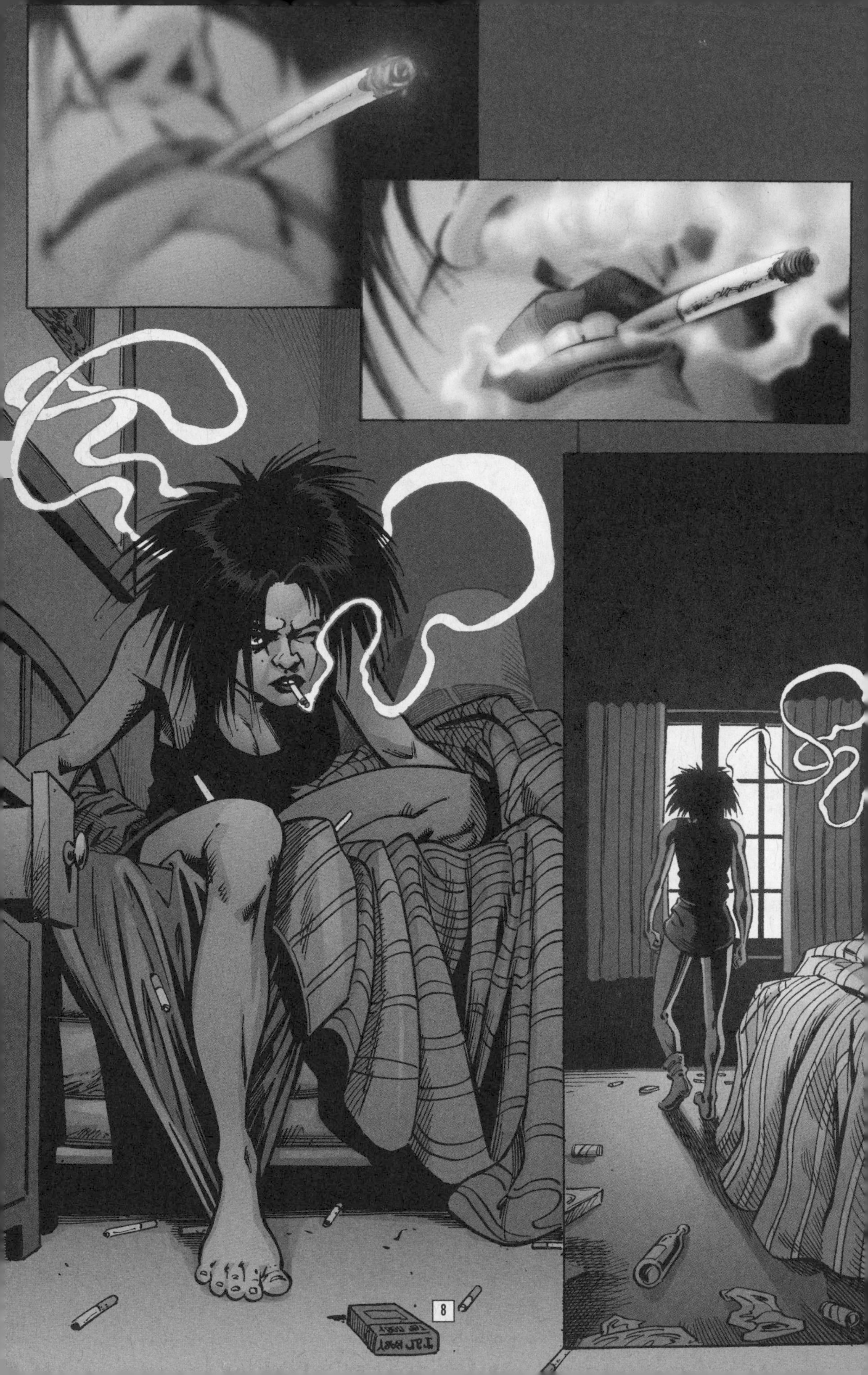

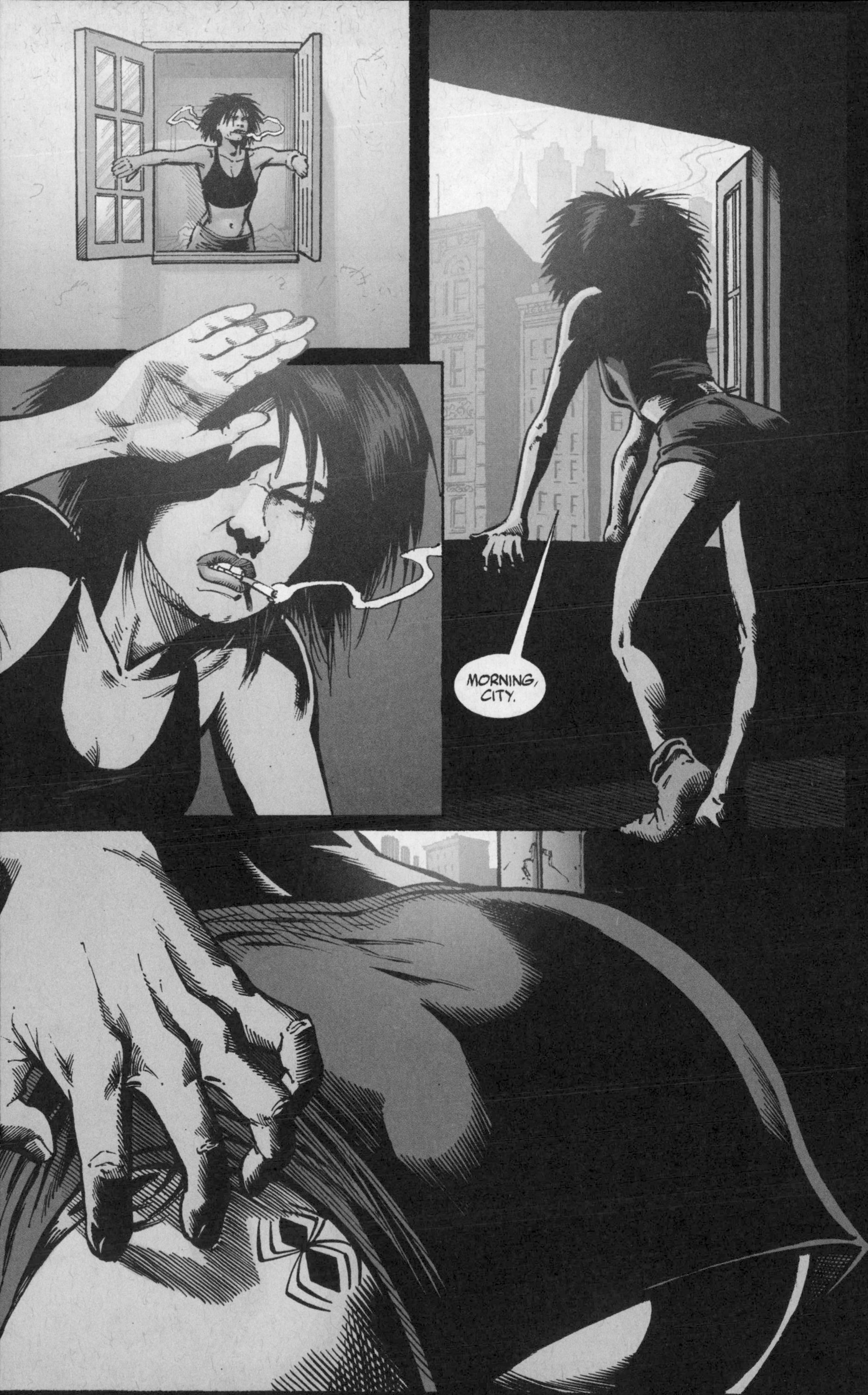
MORNING, CITY.

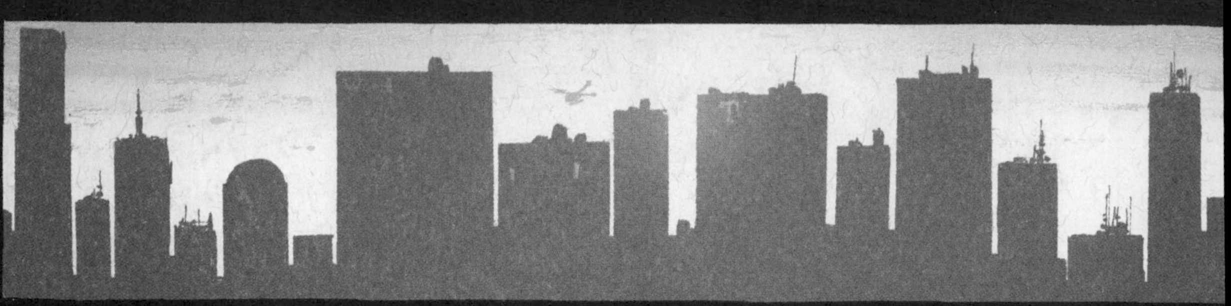

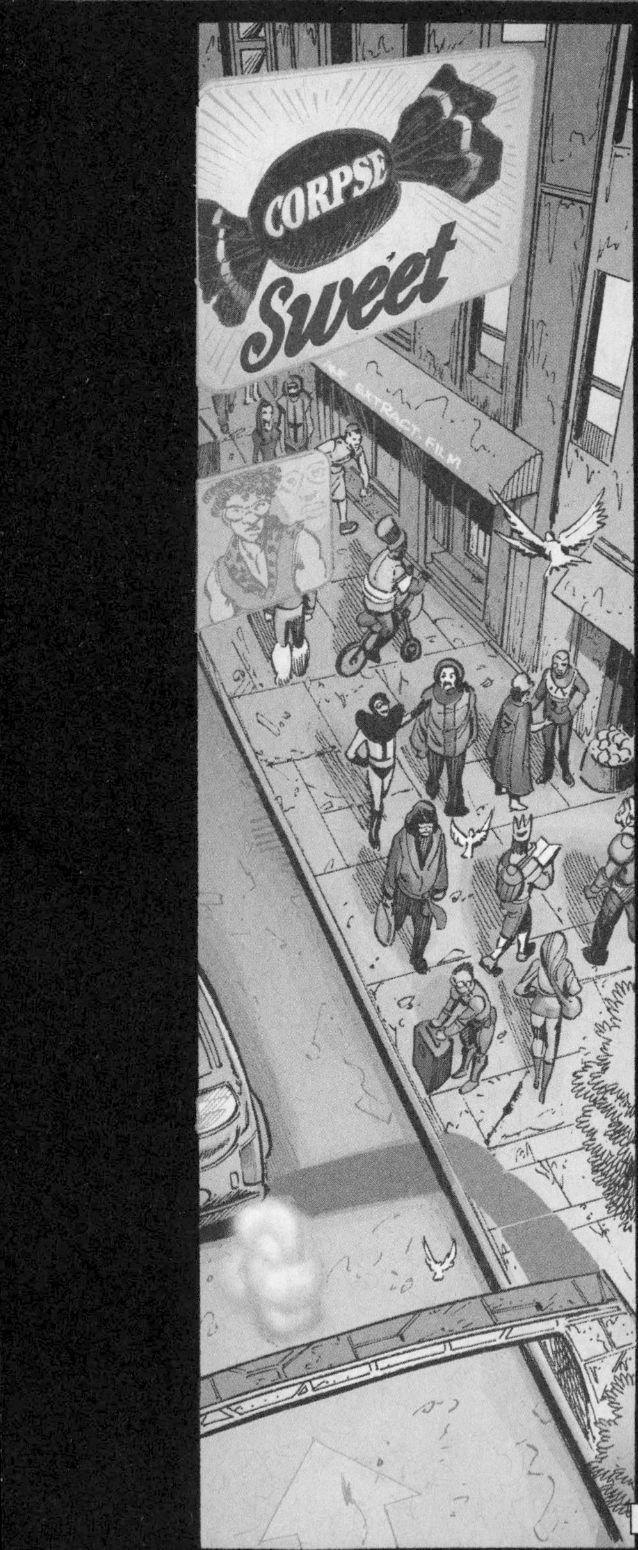
CORPSE
Sweet
EXTRACT · FILM

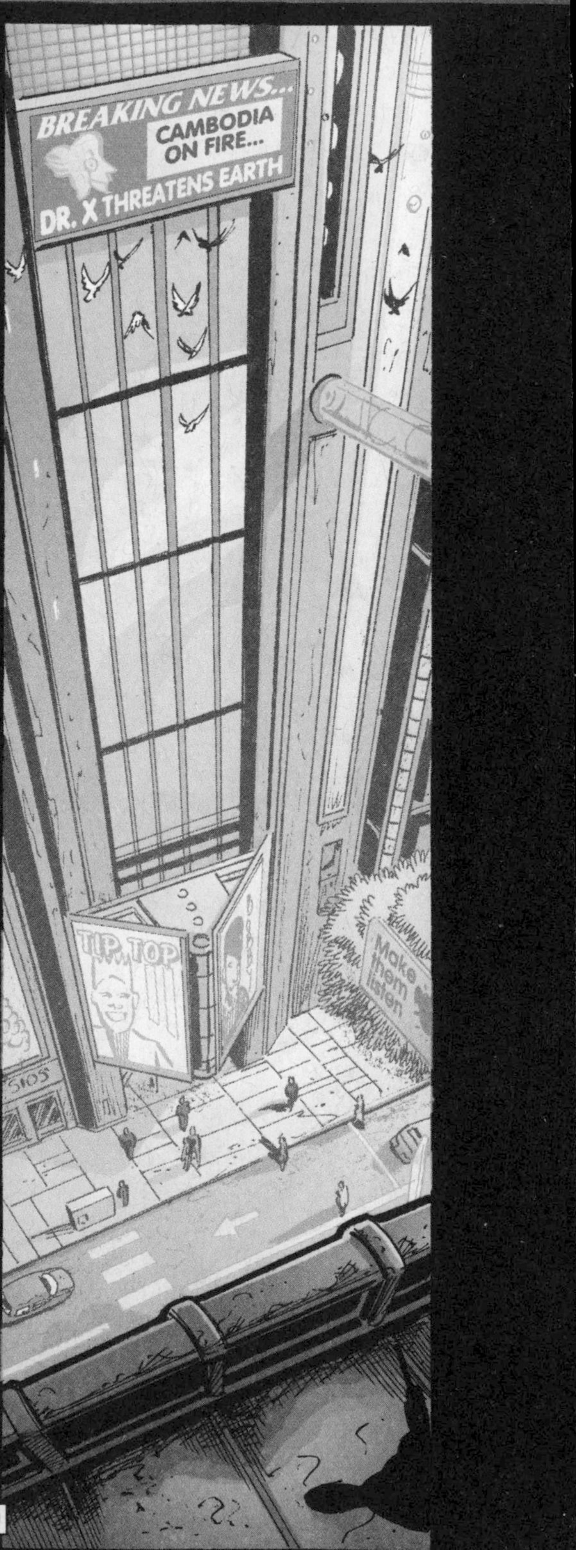
BREAKING NEWS...
CAMBODIA ON FIRE...
DR. X THREATENS EARTH
TIP TOP
Make them listen

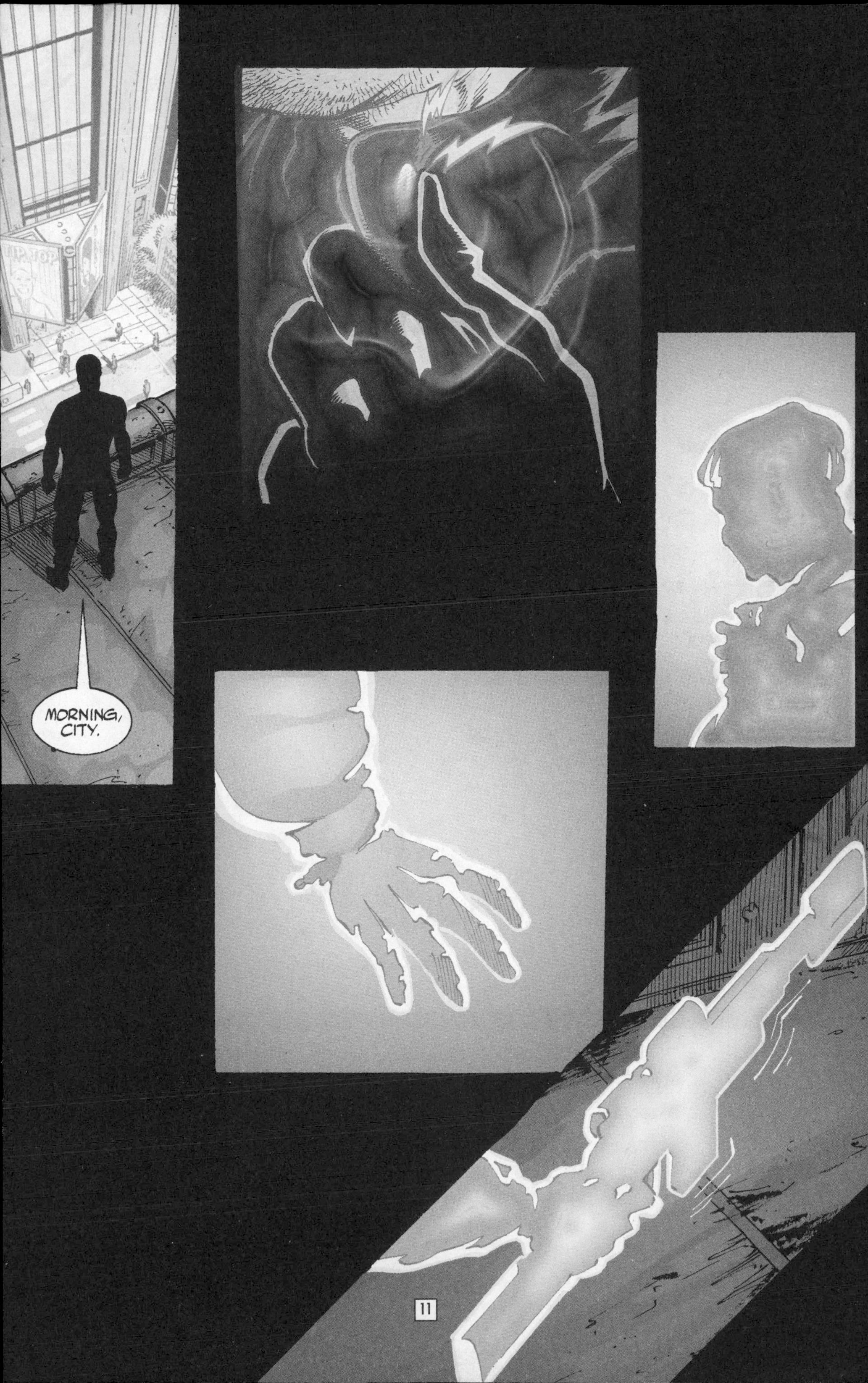
MORNING, CITY.

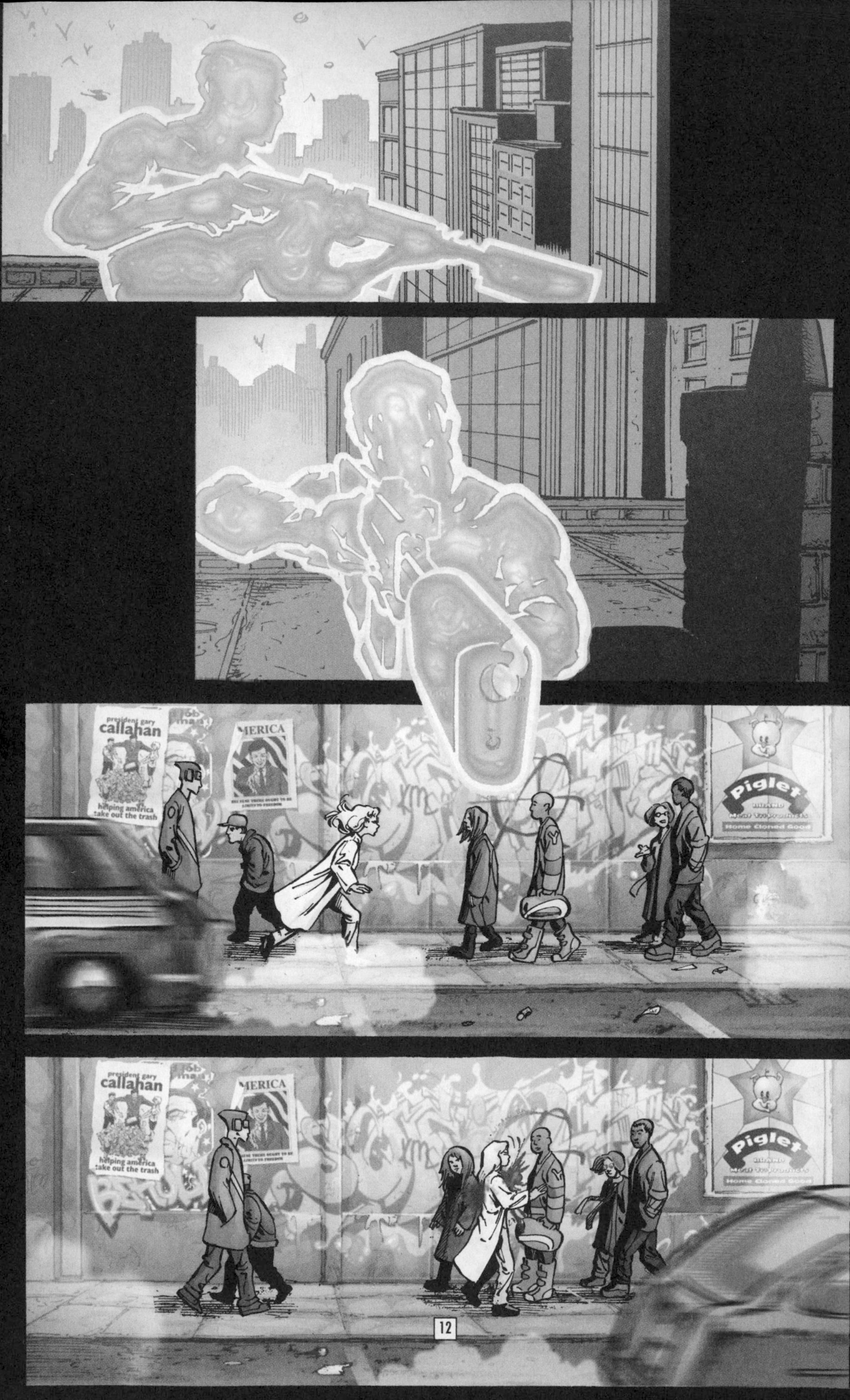
president gary
callahan
helping america
take out the trash
MERICA
Piglet
Home Cloned Good

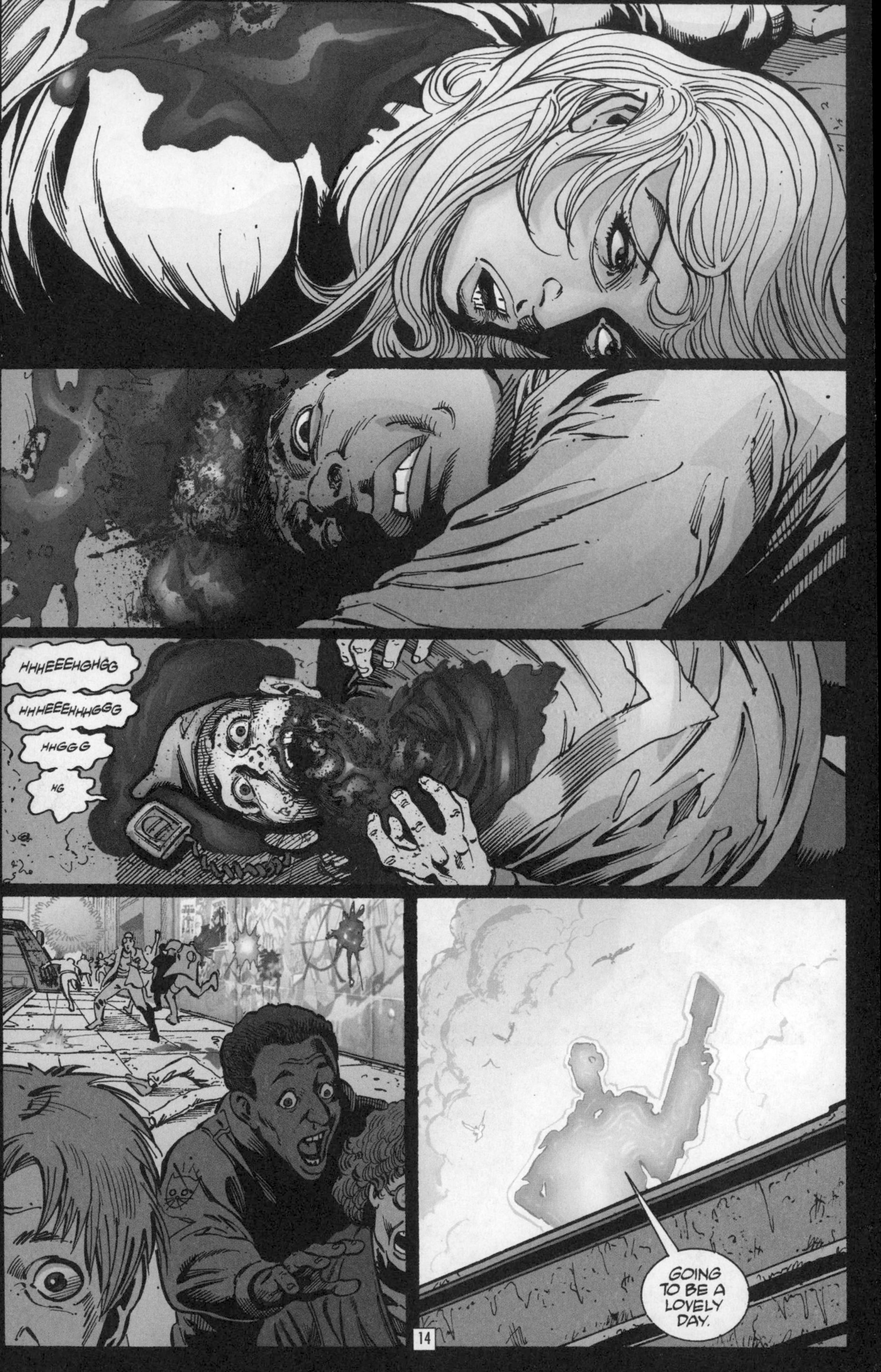
HHHEEEHGHGG
HHHEEEHHHGGG
HHGGG
HG
GOING TO BE A LOVELY DAY.

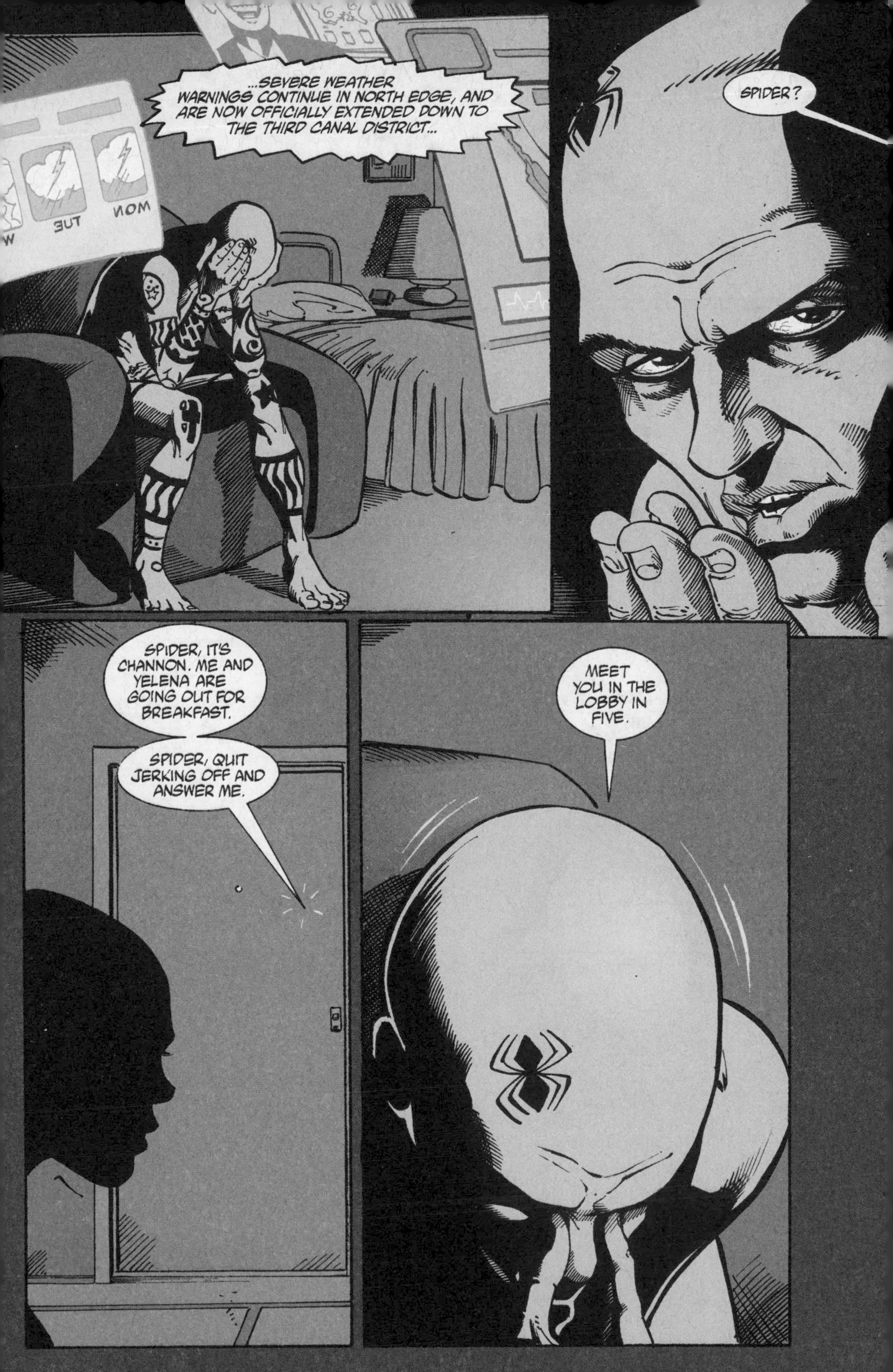
...SEVERE WEATHER WARNINGS CONTINUE IN NORTH EDGE, AND ARE NOW OFFICIALLY EXTENDED DOWN TO THE THIRD CANAL DISTRICT...
MON
TUE
SPIDER?
SPIDER, IT'S CHANNON. ME AND YELENA ARE GOING OUT FOR BREAKFAST.
SPIDER, QUIT JERKING OFF AND ANSWER ME.
MEET YOU IN THE LOBBY IN FIVE.

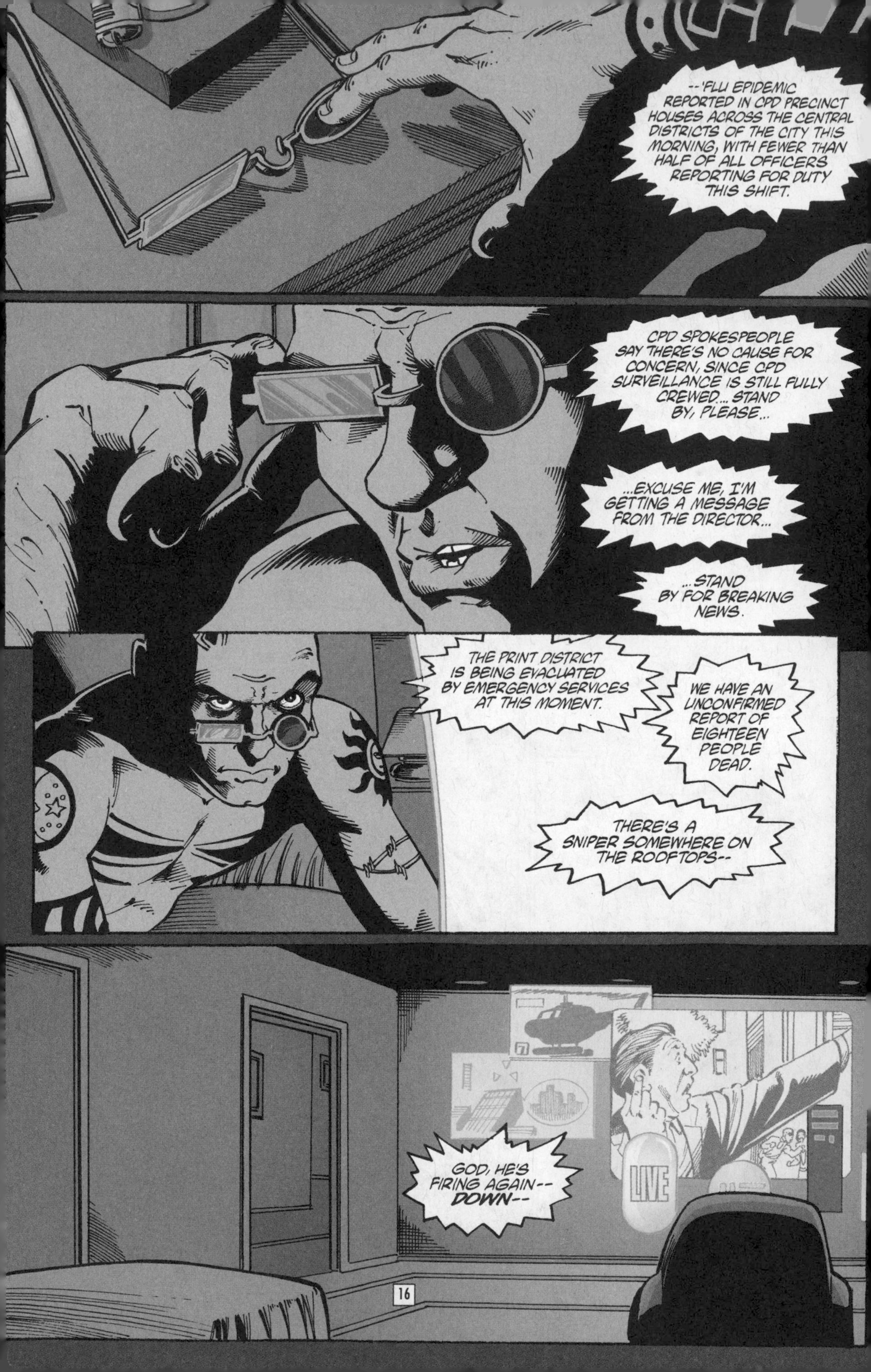
--'FLU EPIDEMIC REPORTED IN CPD PRECINCT HOUSES ACROSS THE CENTRAL DISTRICTS OF THE CITY THIS MORNING, WITH FEWER THAN HALF OF ALL OFFICERS REPORTING FOR DUTY THIS SHIFT.
CPD SPOKESPEOPLE SAY THERE'S NO CAUSE FOR CONCERN, SINCE CPD SURVEILLANCE IS STILL FULLY CREWED... STAND BY, PLEASE...
...EXCUSE ME, I'M GETTING A MESSAGE FROM THE DIRECTOR...
...STAND BY FOR BREAKING NEWS.
THE PRINT DISTRICT IS BEING EVACUATED BY EMERGENCY SERVICES AT THIS MOMENT.
WE HAVE AN UNCONFIRMED REPORT OF EIGHTEEN PEOPLE DEAD.
THERE'S A SNIPER SOMEWHERE ON THE ROOFTOPS--
LIVE
GOD, HE'S FIRING AGAIN-- DOWN--

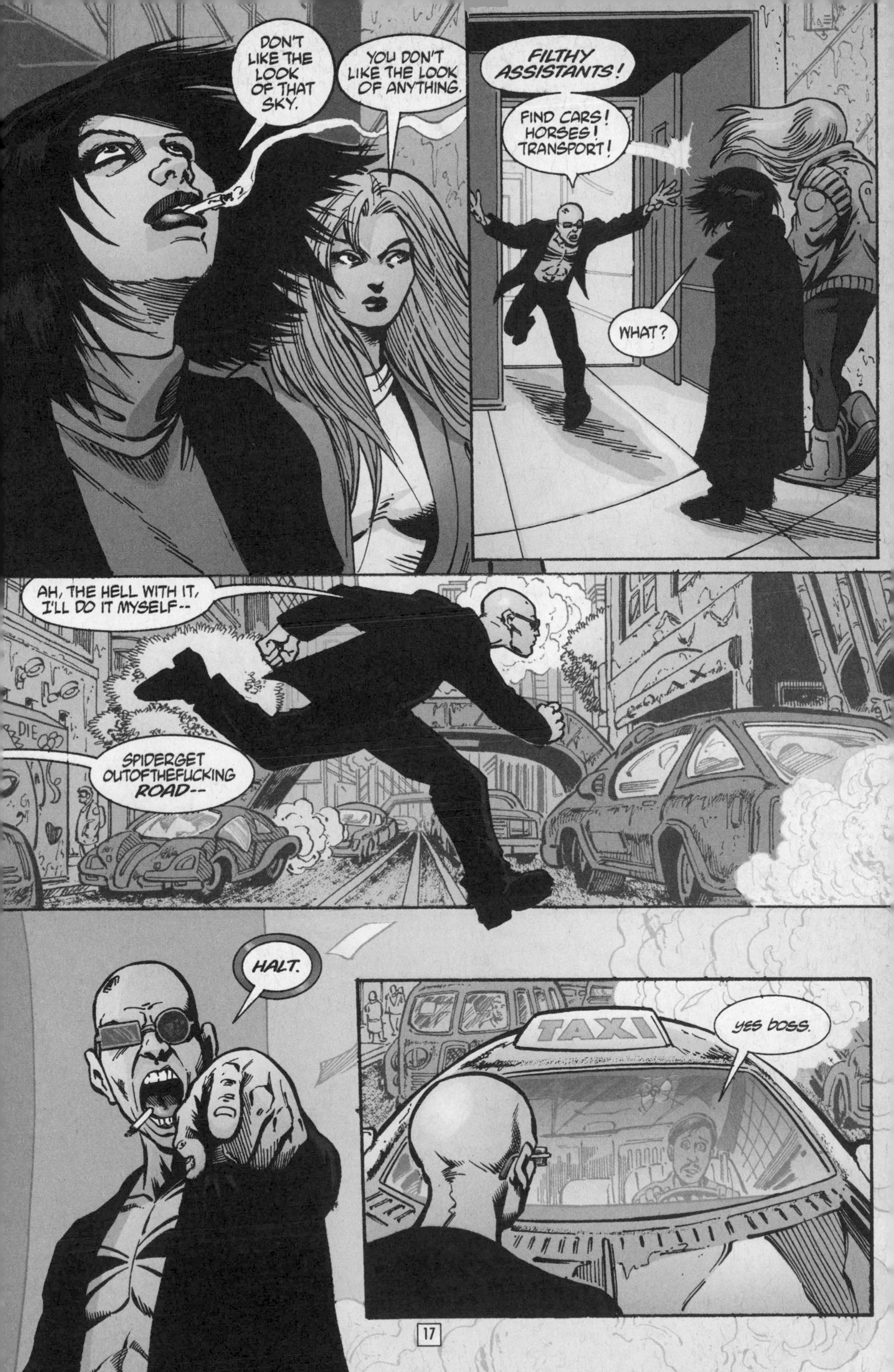
DON'T LIKE THE LOOK OF THAT SKY.
YOU DON'T LIKE THE LOOK OF ANYTHING.
FILTHY ASSISTANTS!
FIND CARS! HORSES! TRANSPORT!
WHAT?
AH, THE HELL WITH IT, I'LL DO IT MYSELF--
SPIDERGET OUTOFTHEFUCKING ROAD--
HALT.
TAXI
yes boss.

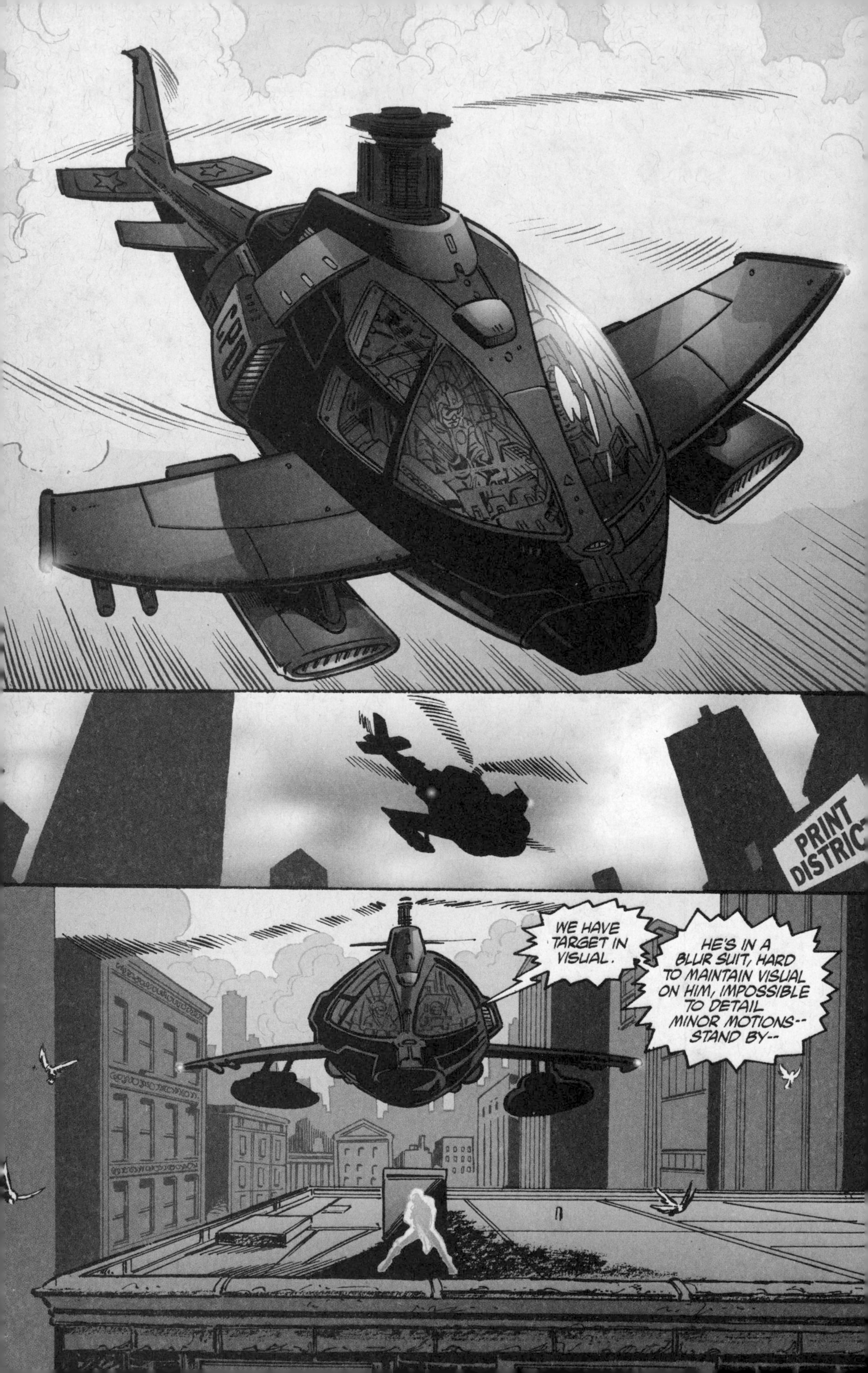
CPD
PRINT DISTRICT
WE HAVE TARGET IN VISUAL.
HE'S IN A BLUR SUIT, HARD TO MAINTAIN VISUAL ON HIM, IMPOSSIBLE TO DETAIL MINOR MOTIONS-- STAND BY--

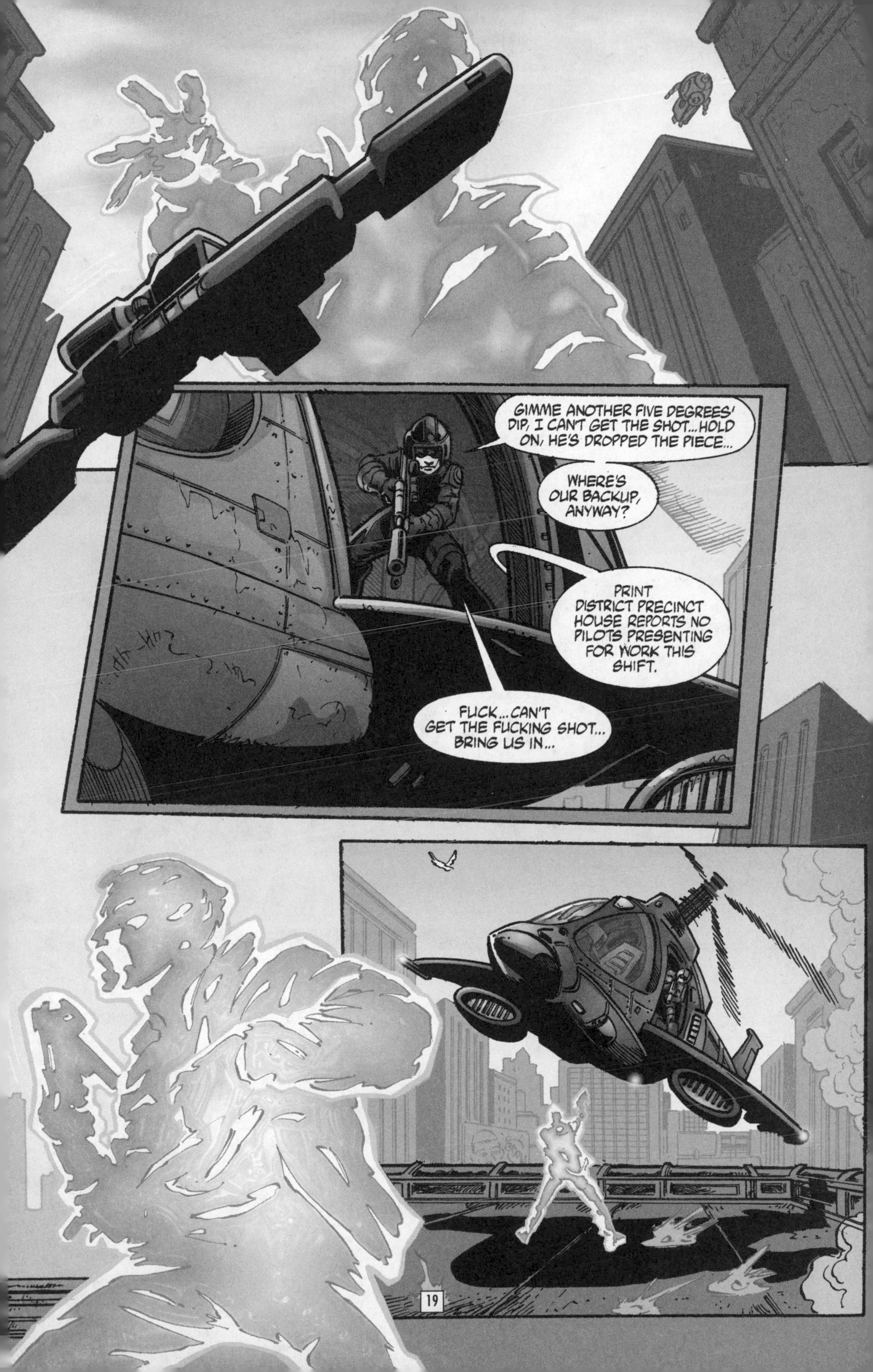
GIMME ANOTHER FIVE DEGREES' DIP, I CAN'T GET THE SHOT...HOLD ON, HE'S DROPPED THE PIECE...
WHERE'S OUR BACKUP, ANYWAY?
PRINT DISTRICT PRECINCT HOUSE REPORTS NO PILOTS PRESENTING FOR WORK THIS SHIFT.
FUCK...CAN'T GET THE FUCKING SHOT... BRING US IN...

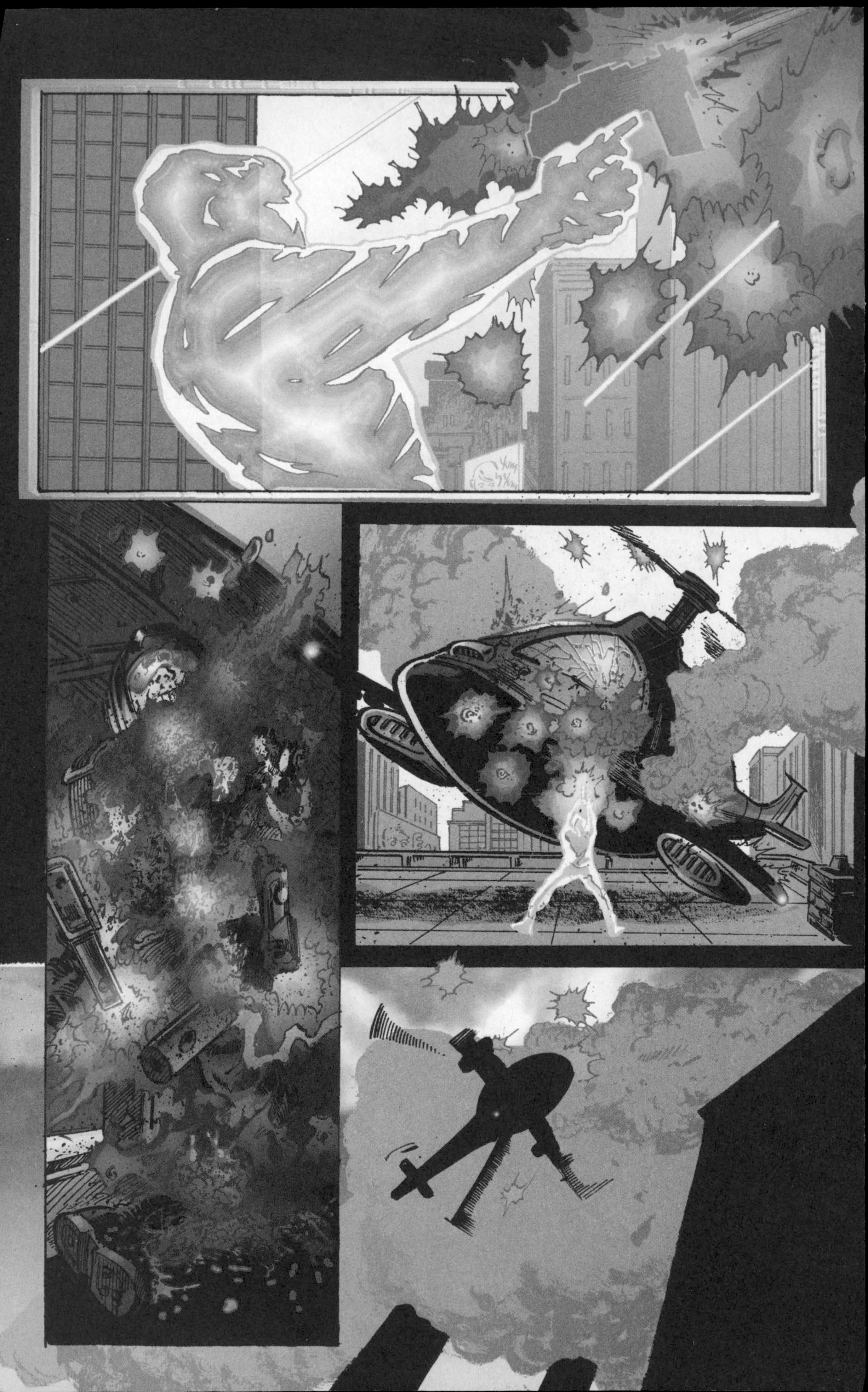

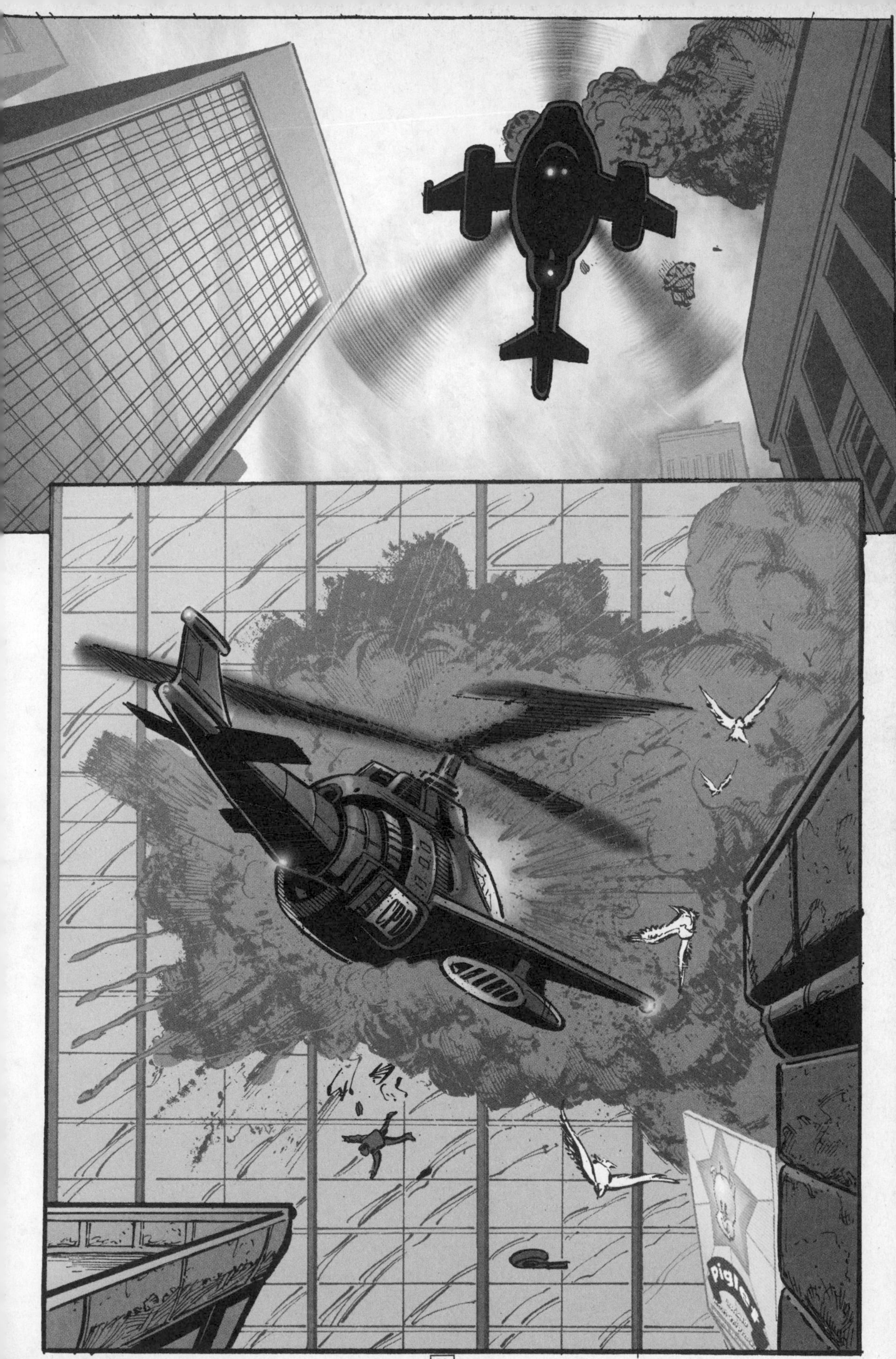
CPD

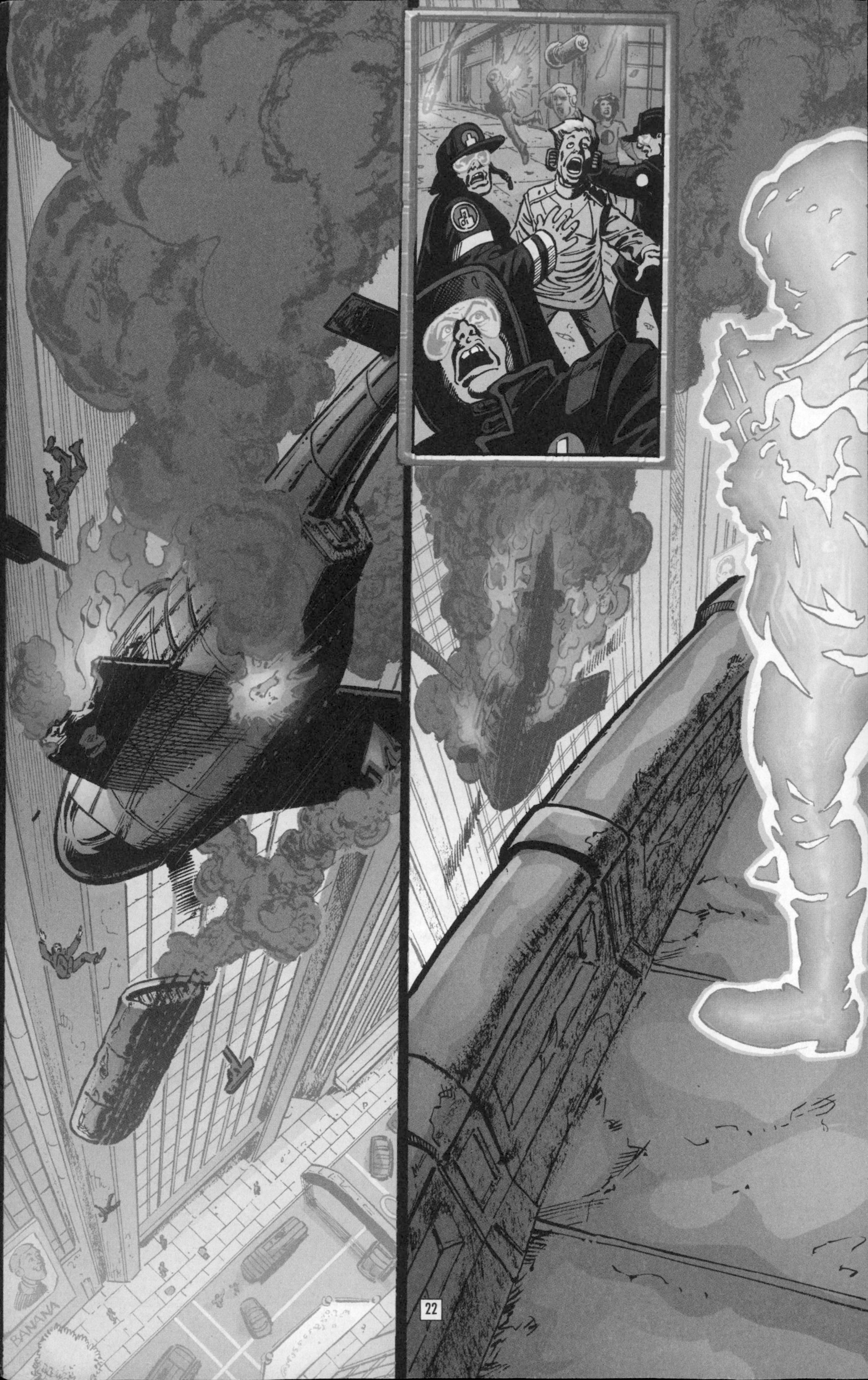
BANANA

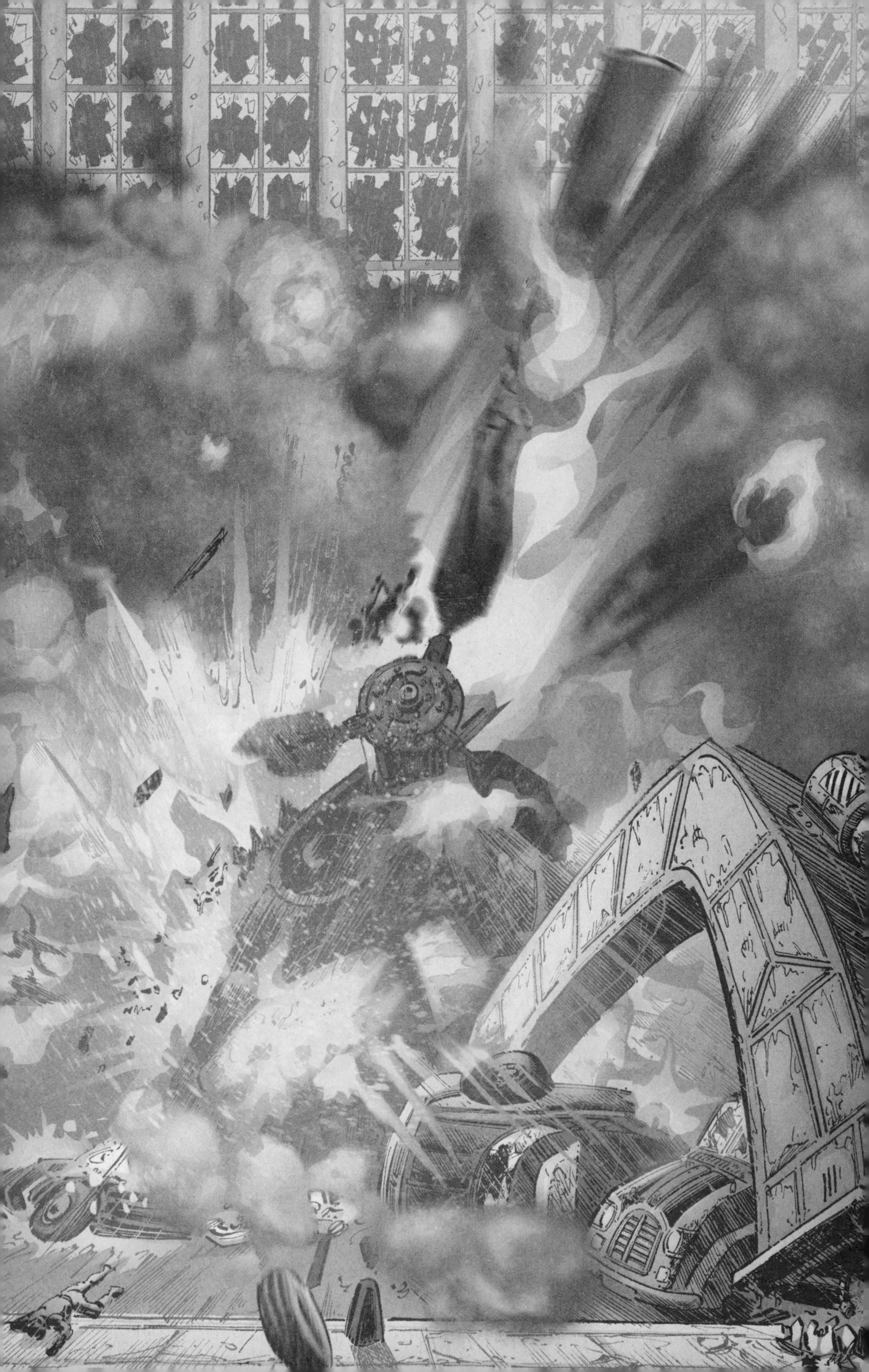

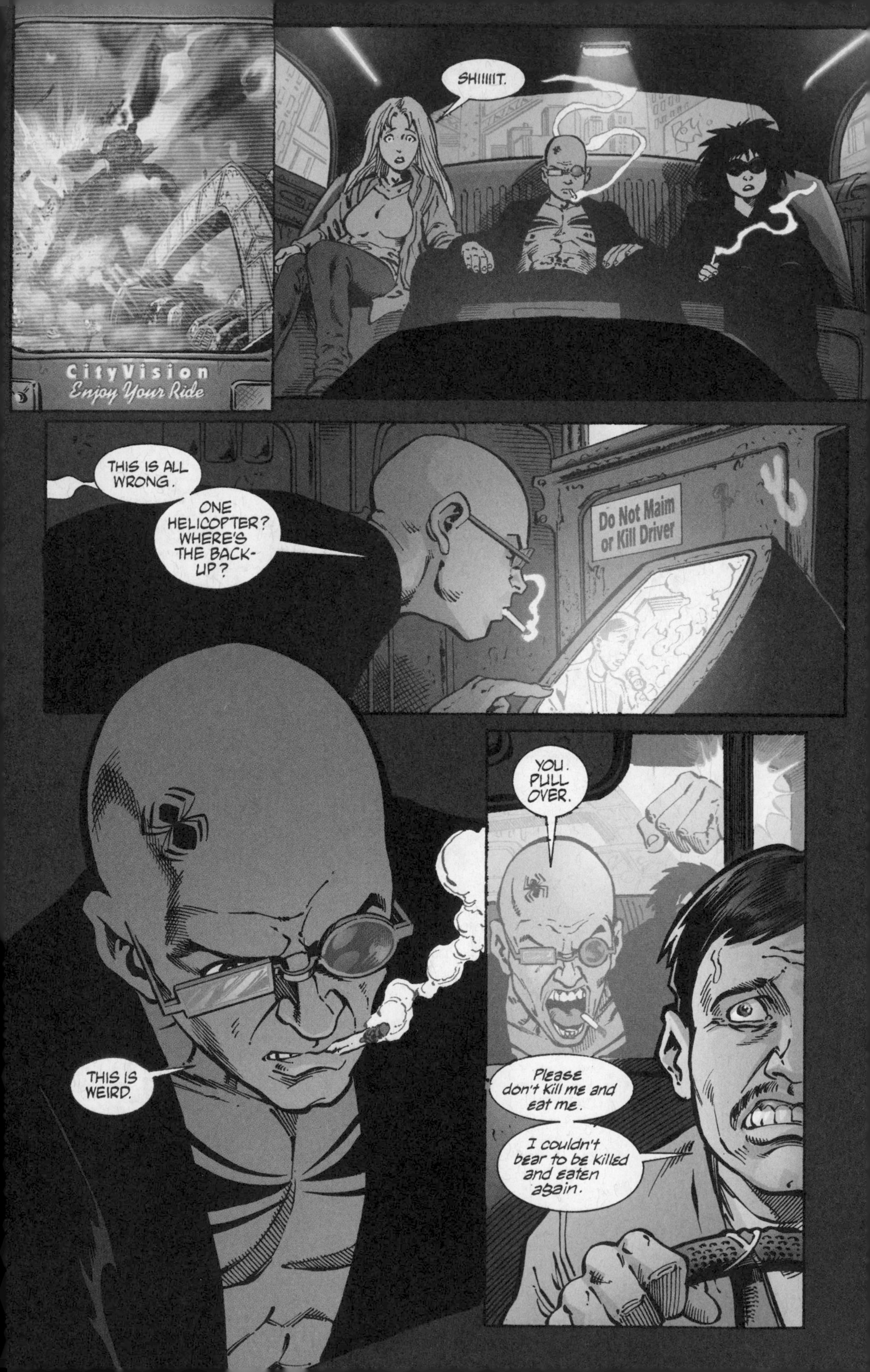

CityVision
Enjoy Your Ride
SHIIIIIT.
THIS IS ALL WRONG.
ONE HELICOPTER? WHERE'S THE BACK-UP?
Do Not Maim or Kill Driver
THIS IS WEIRD.
YOU. PULL OVER.
Please don't kill me and eat me.
I couldn't bear to be killed and eaten again.

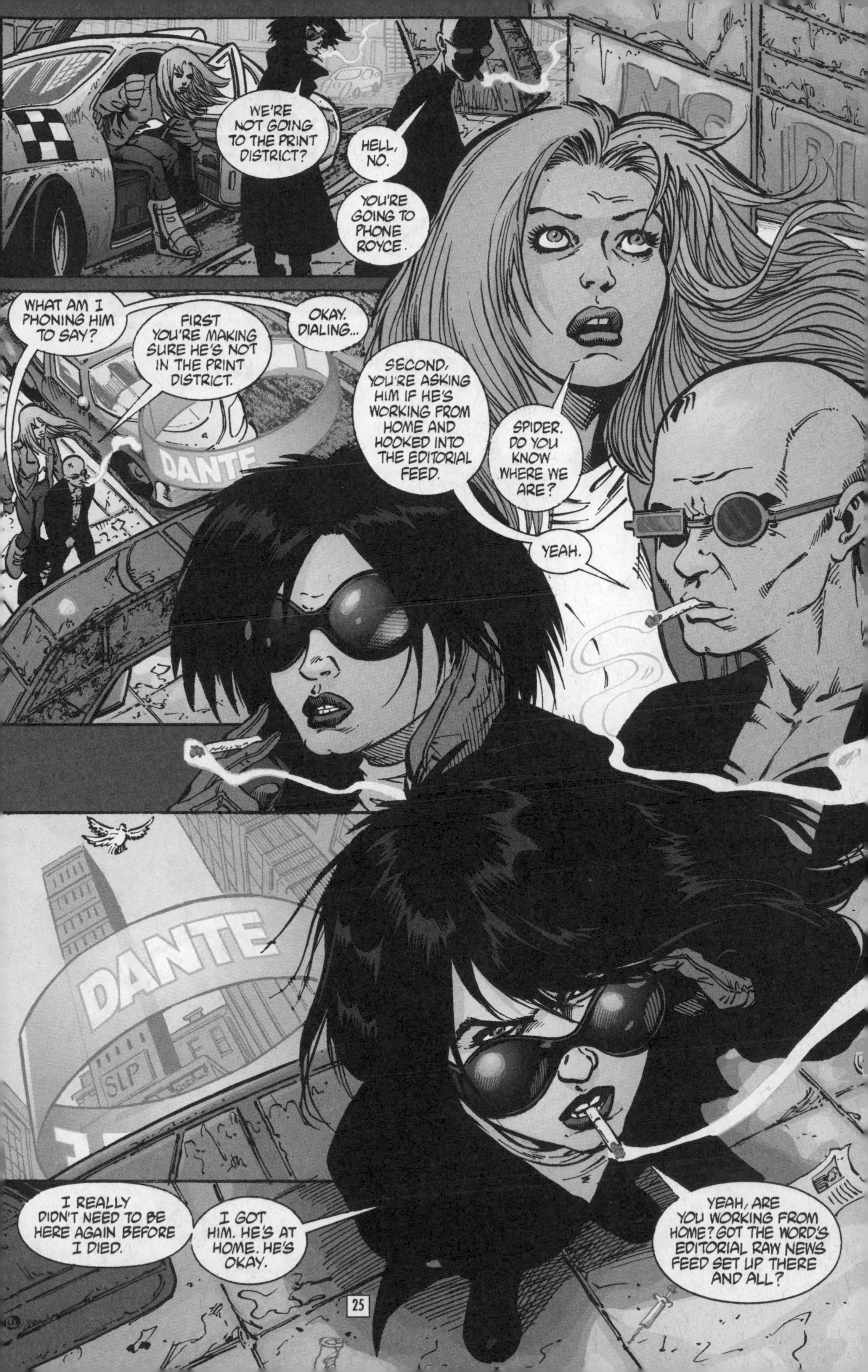

WE'RE NOT GOING TO THE PRINT DISTRICT?
HELL, NO.
YOU'RE GOING TO PHONE ROYCE.
WHAT AM I PHONING HIM TO SAY?
FIRST YOU'RE MAKING SURE HE'S NOT IN THE PRINT DISTRICT.
OKAY. DIALING...
SECOND, YOU'RE ASKING HIM IF HE'S WORKING FROM HOME AND HOOKED INTO THE EDITORIAL FEED.
DANTE
SPIDER. DO YOU KNOW WHERE WE ARE?
YEAH.
DANTE
SLP
YEAH, ARE YOU WORKING FROM HOME? GOT THE WORD'S EDITORIAL RAW NEWS FEED SET UP THERE AND ALL?
I GOT HIM. HE'S AT HOME. HE'S OKAY.
I REALLY DIDN'T NEED TO BE HERE AGAIN BEFORE I DIED.

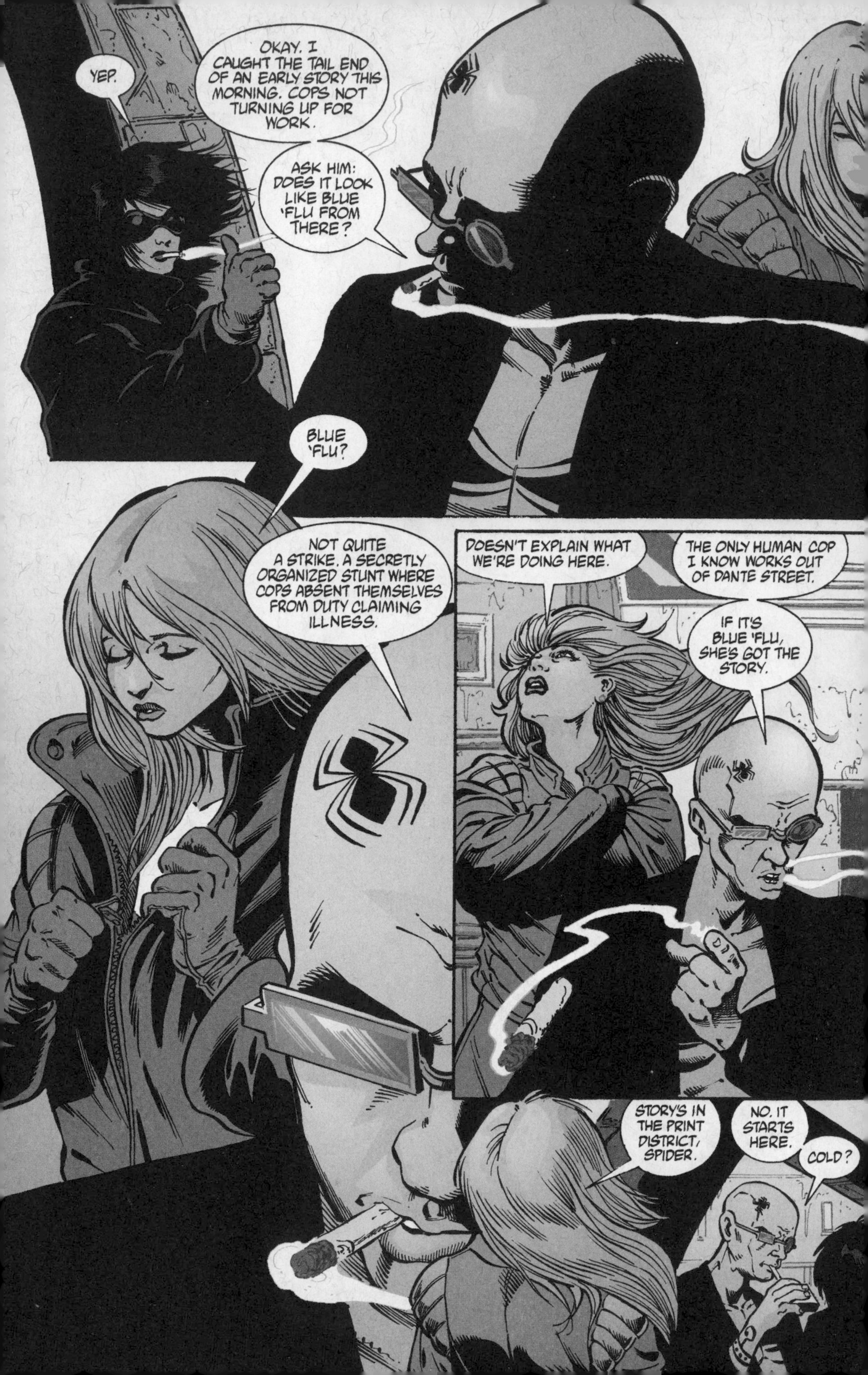
YEP.
OKAY. I CAUGHT THE TAIL END OF AN EARLY STORY THIS MORNING. COPS NOT TURNING UP FOR WORK.
ASK HIM: DOES IT LOOK LIKE BLUE 'FLU FROM THERE?
BLUE 'FLU?
NOT QUITE A STRIKE. A SECRETLY ORGANIZED STUNT WHERE COPS ABSENT THEMSELVES FROM DUTY CLAIMING ILLNESS.
DOESN'T EXPLAIN WHAT WE'RE DOING HERE.
THE ONLY HUMAN COP I KNOW WORKS OUT OF DANTE STREET.
IF IT'S BLUE 'FLU, SHE'S GOT THE STORY.
STORY'S IN THE PRINT DISTRICT, SPIDER.
NO. IT STARTS HERE.
COLD?

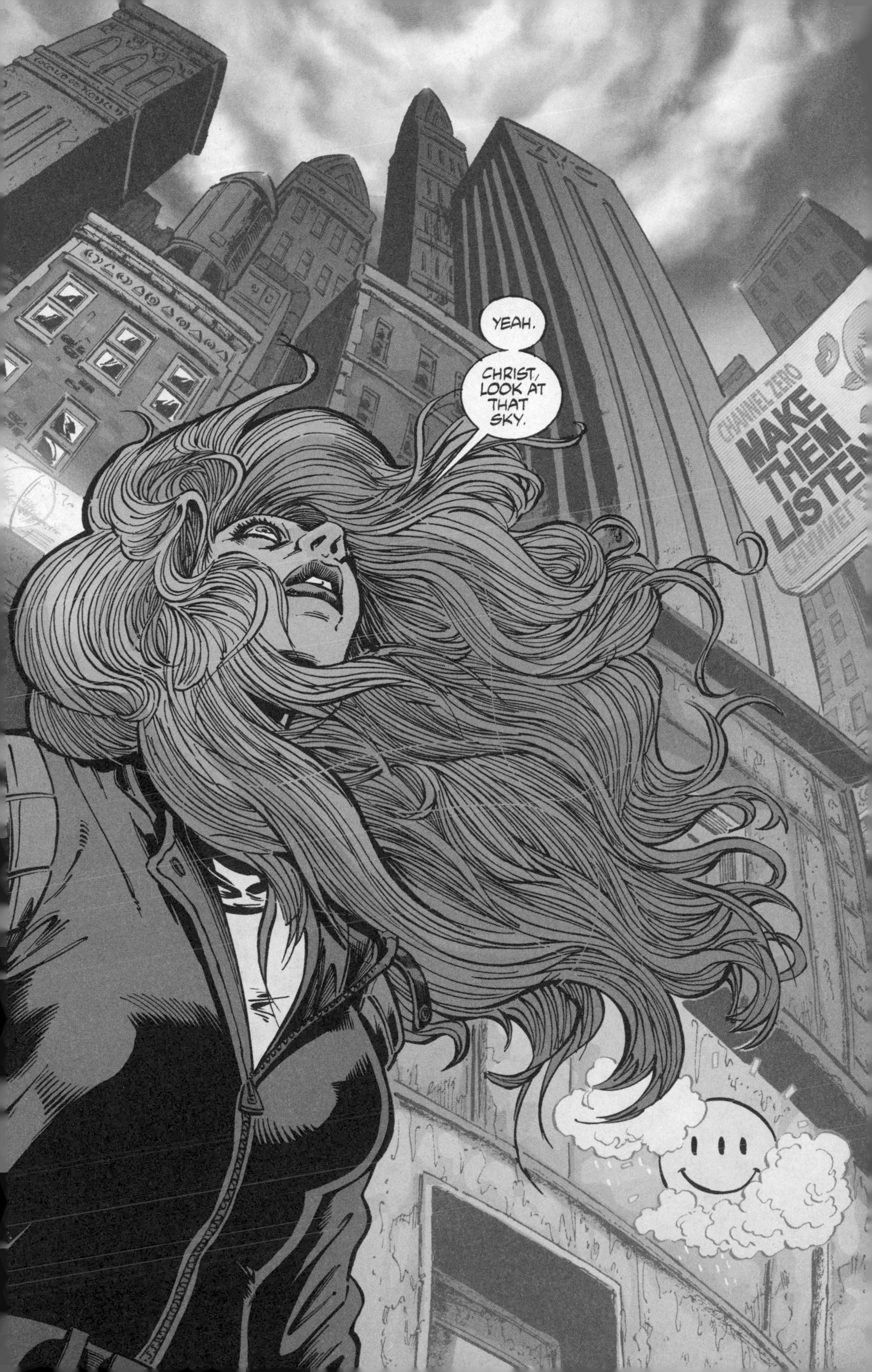

YEAH.
CHRIST, LOOK AT THAT SKY.
CHANNEL ZERO
MAKE THEM LISTEN

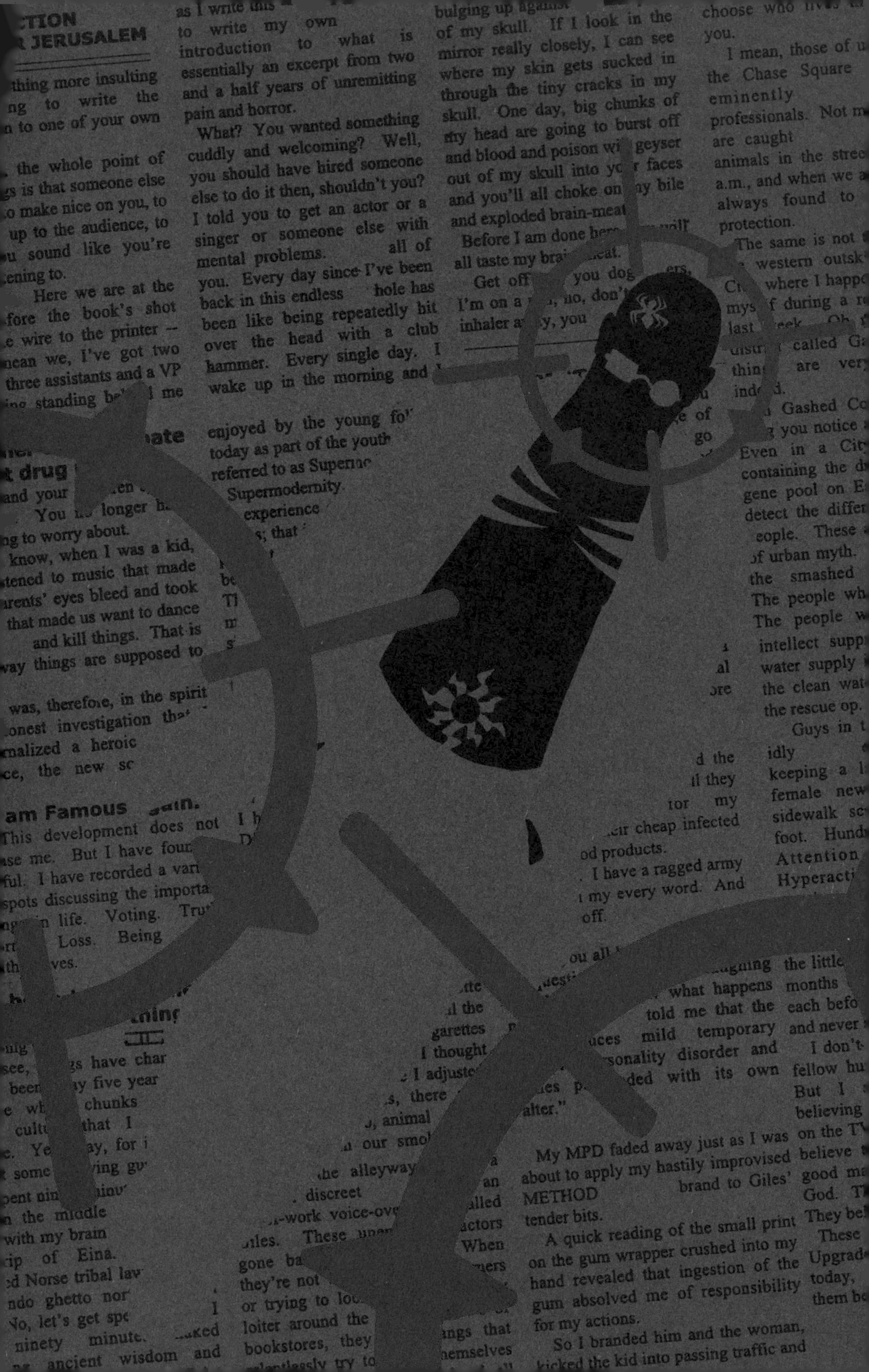

as I write this
to write my own introduction to what is essentially an excerpt from two and a half years of unremitting pain and horror.
What? You wanted something cuddly and welcoming? Well, you should have hired someone else to do it then, shouldn't you? I told you to get an actor or a singer or someone else with mental problems.
you. Every day since I've been back in this endless hole has been like being repeatedly hit over the head with a club hammer. Every single day. I wake up in the morning and
enjoyed by the young fo
today as part of the youth
referred to as Supermo
Supermodernity.
experience
bulging up against
of my skull. If I look in the mirror really closely, I can see where my skin gets sucked in through the tiny cracks in my skull. One day, big chunks of my head are going to burst off and blood and poison will geyser out of my skull into your faces and you'll all choke on my bile and exploded brain-meat.
Before I am done here you will all taste my brain-meat.
Get off you dog
I'm on a no, don't
inhaler a y, you
choose who lives
you.
I mean, those of u
the Chase Square
eminently
professionals. Not m
are caught
animals in the stree
a.m., and when we a
always found to
protection.
The same is not
western outsk
Ci where I happe
mys f during a r
last week
called G
thin are ver
ind d.
Gashed C
you notice
Even in a Cit
containing the d
gene pool on E
detect the differ
eople. These
of urban myth.
the smashed
The people wh
The people w
intellect supp
water supply
the clean wat
the rescue op.
Guys in t
idly
keeping a l
female new
sidewalk sc
foot. Hund
Attention
Hyperacti
thing more insulting
ng to write the
n to one of your own
the whole point of
s is that someone else
o make nice on you, to
up to the audience, to
u sound like you're
ening to.
Here we are at the
fore the book's shot
e wire to the printer --
nean we, I've got two
three assistants and a VP
standing b me
hate
t drug
and your
You longer h
ng to worry about.
know, when I was a kid,
tened to music that made
arents' eyes bleed and took
that made us want to dance
and kill things. That is
way things are supposed to
was, therefore, in the spirit
onest investigation that
nalized a heroic
ce, the new sc
am Famous
This development does not
se me. But I have foun
ful. I have recorded a vari
spots discussing the importa
in life. Voting. Tru
Loss. Being
ves.
have char
ay five year
chunks
that I
ay, for i
ving gu
the middle
with my brain
of Eina.
Norse tribal lav
ndo ghetto nor
No, let's get spe
ninety minute.
ancient wisdom and
d the
ll they
tor my
eir cheap infected
od products.
I have a ragged army
my every word. And
off.
ou all
what happens
told me that the
uces mild temporary
sonality disorder and
ded with its own
alter."
the little
months
each befo
and never
I don't
fellow hu
But I
believing
on the TV
believe
good ma
God. T
They be
These
Upgrad
today,
them be
My MPD faded away just as I was about to apply my hastily improvised METHOD brand to Giles' tender bits.
A quick reading of the small print on the gum wrapper crushed into my hand revealed that ingestion of the responsibility gum absolved me of responsibility for my actions.
So I branded him and the woman, kicked the kid into passing traffic and
l the
garettes
I thought
I adjuste
s, there
animal
our smo
the alleyway
discreet
work voice-ove
les. These
gone ba
they're not
or trying to loo
loiter around the
bookstores, they
an
alled
actors
When
ngs that
emselves

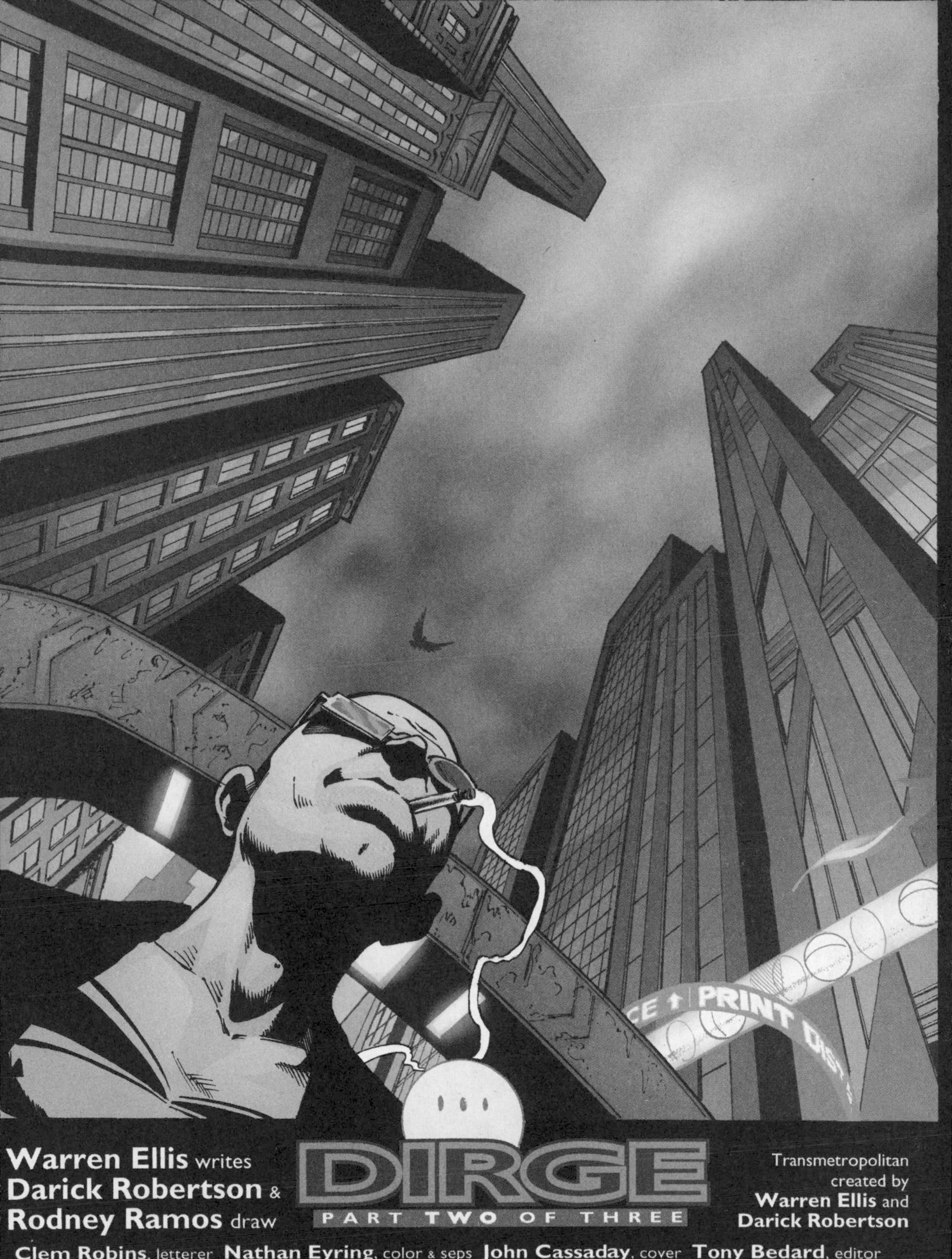
CE ↑ PRINT DIST

Warren Ellis writes
Darick Robertson &
Rodney Ramos draw

DIRGE
PART TWO OF THREE

Transmetropolitan
created by
Warren Ellis and
Darick Robertson

Clem Robins, letterer **Nathan Eyring**, color & seps **John Cassaday**, cover **Tony Bedard**, editor

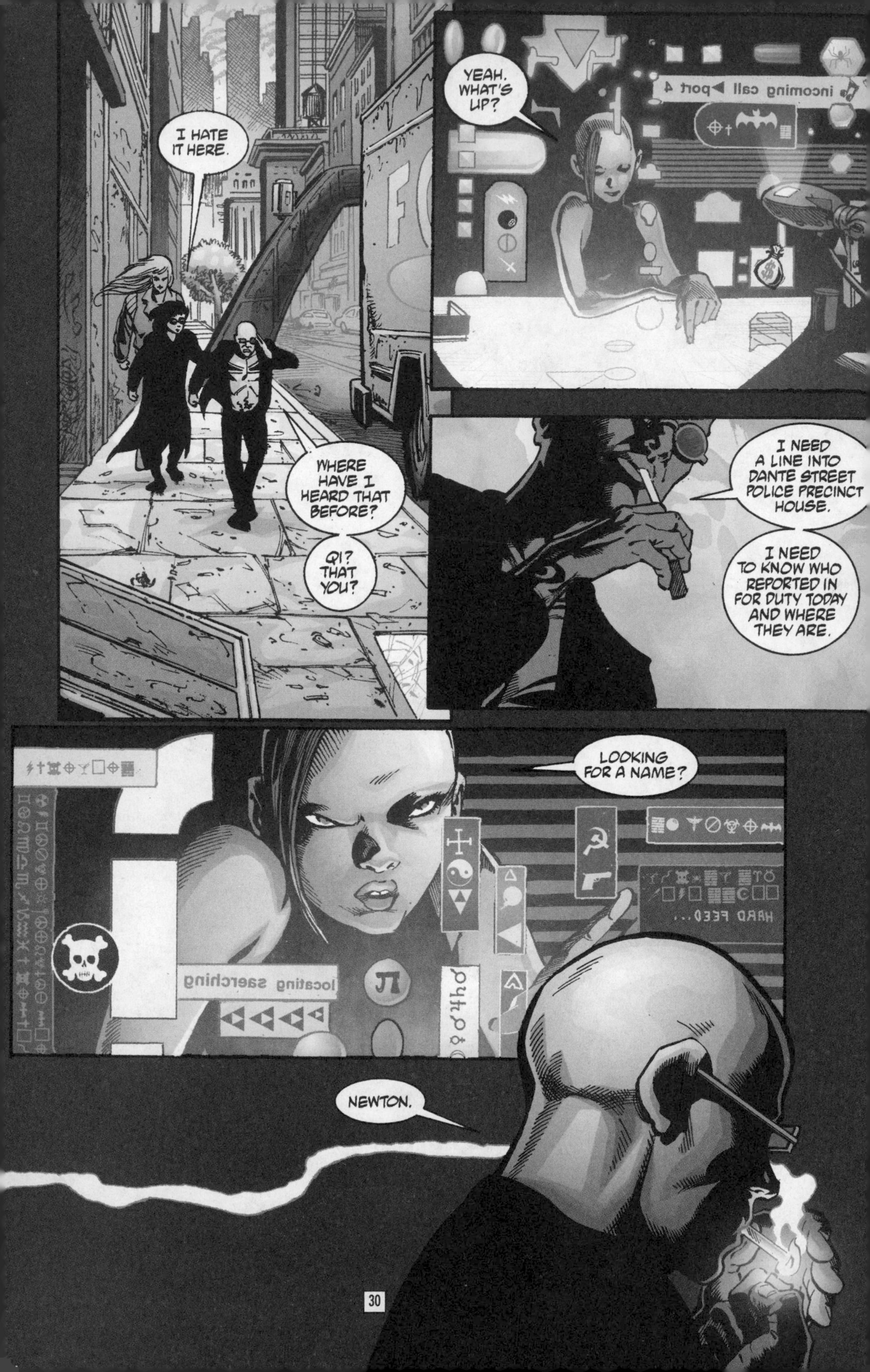
I HATE IT HERE.
WHERE HAVE I HEARD THAT BEFORE?
QI? THAT YOU?
YEAH. WHAT'S UP?
incoming call ▶port 4
I NEED A LINE INTO DANTE STREET POLICE PRECINCT HOUSE.
I NEED TO KNOW WHO REPORTED IN FOR DUTY TODAY AND WHERE THEY ARE.
LOOKING FOR A NAME?
locating sarching
HARD FEED...
NEWTON.

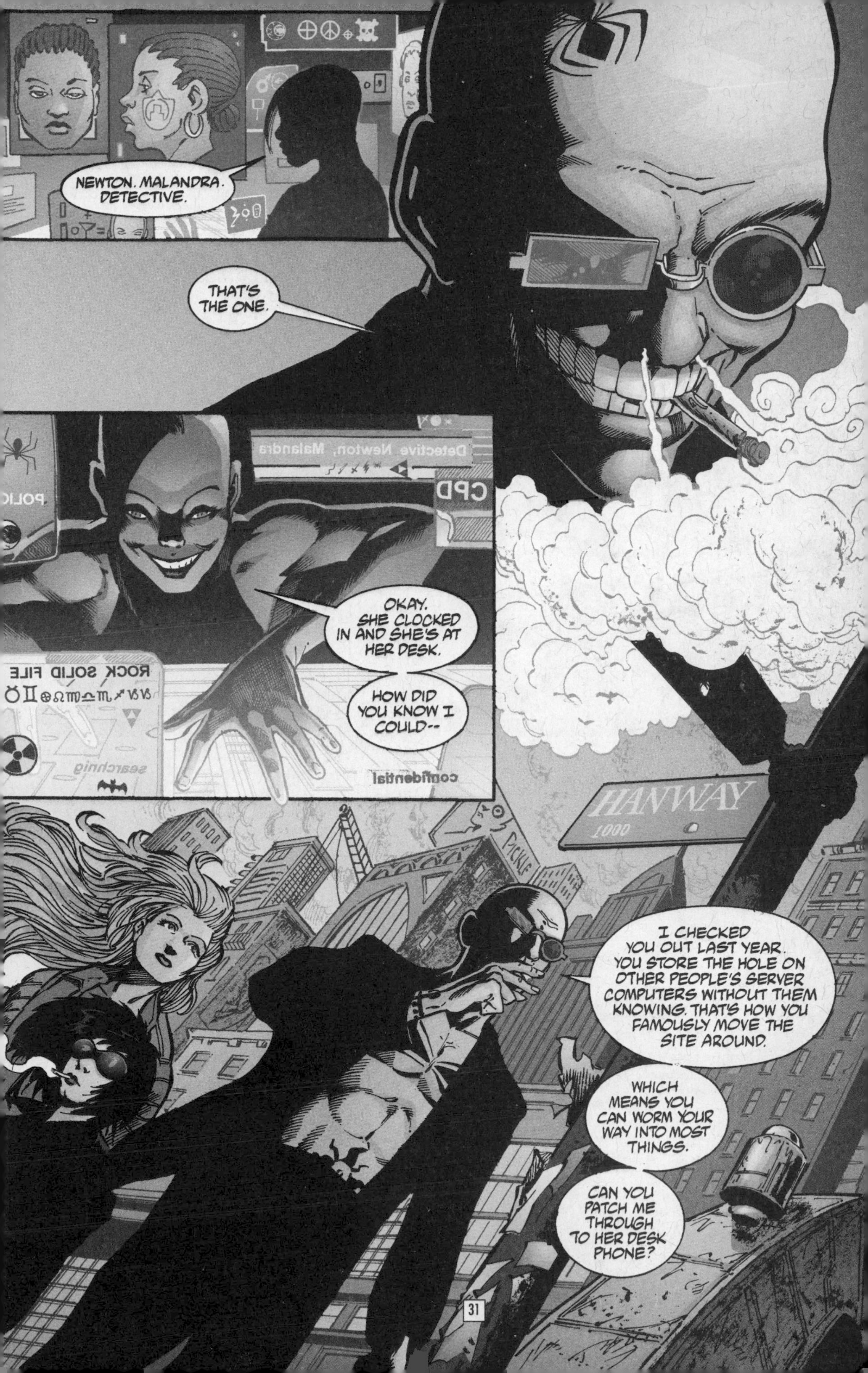
NEWTON. MALANDRA. DETECTIVE.
THAT'S THE ONE.
OKAY. SHE CLOCKED IN AND SHE'S AT HER DESK.
HOW DID YOU KNOW I COULD--
HANWAY
1000
I CHECKED YOU OUT LAST YEAR. YOU STORE THE HOLE ON OTHER PEOPLE'S SERVER COMPUTERS WITHOUT THEM KNOWING. THAT'S HOW YOU FAMOUSLY MOVE THE SITE AROUND.
WHICH MEANS YOU CAN WORM YOUR WAY INTO MOST THINGS.
CAN YOU PATCH ME THROUGH TO HER DESK PHONE?

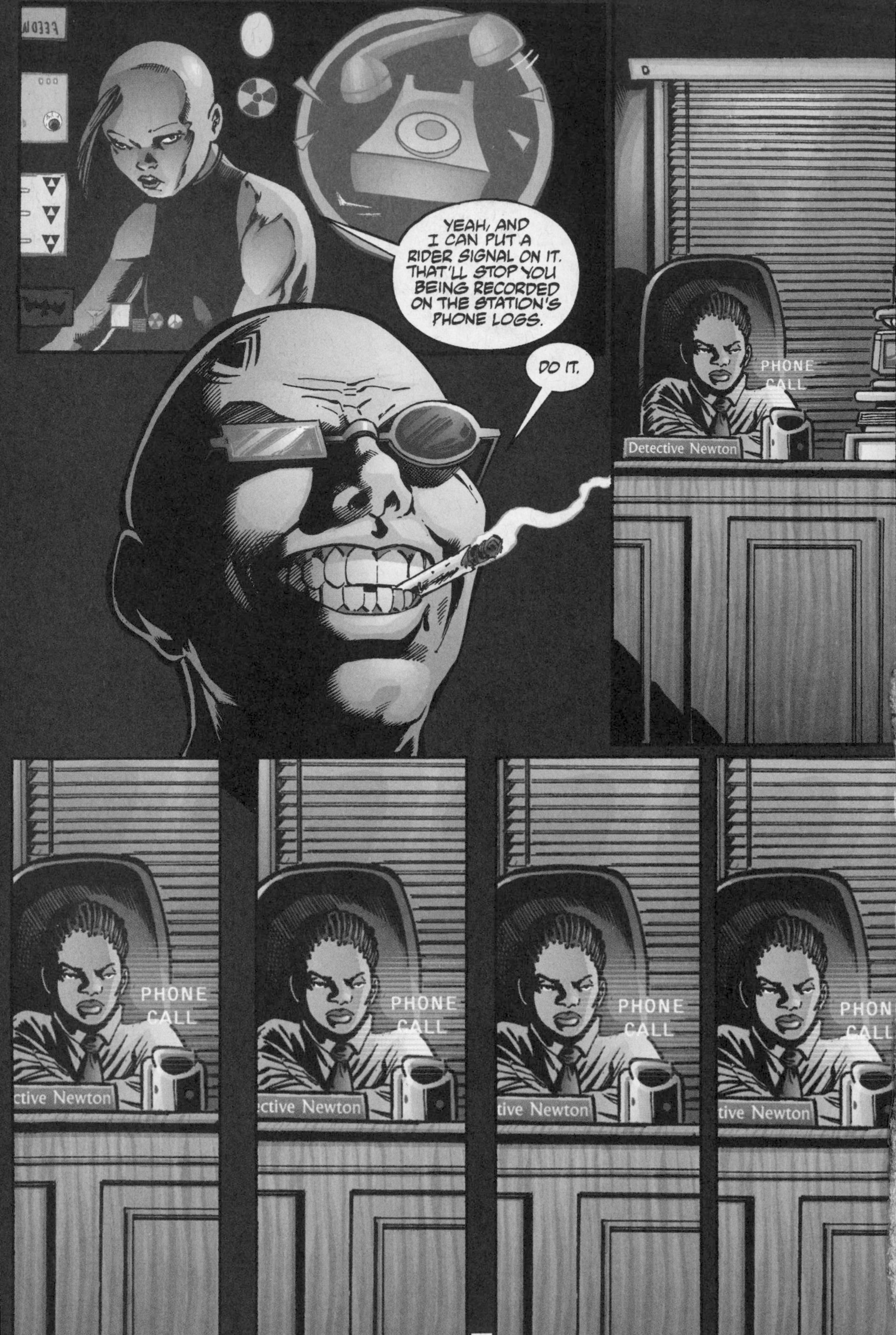

YEAH, AND I CAN PUT A RIDER SIGNAL ON IT. THAT'LL STOP YOU BEING RECORDED ON THE STATION'S PHONE LOGS.
DO IT.
PHONE CALL
Detective Newton
PHONE CALL
ctive Newton
PHONE CALL
ective Newton
PHONE CALL
tive Newton
tive Newton

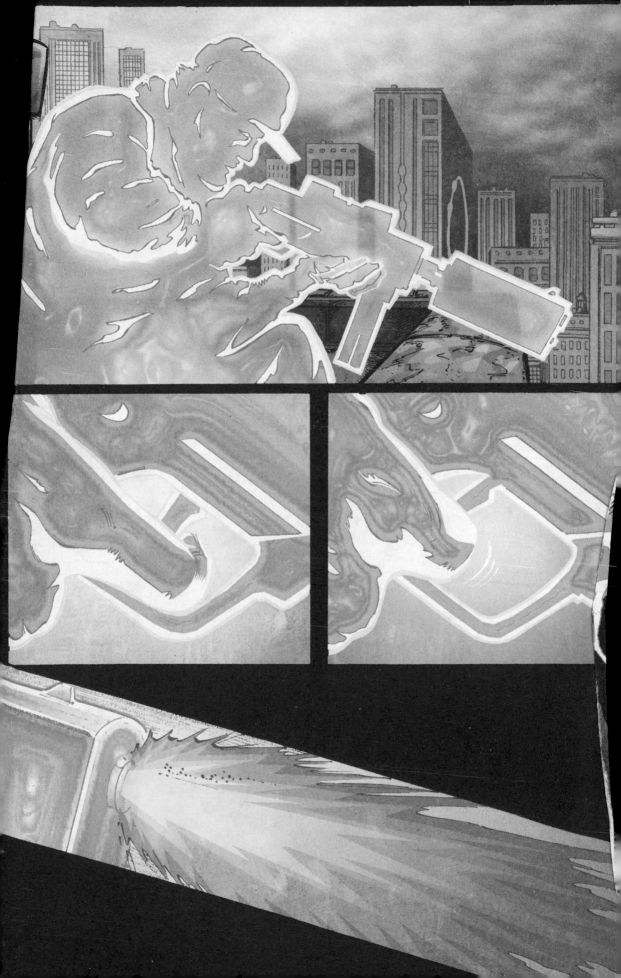

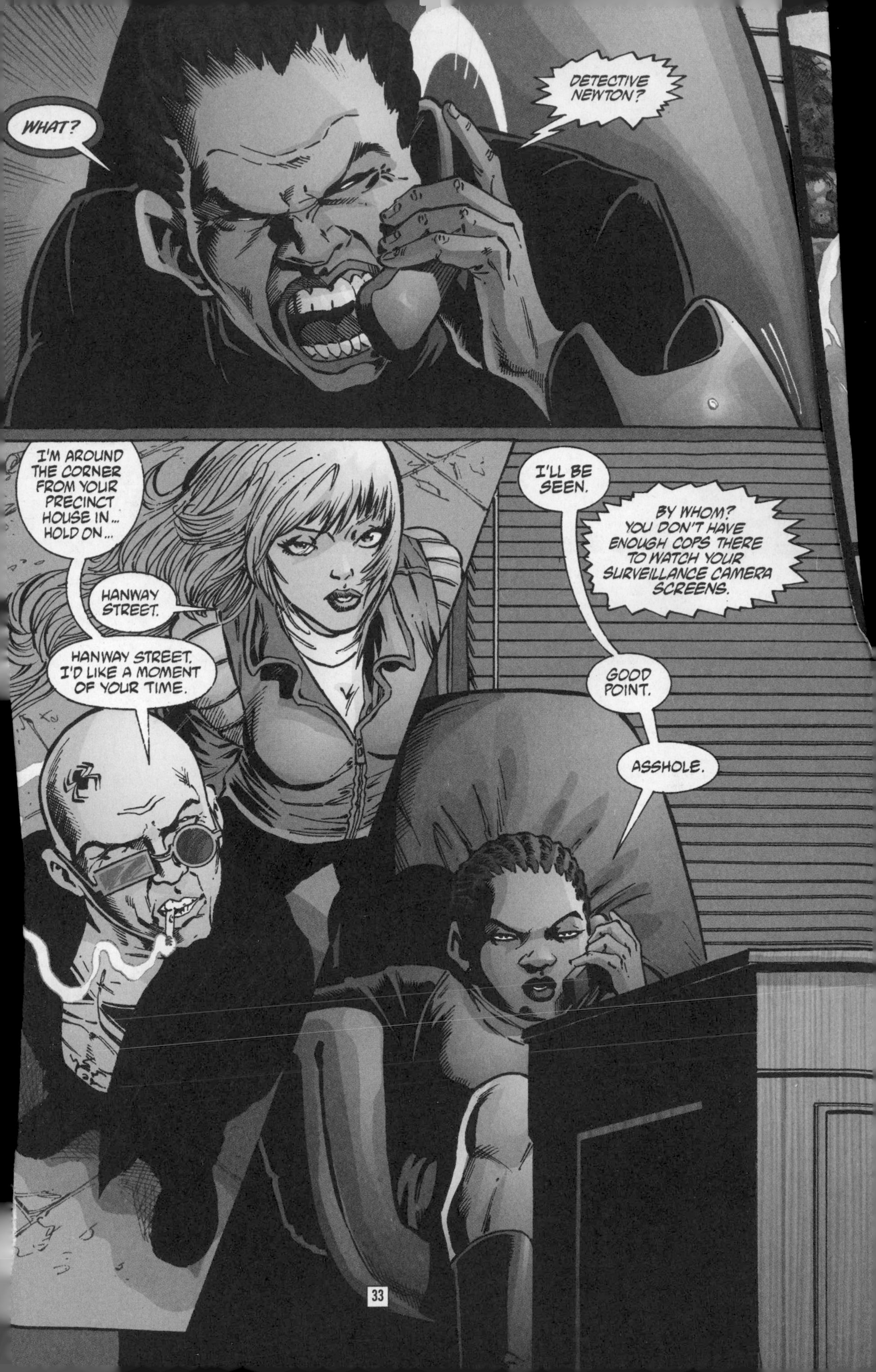
WHAT?
DETECTIVE NEWTON?
I'M AROUND THE CORNER FROM YOUR PRECINCT HOUSE IN... HOLD ON...
HANWAY STREET.
HANWAY STREET. I'D LIKE A MOMENT OF YOUR TIME.
I'LL BE SEEN.
BY WHOM? YOU DON'T HAVE ENOUGH COPS THERE TO WATCH YOUR SURVEILLANCE CAMERA SCREENS.
GOOD POINT.
ASSHOLE.

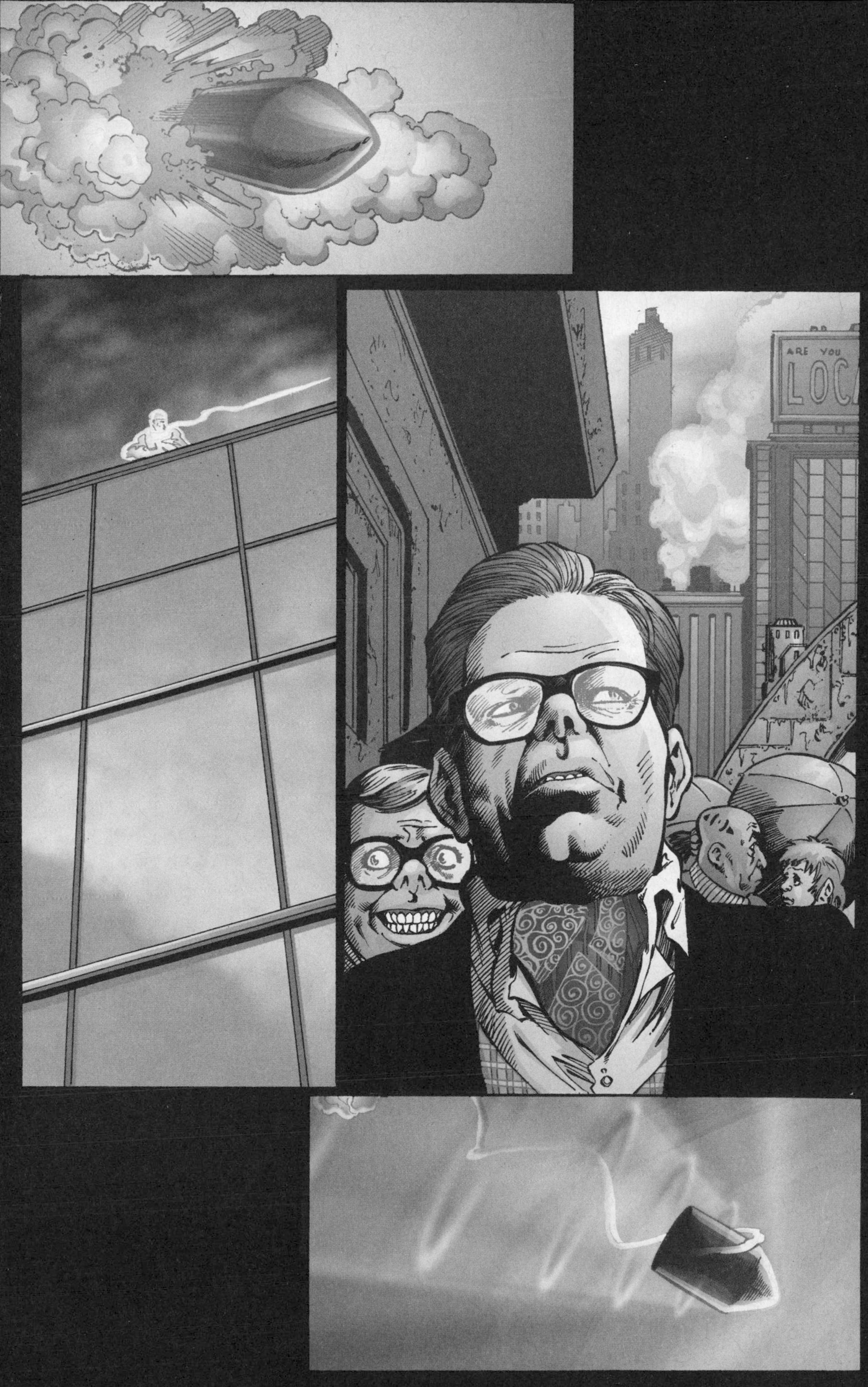
ARE YOU
LOCA

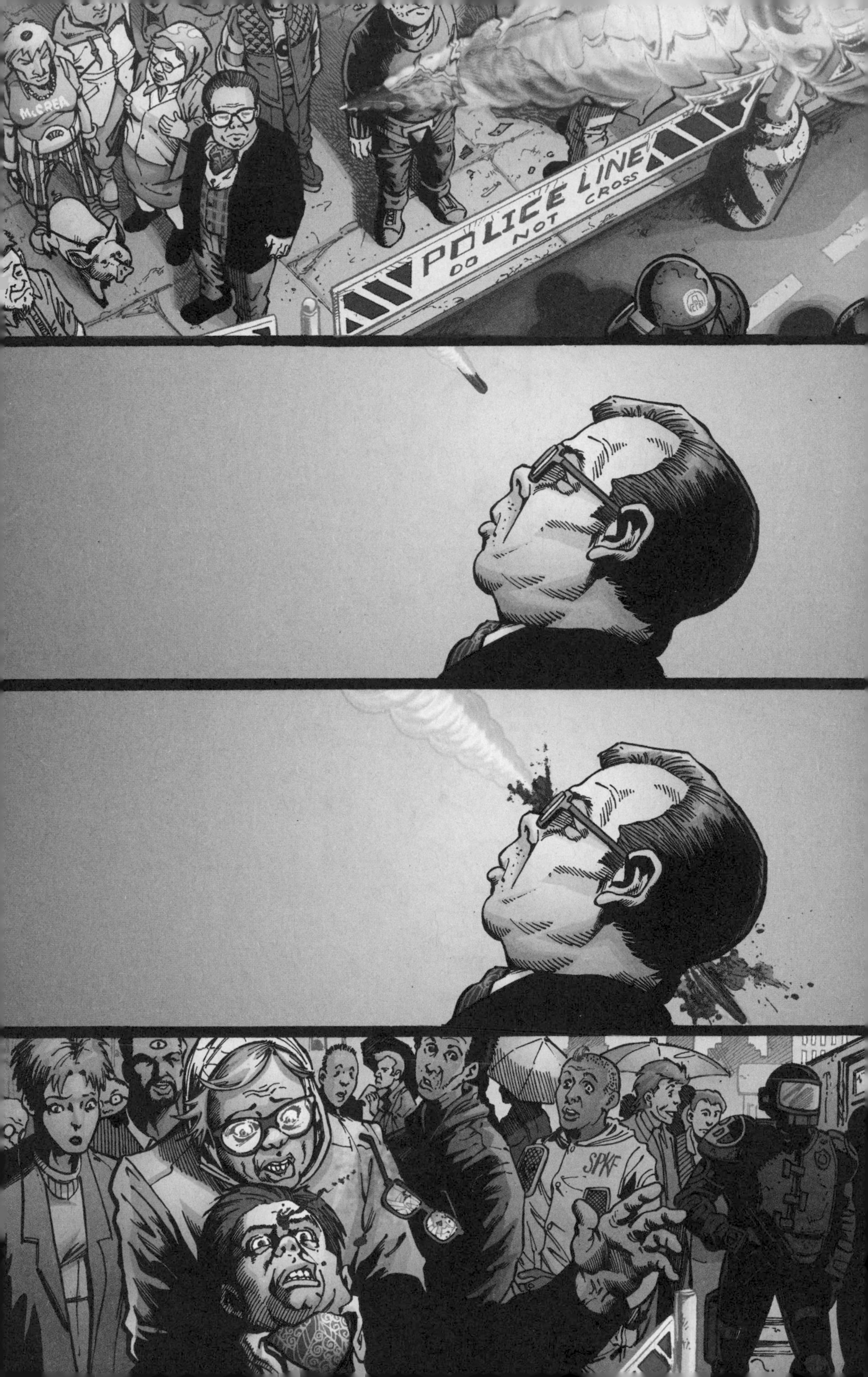
McCREA
POLICE LINE
DO NOT CROSS
SPKF

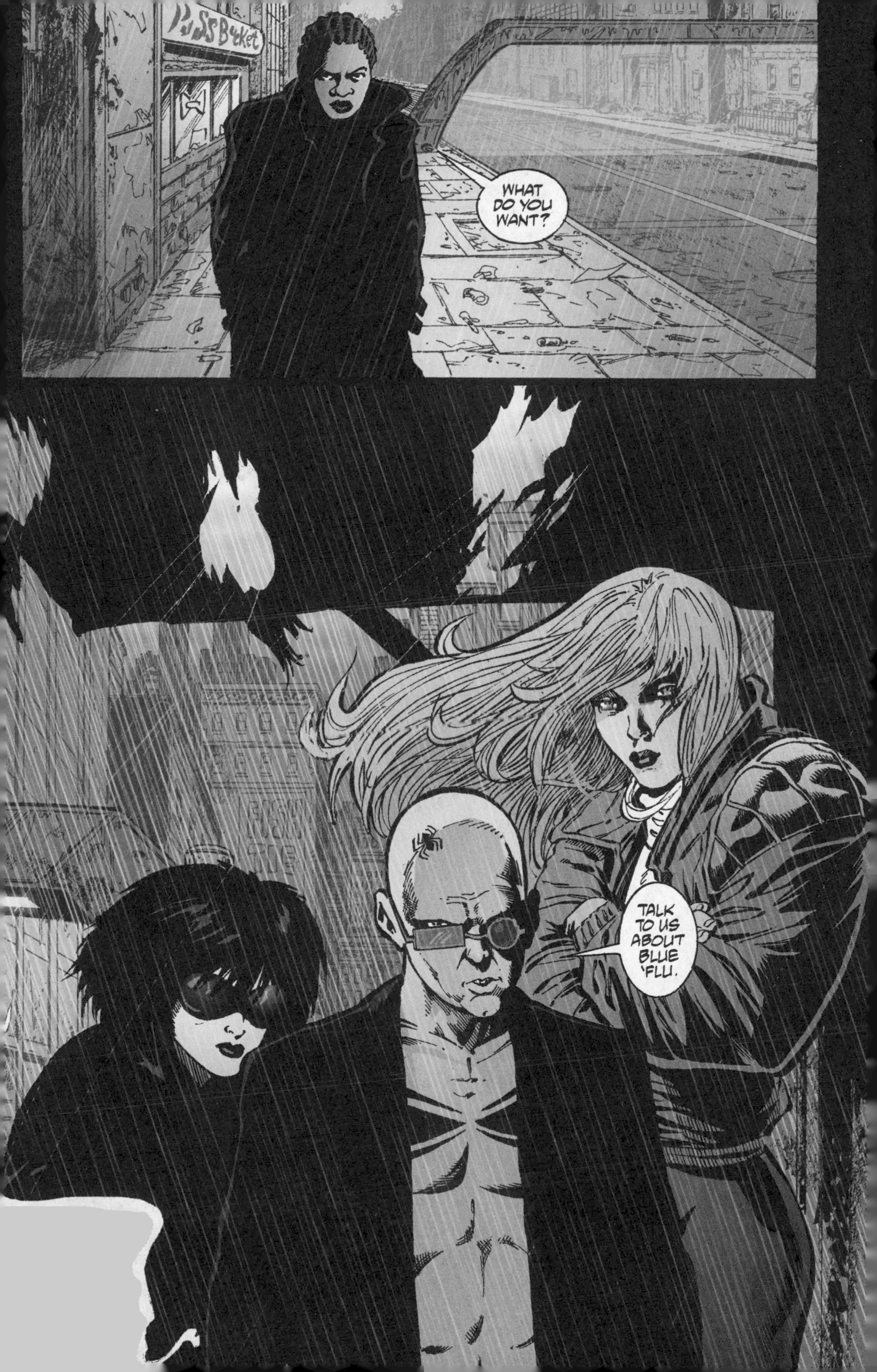
PUSSBUCKET
WHAT DO YOU WANT?
TALK TO US ABOUT BLUE 'FLU.

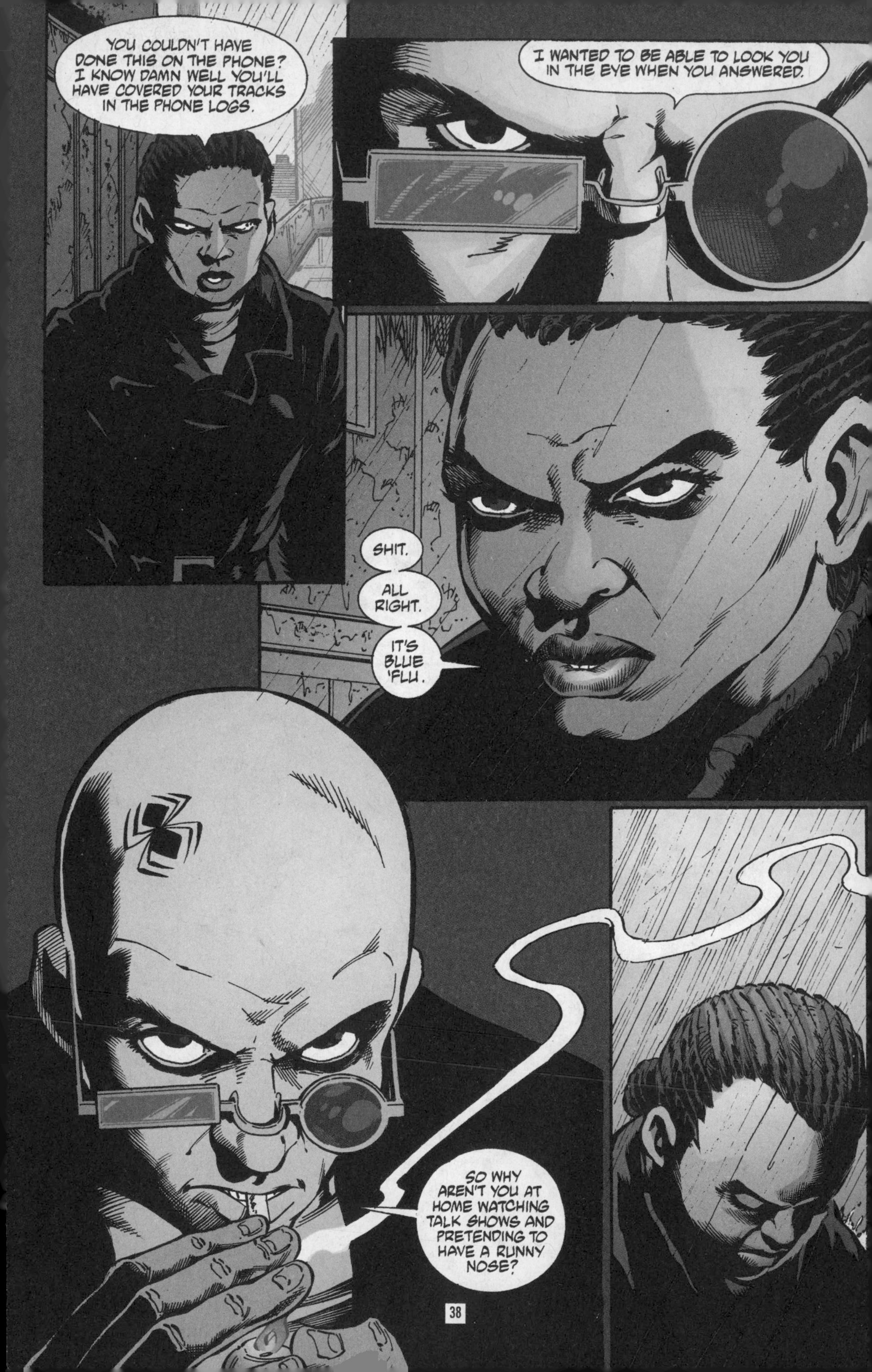
YOU COULDN'T HAVE DONE THIS ON THE PHONE? I KNOW DAMN WELL YOU'LL HAVE COVERED YOUR TRACKS IN THE PHONE LOGS.
I WANTED TO BE ABLE TO LOOK YOU IN THE EYE WHEN YOU ANSWERED.
SHIT.
ALL RIGHT.
IT'S BLUE 'FLU.
SO WHY AREN'T YOU AT HOME WATCHING TALK SHOWS AND PRETENDING TO HAVE A RUNNY NOSE?

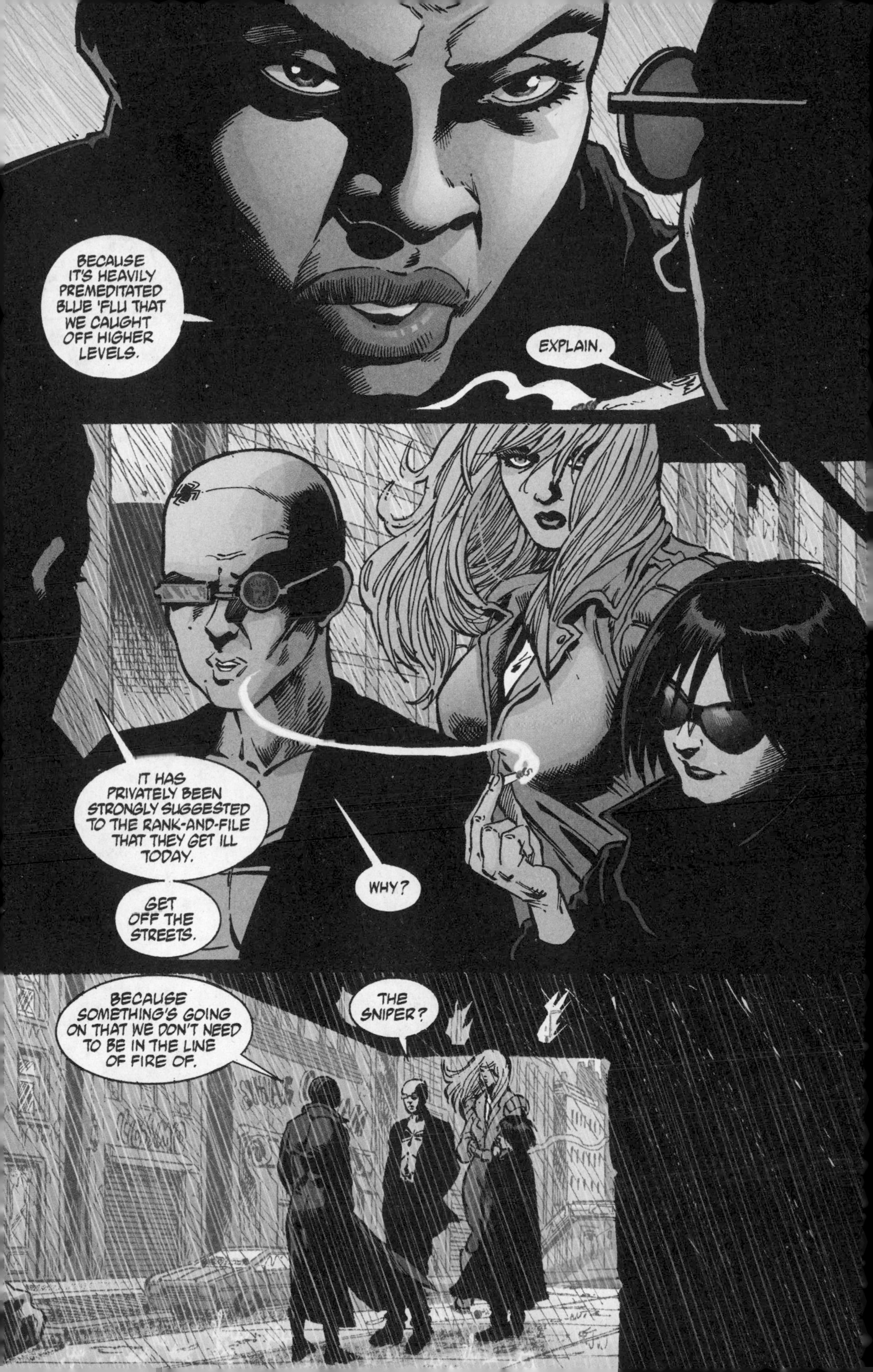
BECAUSE IT'S HEAVILY PREMEDITATED BLUE 'FLU THAT WE CAUGHT OFF HIGHER LEVELS.
EXPLAIN.
IT HAS PRIVATELY BEEN STRONGLY SUGGESTED TO THE RANK-AND-FILE THAT THEY GET ILL TODAY.
WHY?
GET OFF THE STREETS.
BECAUSE SOMETHING'S GOING ON THAT WE DON'T NEED TO BE IN THE LINE OF FIRE OF.
THE SNIPER?

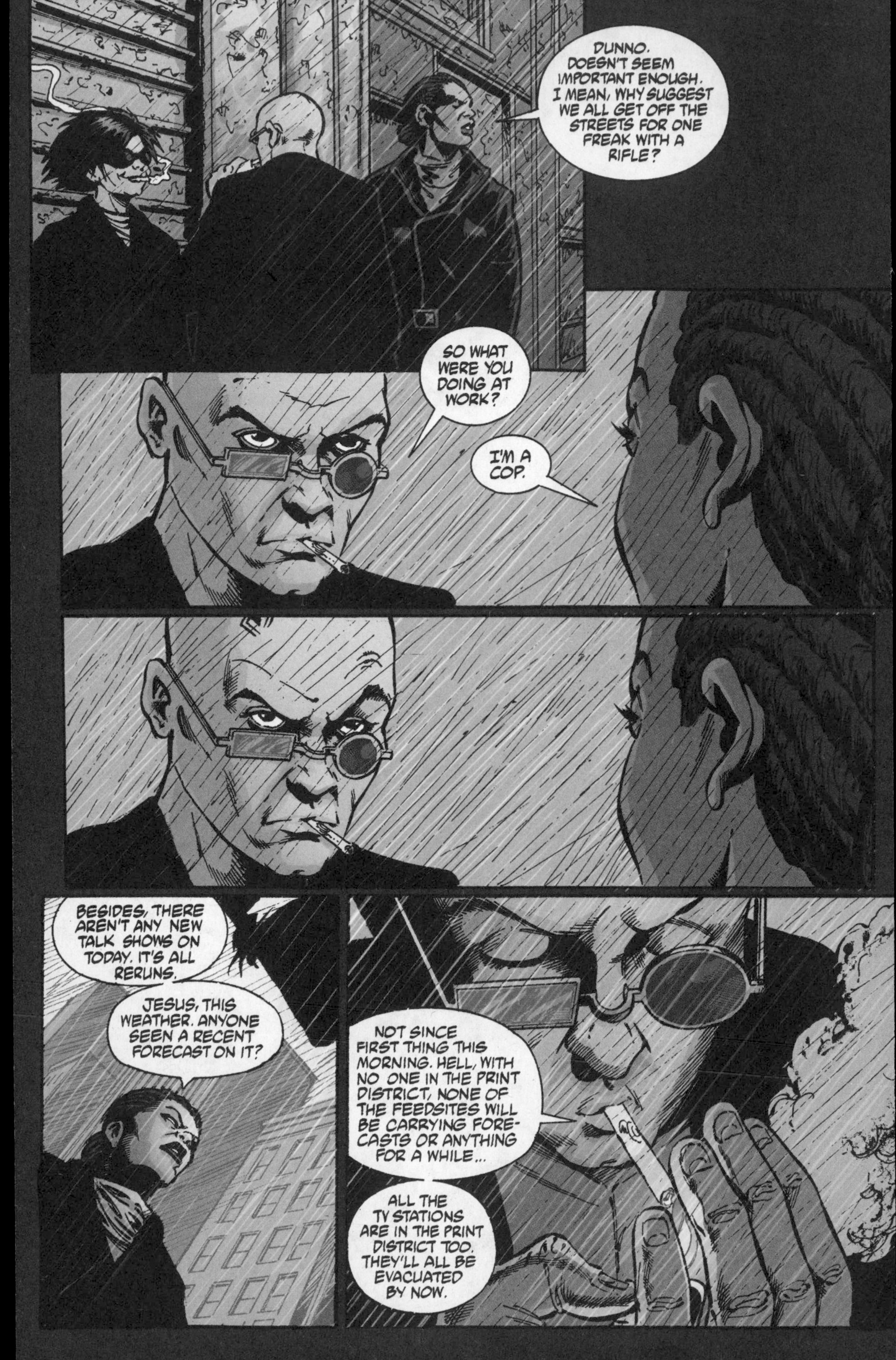
DUNNO. DOESN'T SEEM IMPORTANT ENOUGH. I MEAN, WHY SUGGEST WE ALL GET OFF THE STREETS FOR ONE FREAK WITH A RIFLE?
SO WHAT WERE YOU DOING AT WORK?
I'M A COP.
BESIDES, THERE AREN'T ANY NEW TALK SHOWS ON TODAY. IT'S ALL RERUNS.
JESUS, THIS WEATHER. ANYONE SEEN A RECENT FORECAST ON IT?
NOT SINCE FIRST THING THIS MORNING. HELL, WITH NO ONE IN THE PRINT DISTRICT, NONE OF THE FEEDSITES WILL BE CARRYING FORE-CASTS OR ANYTHING FOR A WHILE...
ALL THE TV STATIONS ARE IN THE PRINT DISTRICT TOO. THEY'LL ALL BE EVACUATED BY NOW.

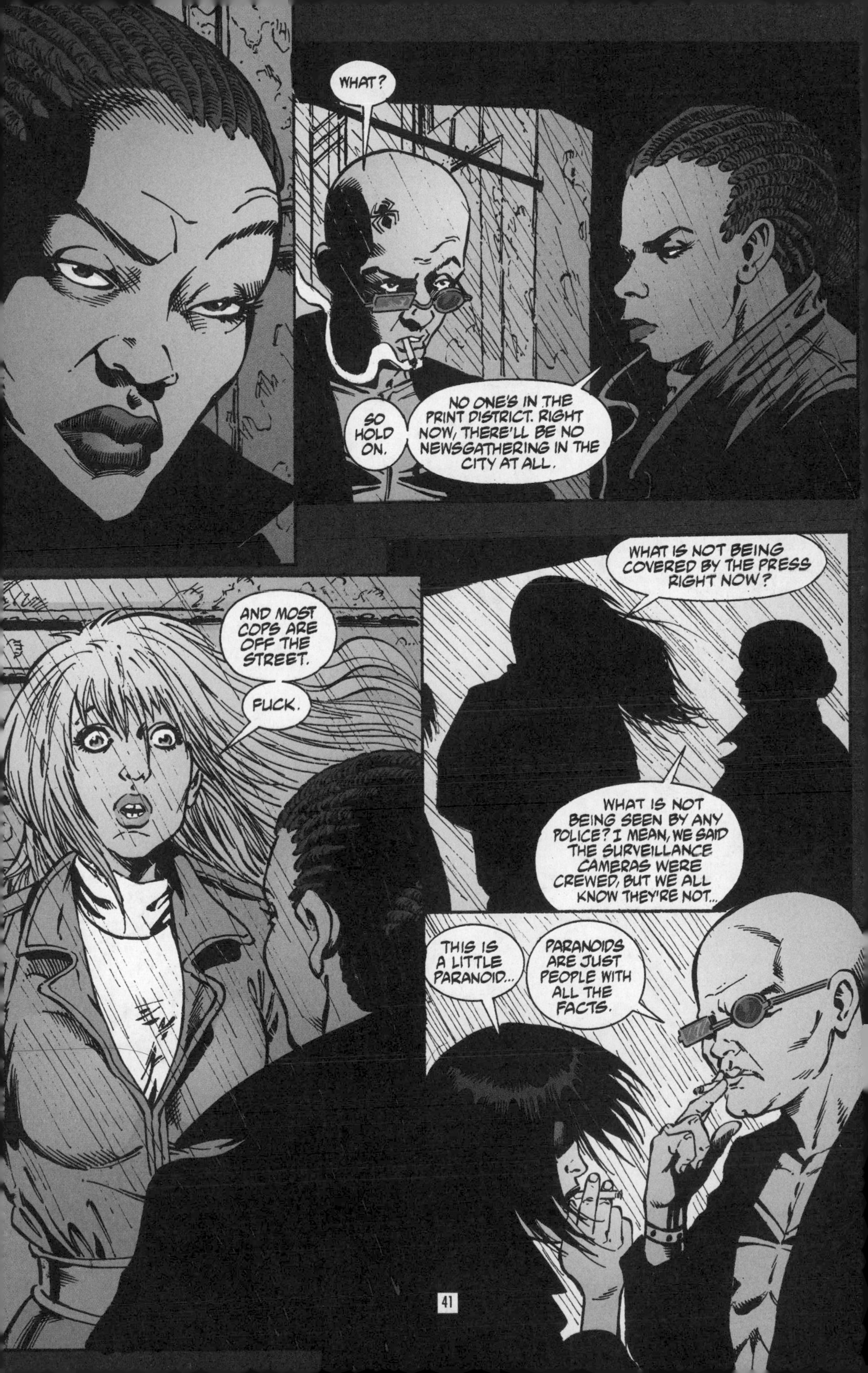
WHAT?
NO ONE'S IN THE PRINT DISTRICT. RIGHT NOW, THERE'LL BE NO NEWSGATHERING IN THE CITY AT ALL.
SO HOLD ON.
AND MOST COPS ARE OFF THE STREET.
FUCK.
WHAT IS NOT BEING COVERED BY THE PRESS RIGHT NOW?
WHAT IS NOT BEING SEEN BY ANY POLICE? I MEAN, WE SAID THE SURVEILLANCE CAMERAS WERE CREWED, BUT WE ALL KNOW THEY'RE NOT...
THIS IS A LITTLE PARANOID...
PARANOIDS ARE JUST PEOPLE WITH ALL THE FACTS.

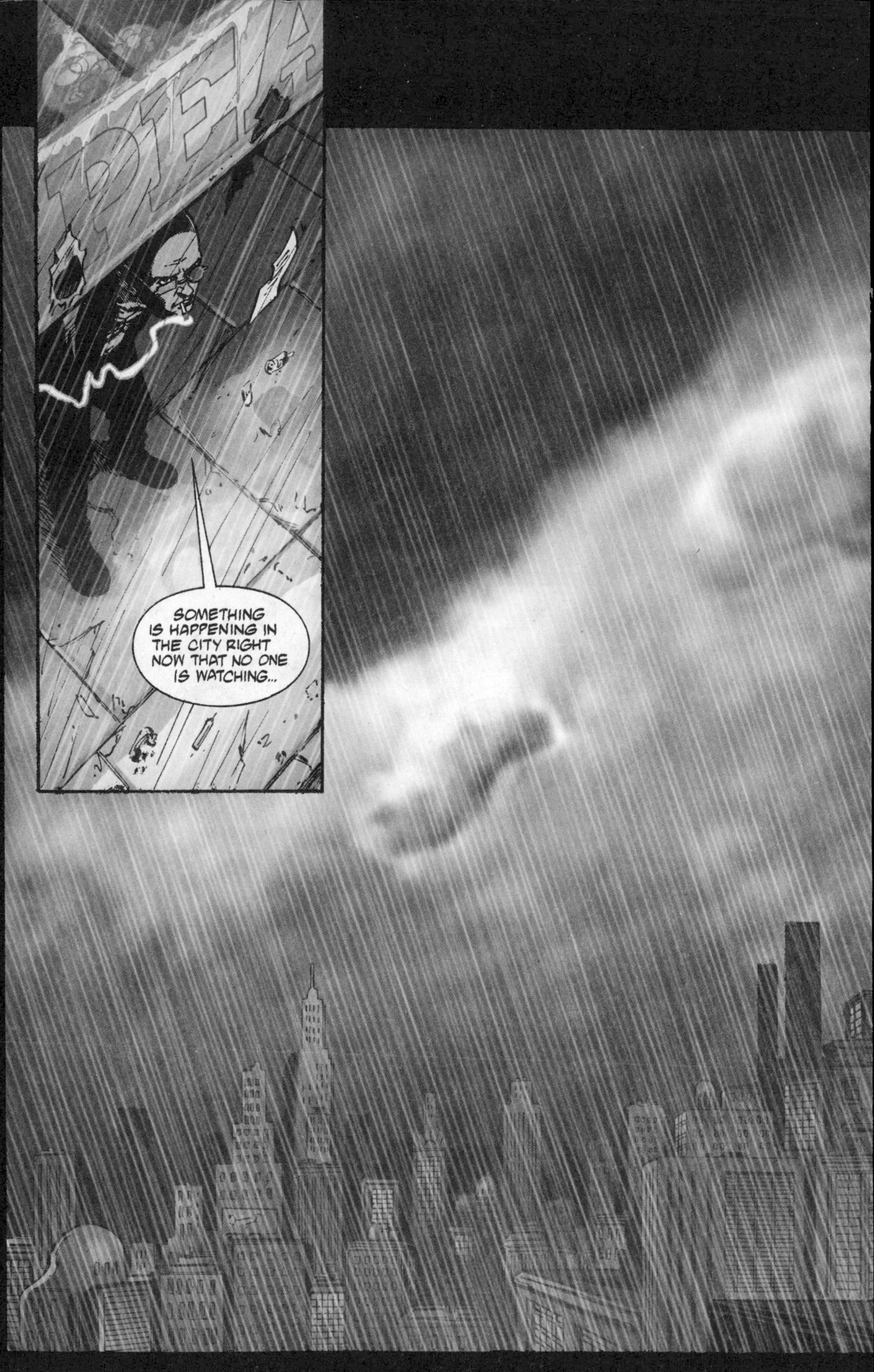
SOMETHING IS HAPPENING IN THE CITY RIGHT NOW THAT NO ONE IS WATCHING...

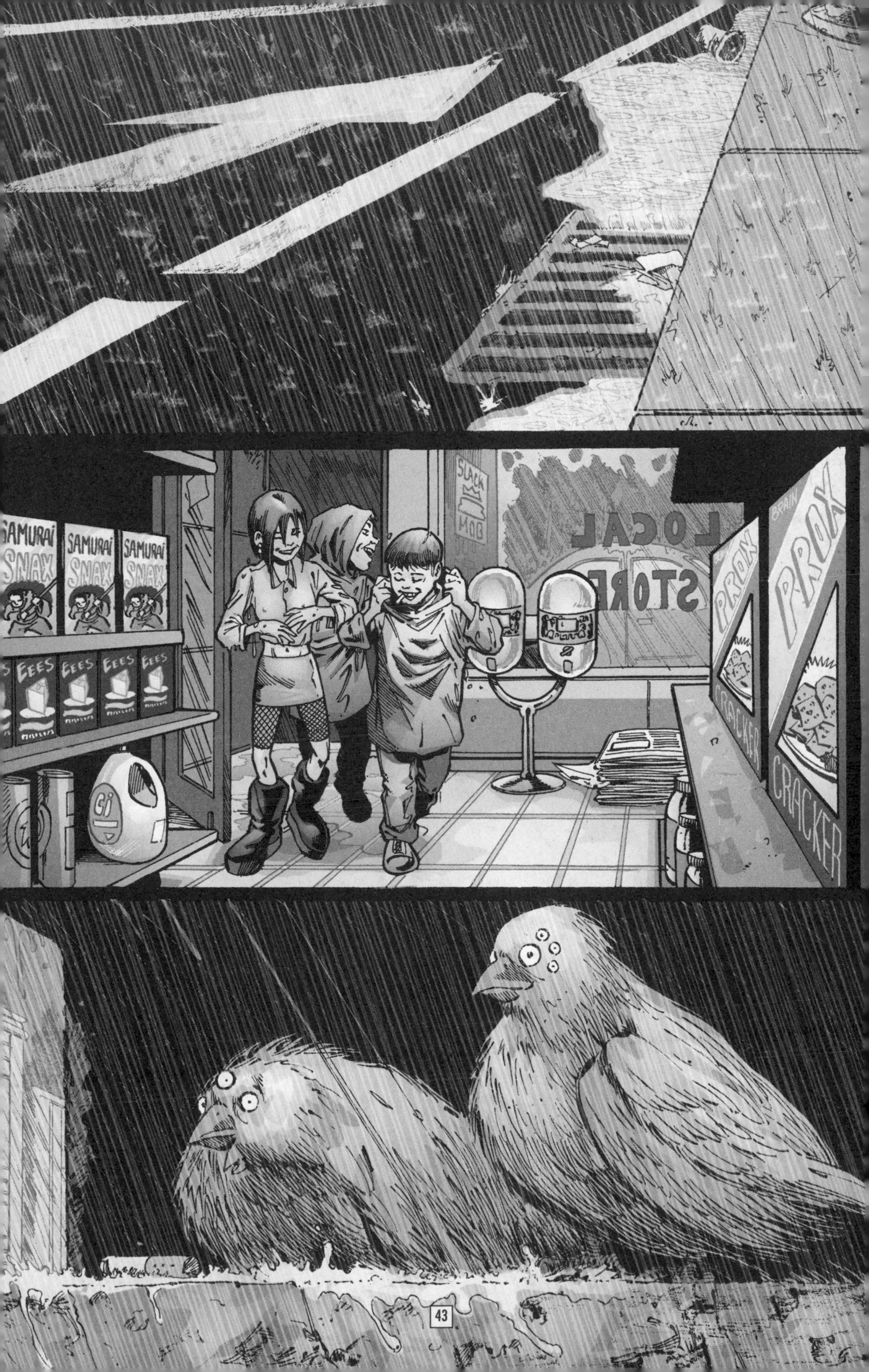
SAMURAI SNAX
SAMURAI SNAX
SAMURAI SNAX
EEES
EEES
EEES
SLACK MOB
LOCAL STORE
BRAIN PROX
PROX
CRACKER
CRACKER

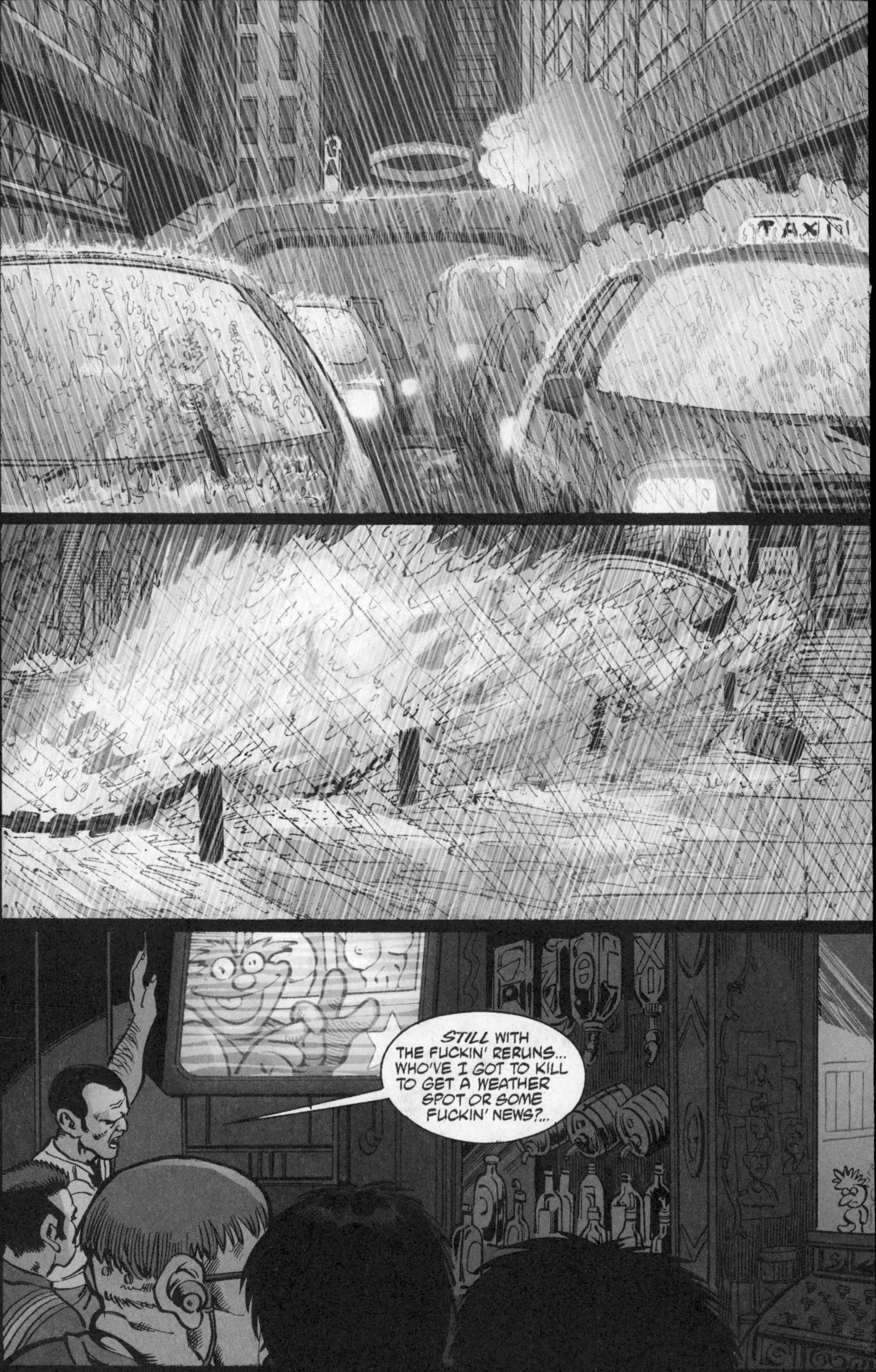
TAXI
STILL WITH THE FUCKIN' RERUNS... WHO'VE I GOT TO KILL TO GET A WEATHER SPOT OR SOME FUCKIN' NEWS?...

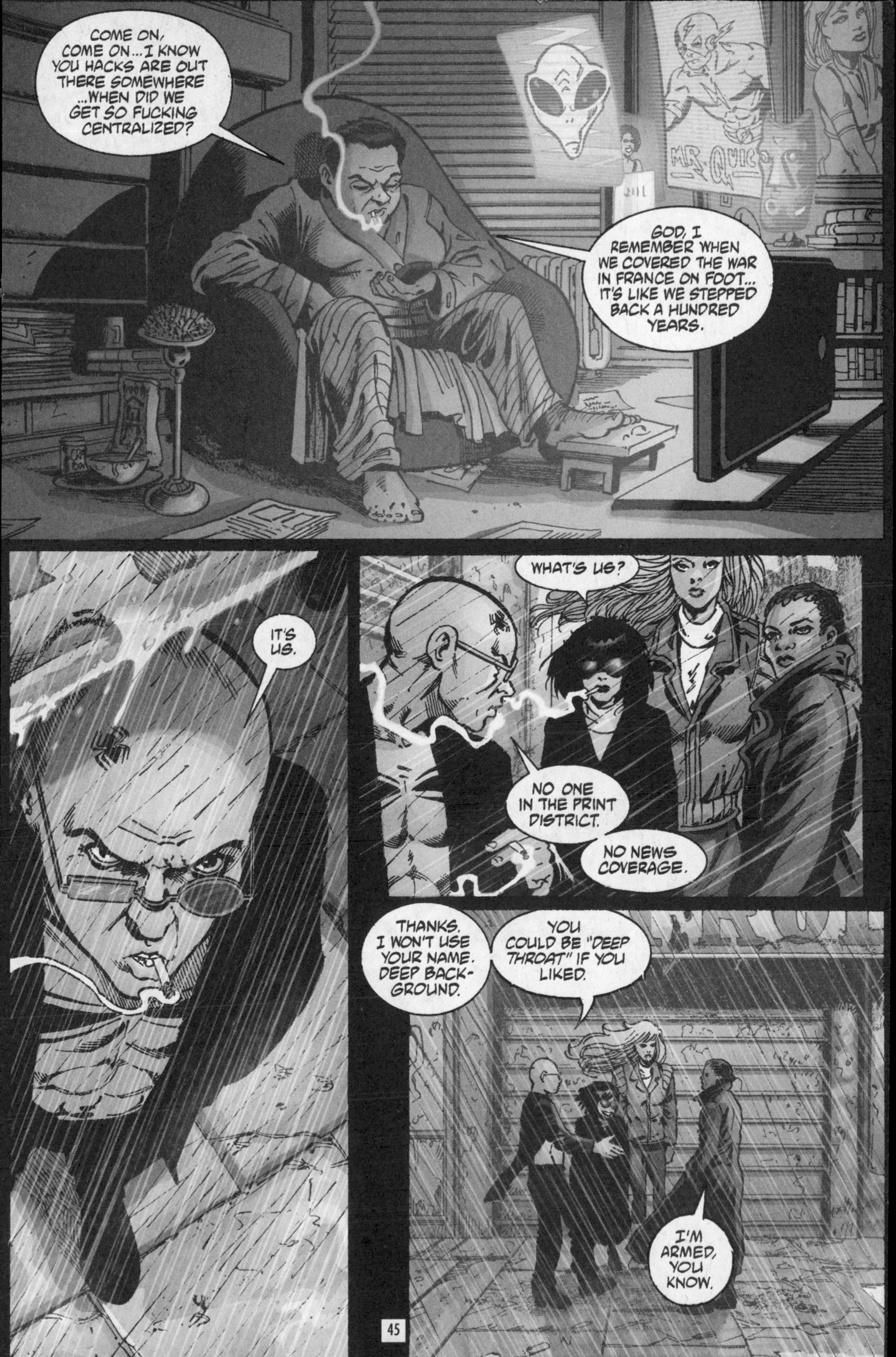
COME ON, COME ON...I KNOW YOU HACKS ARE OUT THERE SOMEWHERE ...WHEN DID WE GET SO FUCKING CENTRALIZED?
MR. QUIC
GOD, I REMEMBER WHEN WE COVERED THE WAR IN FRANCE ON FOOT... IT'S LIKE WE STEPPED BACK A HUNDRED YEARS.
IT'S US.
WHAT'S US?
NO ONE IN THE PRINT DISTRICT.
NO NEWS COVERAGE.
THANKS. I WON'T USE YOUR NAME. DEEP BACK-GROUND.
YOU COULD BE "DEEP THROAT" IF YOU LIKED.
I'M ARMED, YOU KNOW.

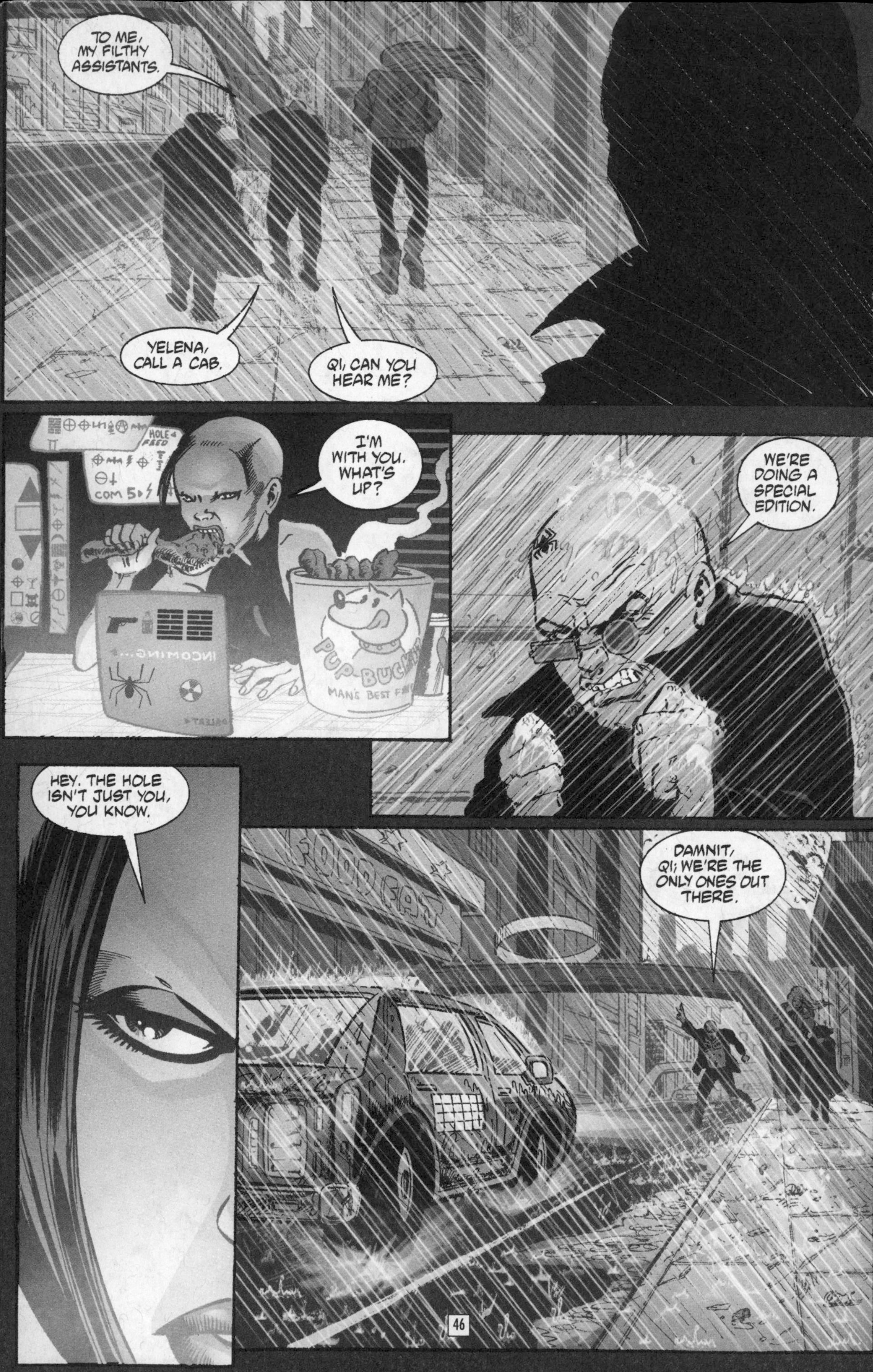
TO ME, MY FILTHY ASSISTANTS.
YELENA, CALL A CAB.
QI, CAN YOU HEAR ME?
HOLE FEED
COM 5
I'M WITH YOU. WHAT'S UP?
INCOMING...
PUP-BUCK
MAN'S BEST F
WE'RE DOING A SPECIAL EDITION.
HEY. THE HOLE ISN'T JUST YOU, YOU KNOW.
DAMNIT, QI; WE'RE THE ONLY ONES OUT THERE.

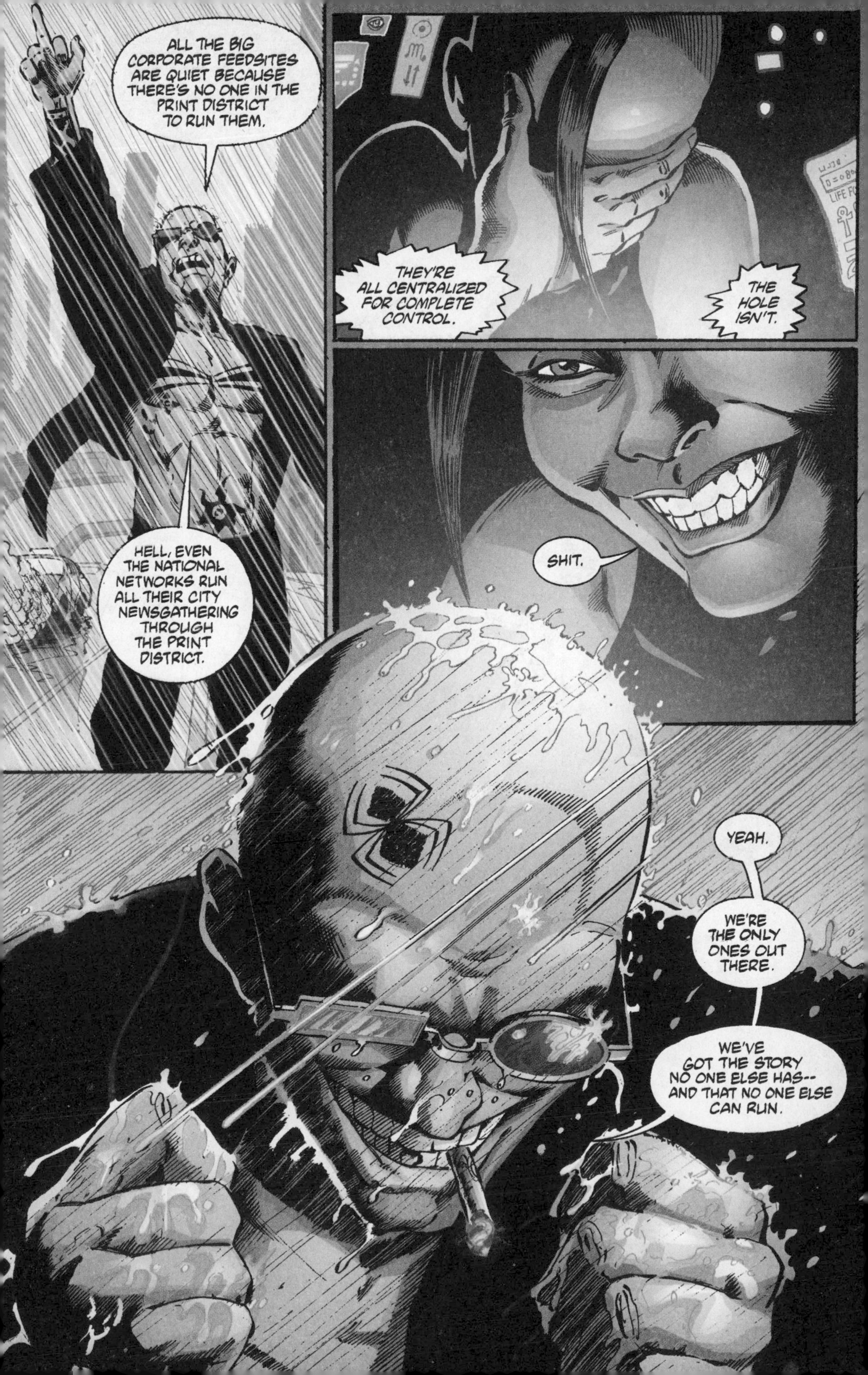
ALL THE BIG CORPORATE FEEDSITES ARE QUIET BECAUSE THERE'S NO ONE IN THE PRINT DISTRICT TO RUN THEM.
THEY'RE ALL CENTRALIZED FOR COMPLETE CONTROL.
THE HOLE ISN'T.
HELL, EVEN THE NATIONAL NETWORKS RUN ALL THEIR CITY NEWSGATHERING THROUGH THE PRINT DISTRICT.
SHIT.
YEAH.
WE'RE THE ONLY ONES OUT THERE.
WE'VE GOT THE STORY NO ONE ELSE HAS-- AND THAT NO ONE ELSE CAN RUN.

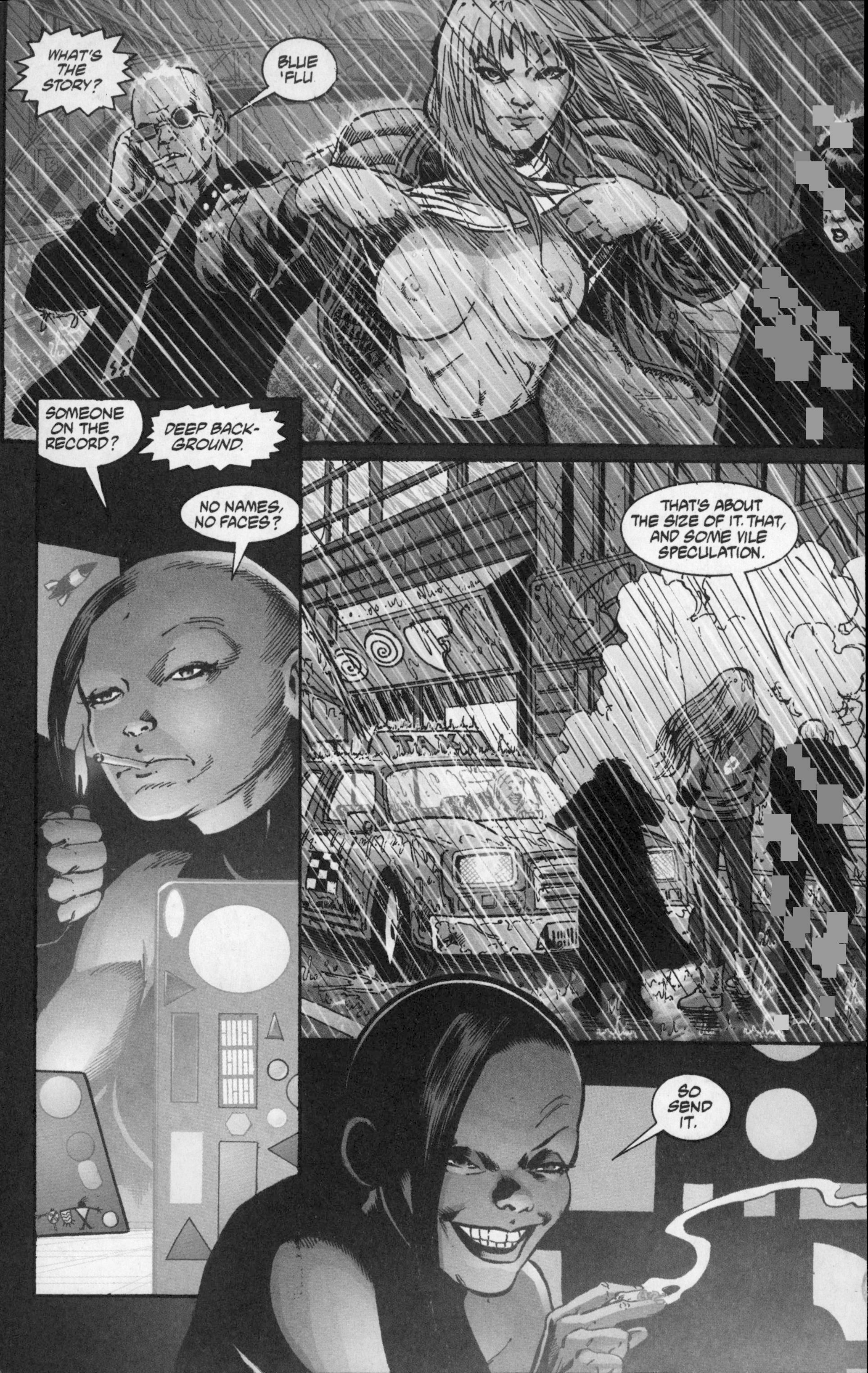
WHAT'S THE STORY?
BLUE 'FLU
SOMEONE ON THE RECORD?
DEEP BACK-GROUND.
NO NAMES, NO FACES?
THAT'S ABOUT THE SIZE OF IT. THAT, AND SOME VILE SPECULATION.
TAXI
SO SEND IT.

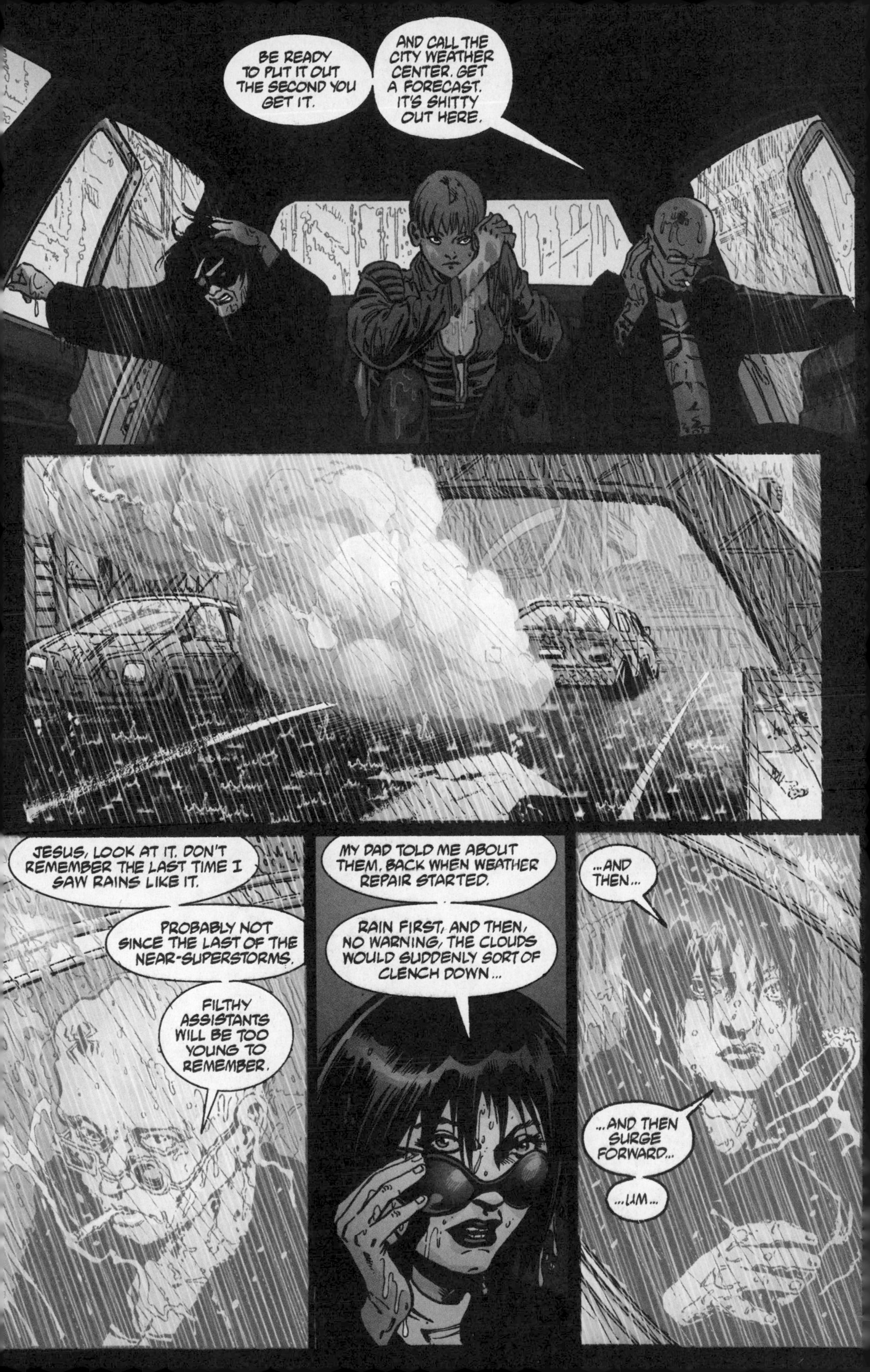
BE READY TO PUT IT OUT THE SECOND YOU GET IT.
AND CALL THE CITY WEATHER CENTER. GET A FORECAST. IT'S SHITTY OUT HERE.
JESUS, LOOK AT IT. DON'T REMEMBER THE LAST TIME I SAW RAINS LIKE IT.
PROBABLY NOT SINCE THE LAST OF THE NEAR-SUPERSTORMS.
FILTHY ASSISTANTS WILL BE TOO YOUNG TO REMEMBER.
MY DAD TOLD ME ABOUT THEM, BACK WHEN WEATHER REPAIR STARTED.
RAIN FIRST, AND THEN, NO WARNING, THE CLOUDS WOULD SUDDENLY SORT OF CLENCH DOWN...
...AND THEN...
...AND THEN SURGE FORWARD...
...UM...

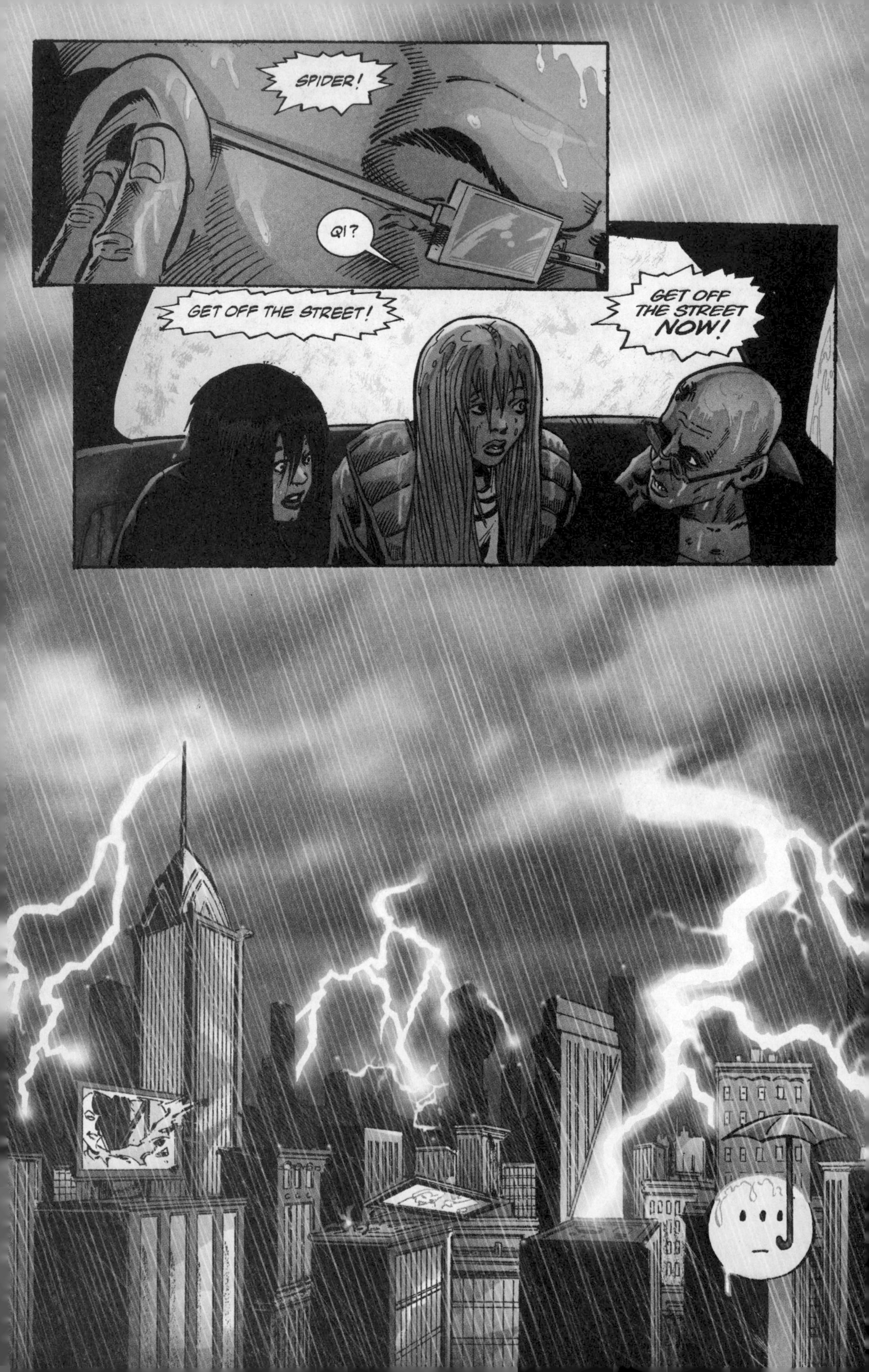
SPIDER!
QI?
GET OFF THE STREET!
GET OFF THE STREET NOW!

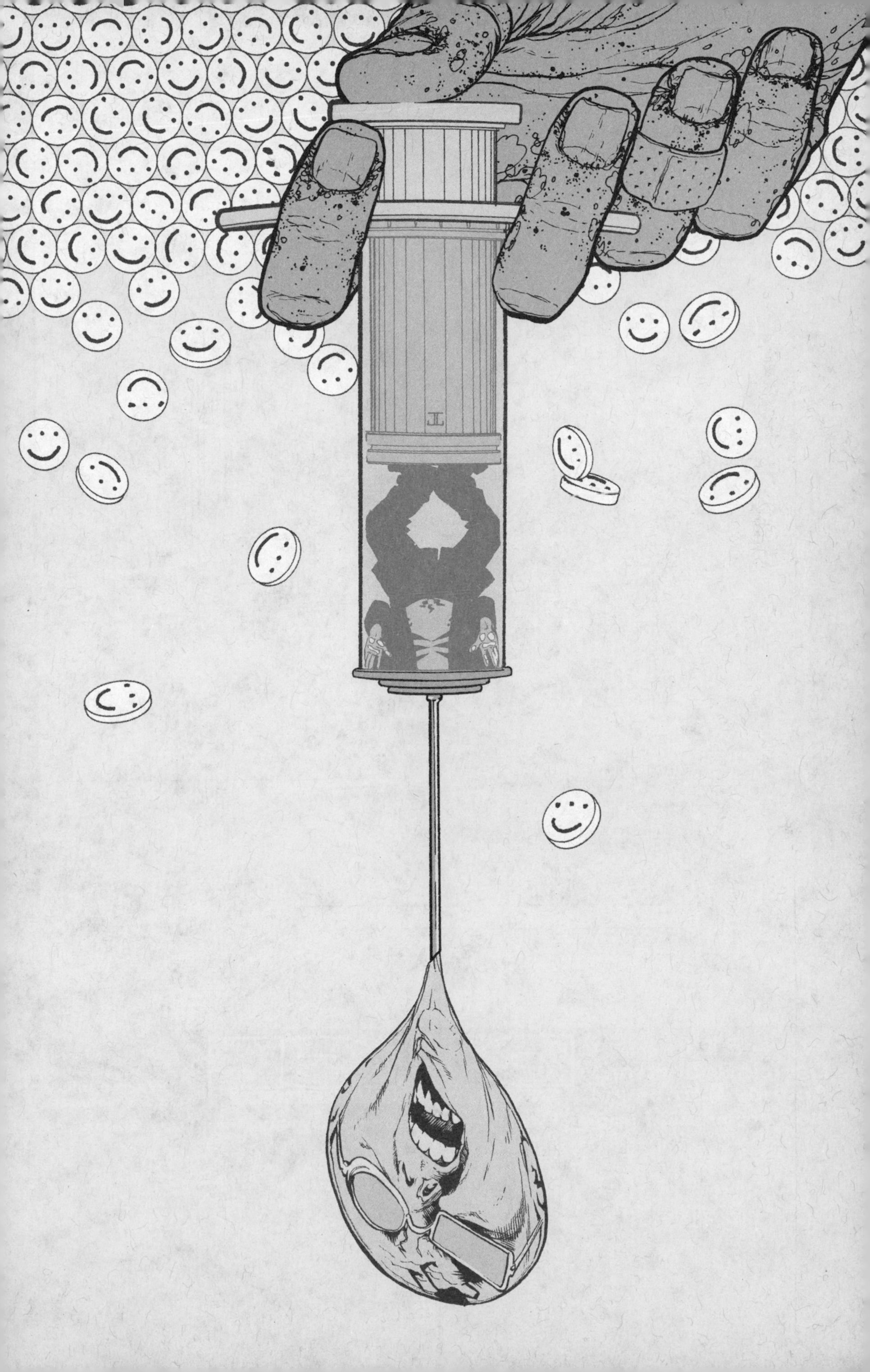

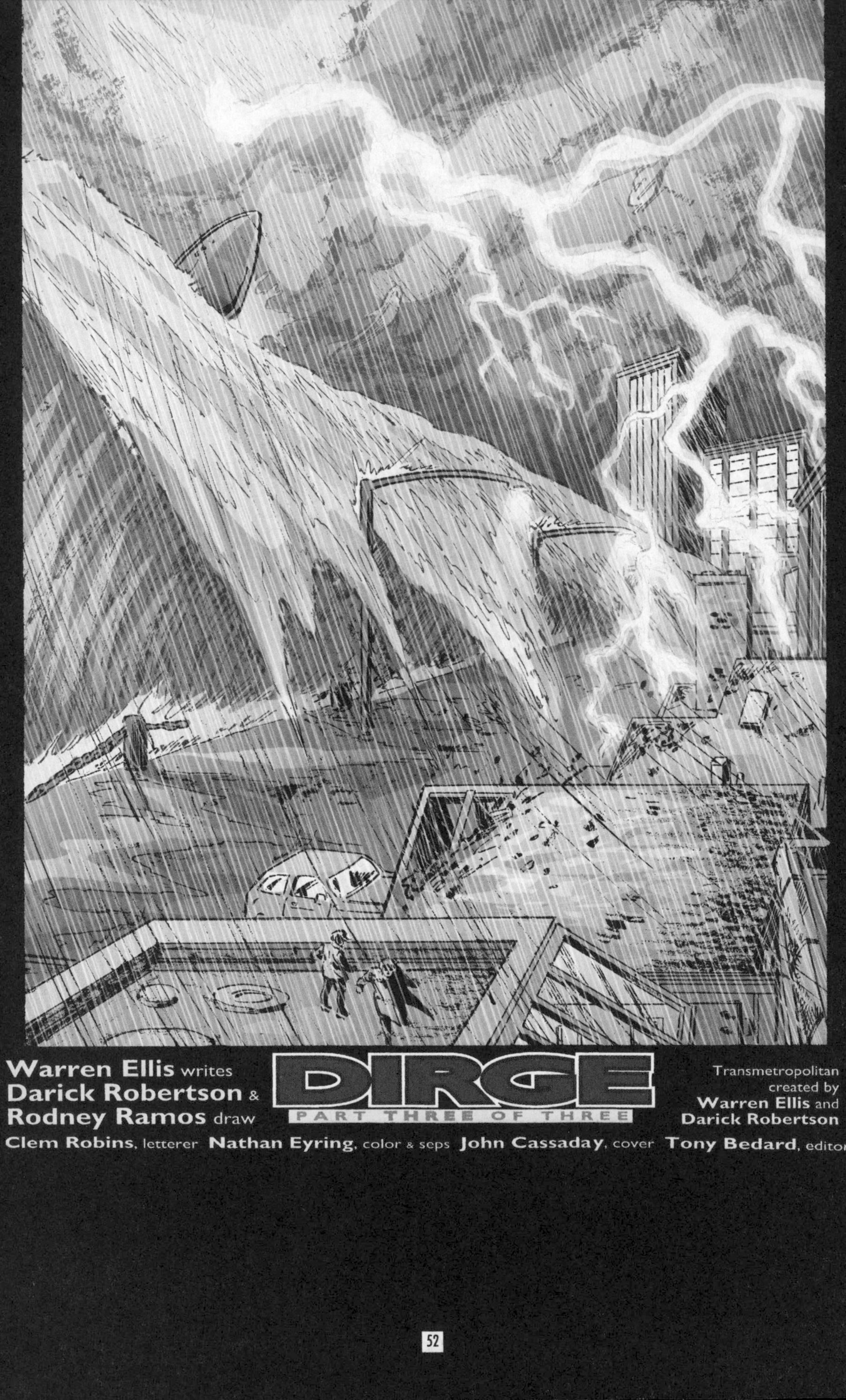

Warren Ellis writes
Darick Robertson &
Rodney Ramos draw

DIRGE
PART THREE OF THREE

Transmetropolitan
created by
Warren Ellis and
Darick Robertson

Clem Robins, letterer **Nathan Eyring**, color & seps **John Cassaday**, cover **Tony Bedard**, editor

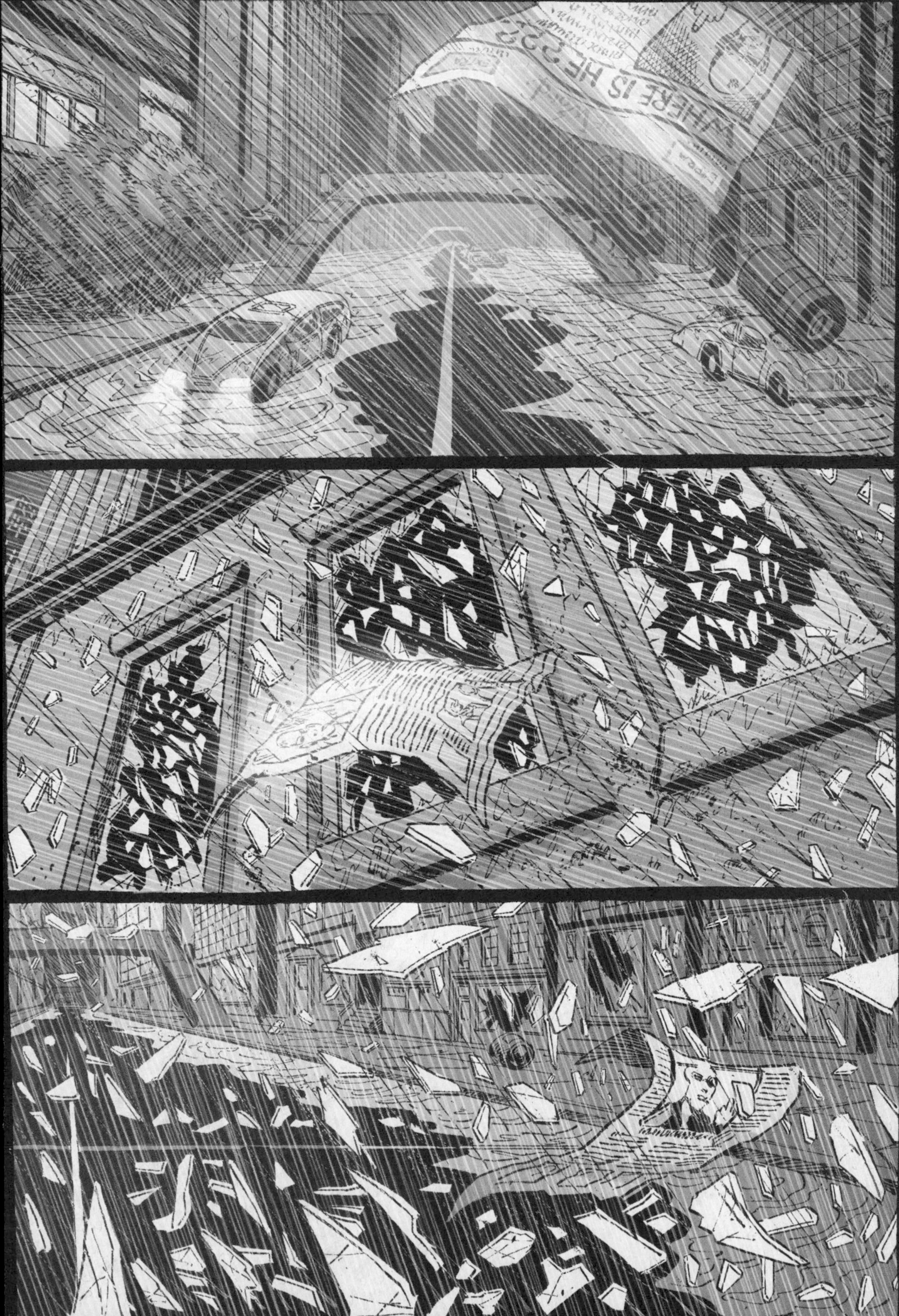

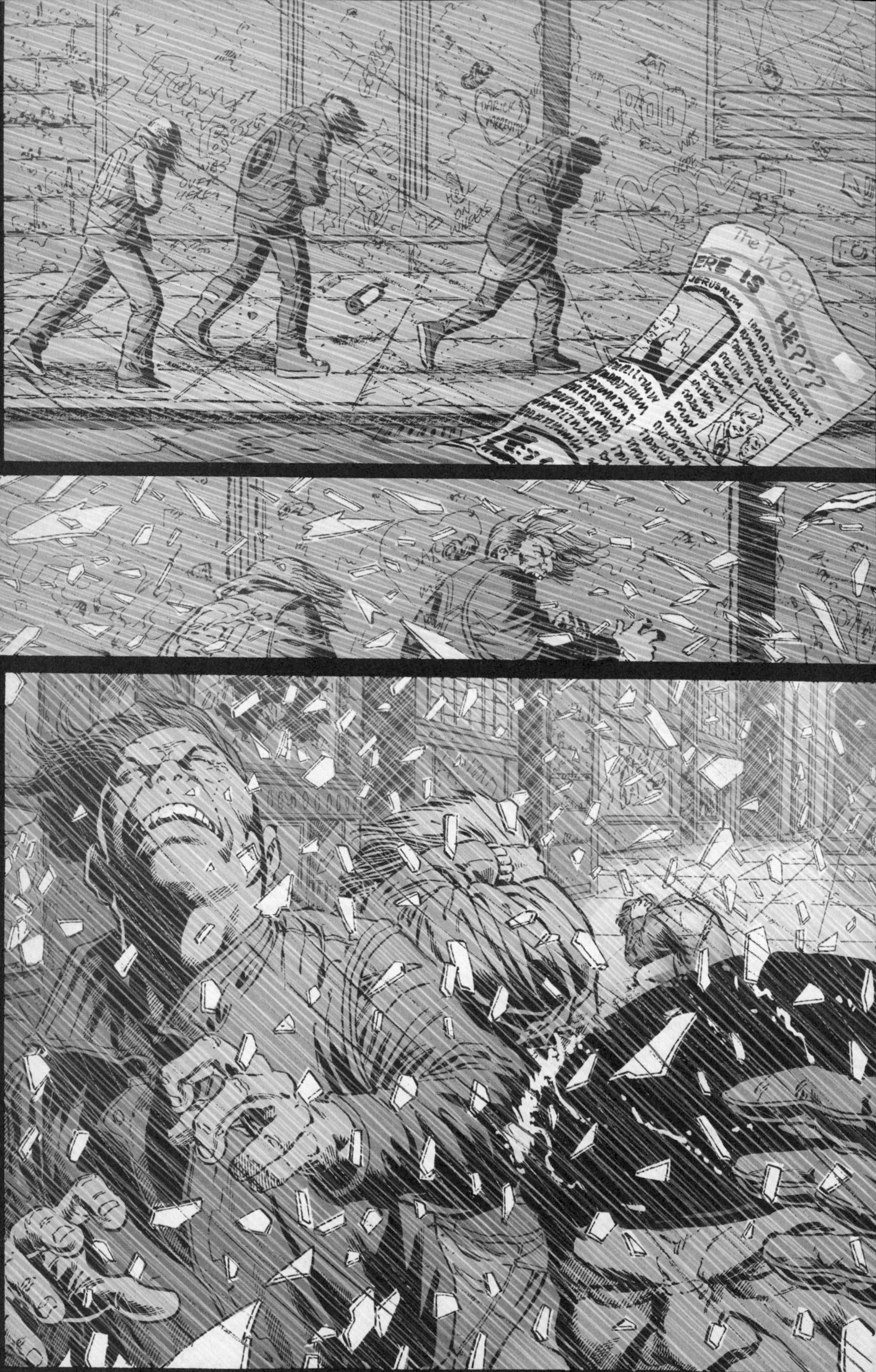
The Word
ERE IS HE??
JERUSALEM

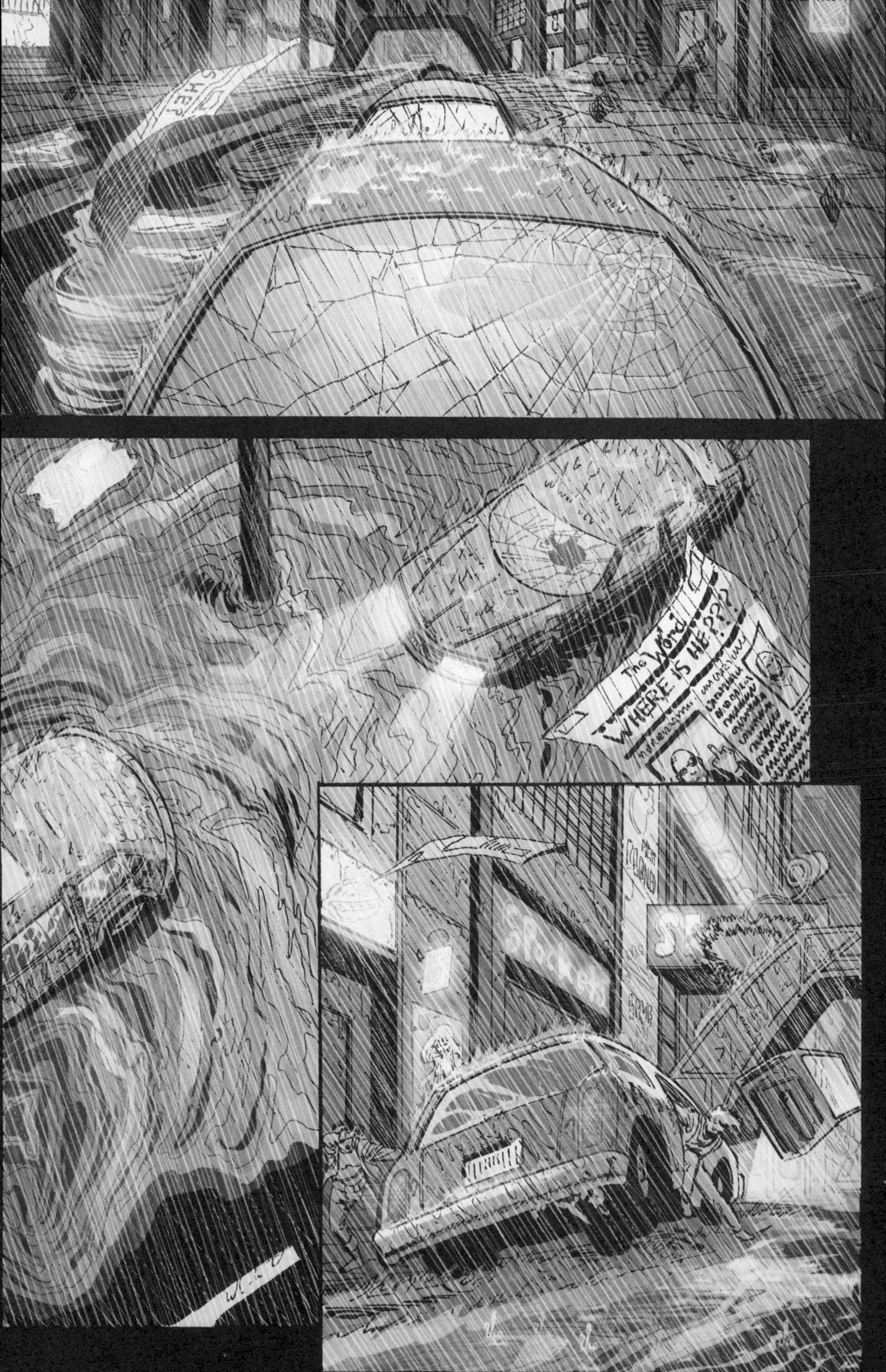
The Word
WHERE IS HE??

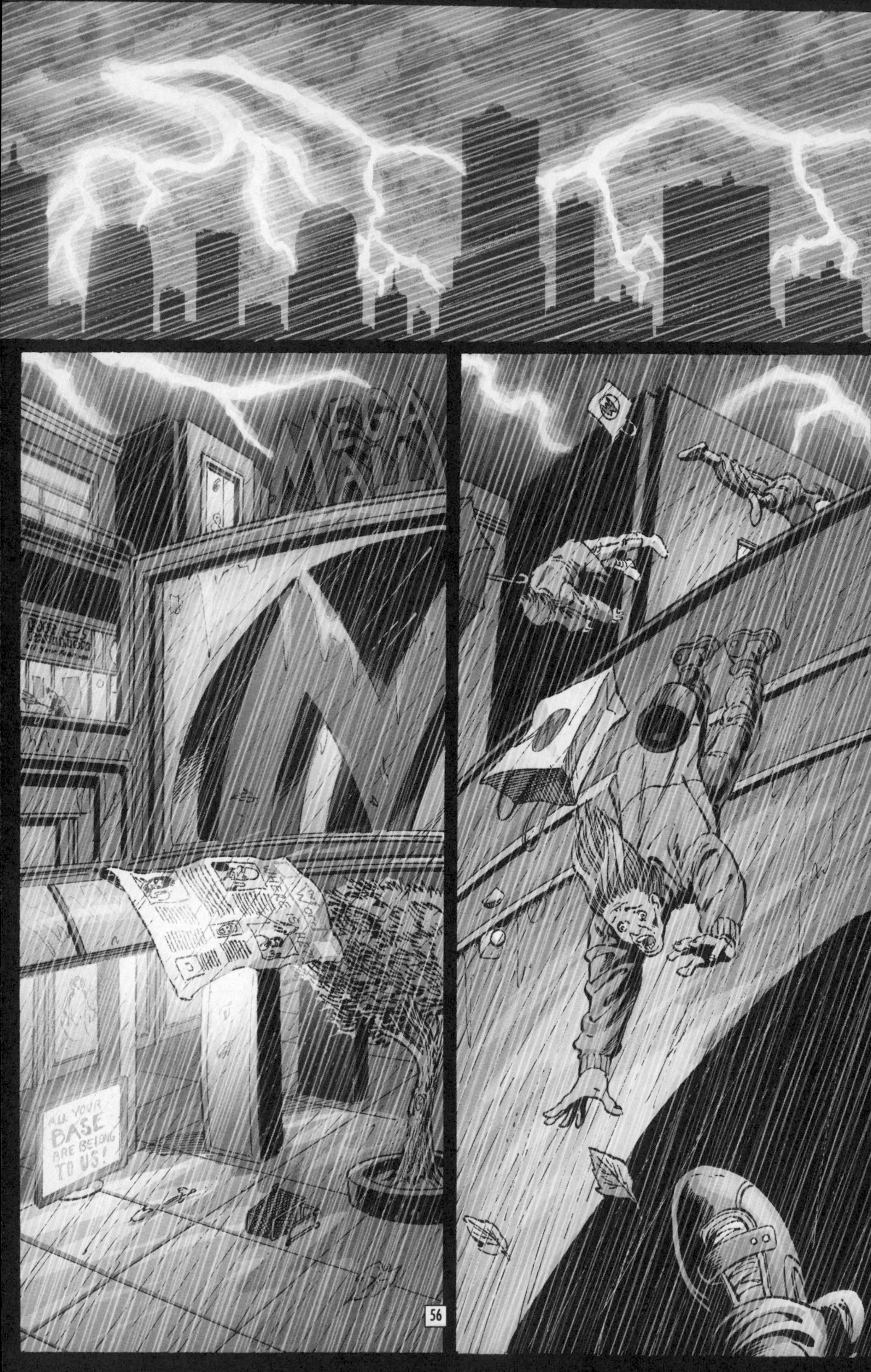
ALL YOUR
BASE
ARE BELONG
TO US!

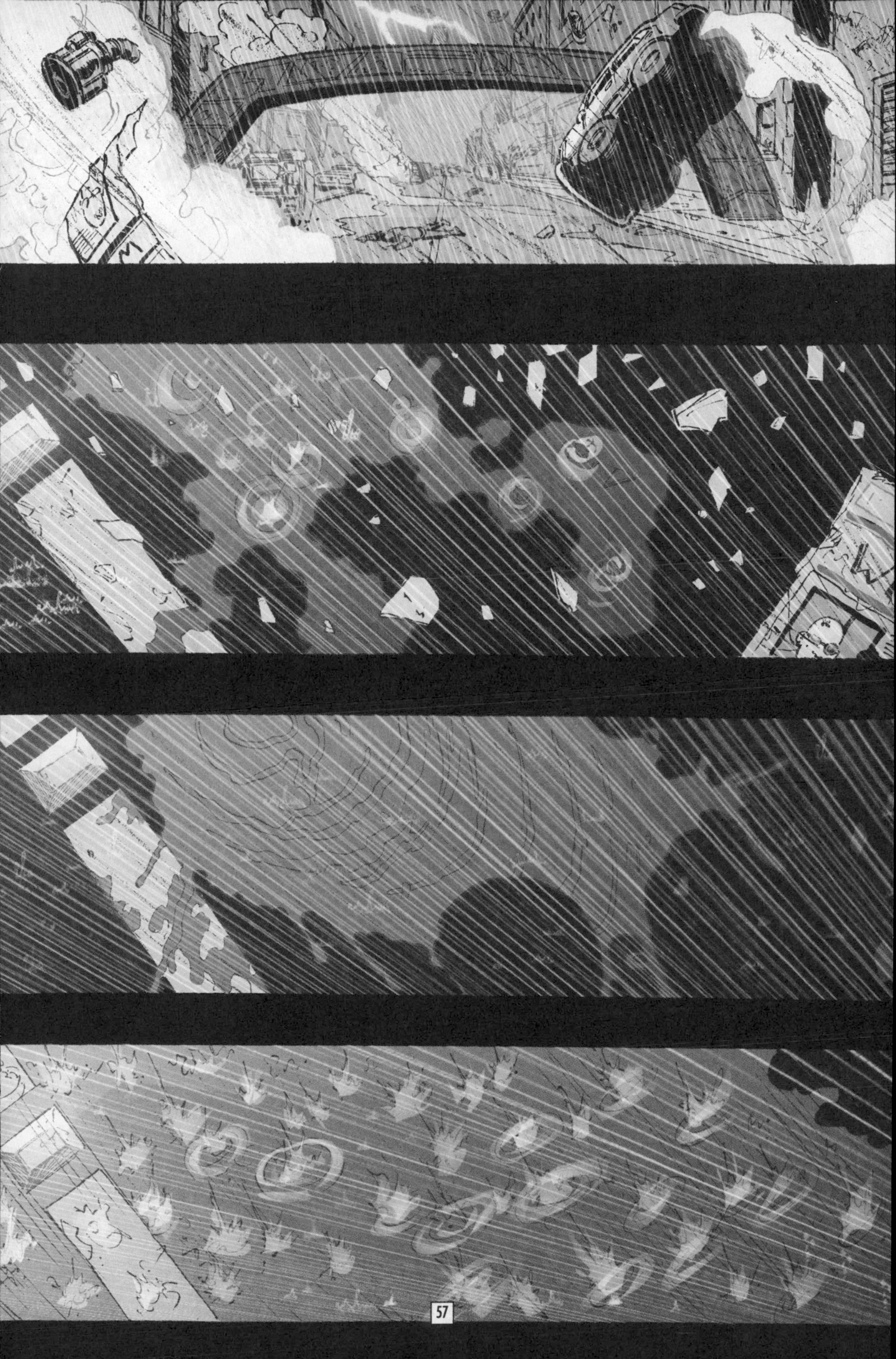

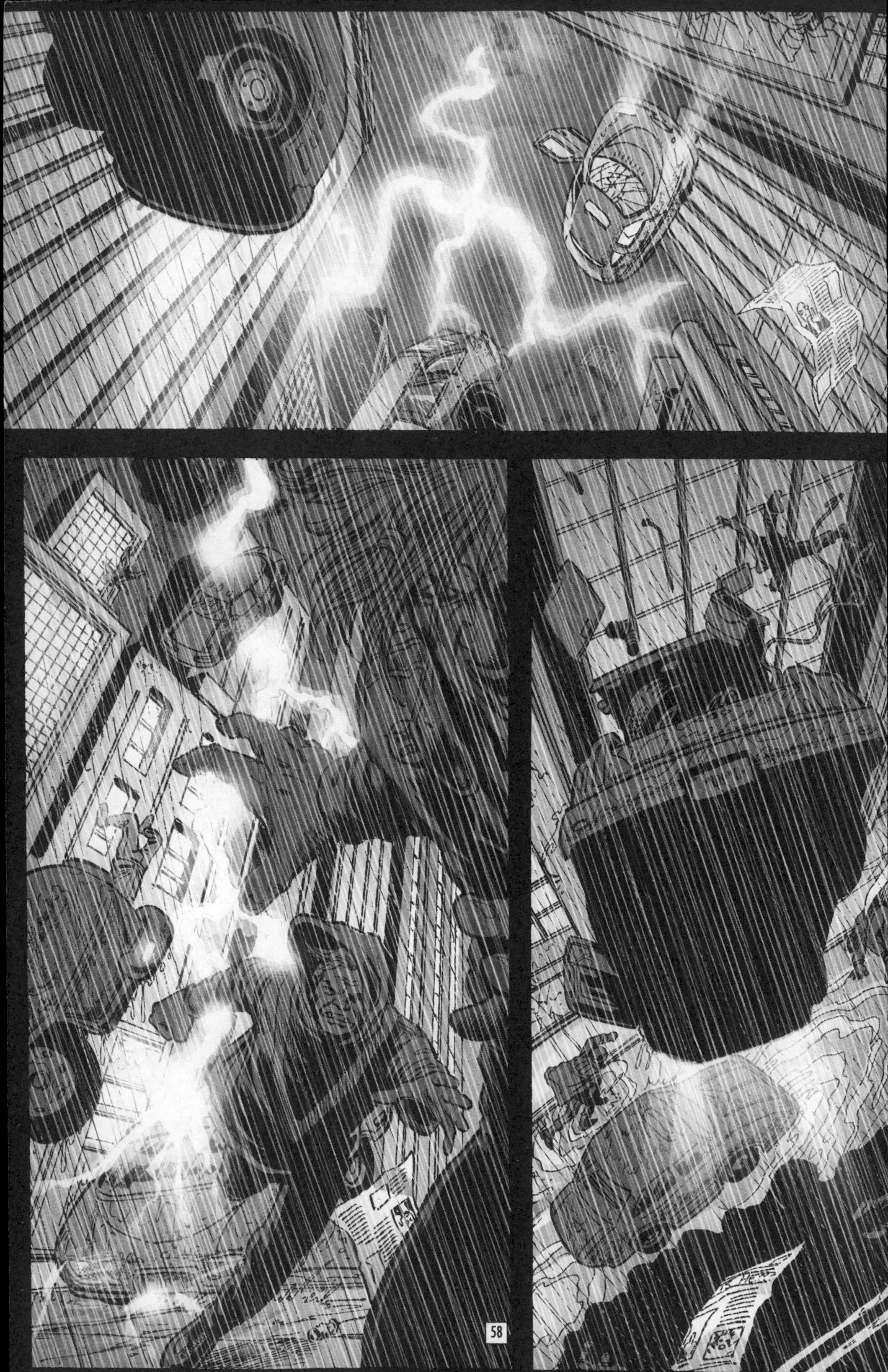

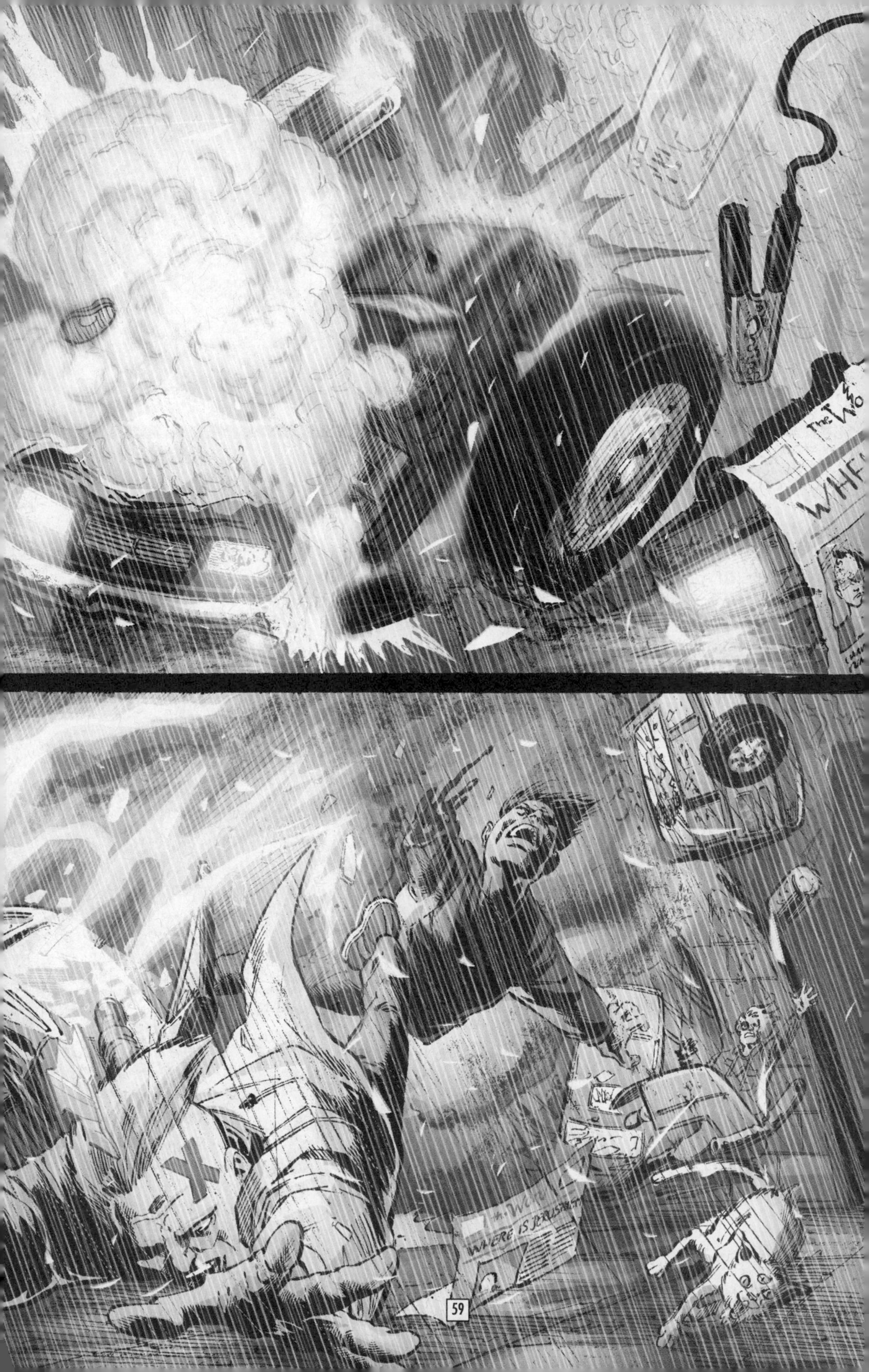
WHERE IS

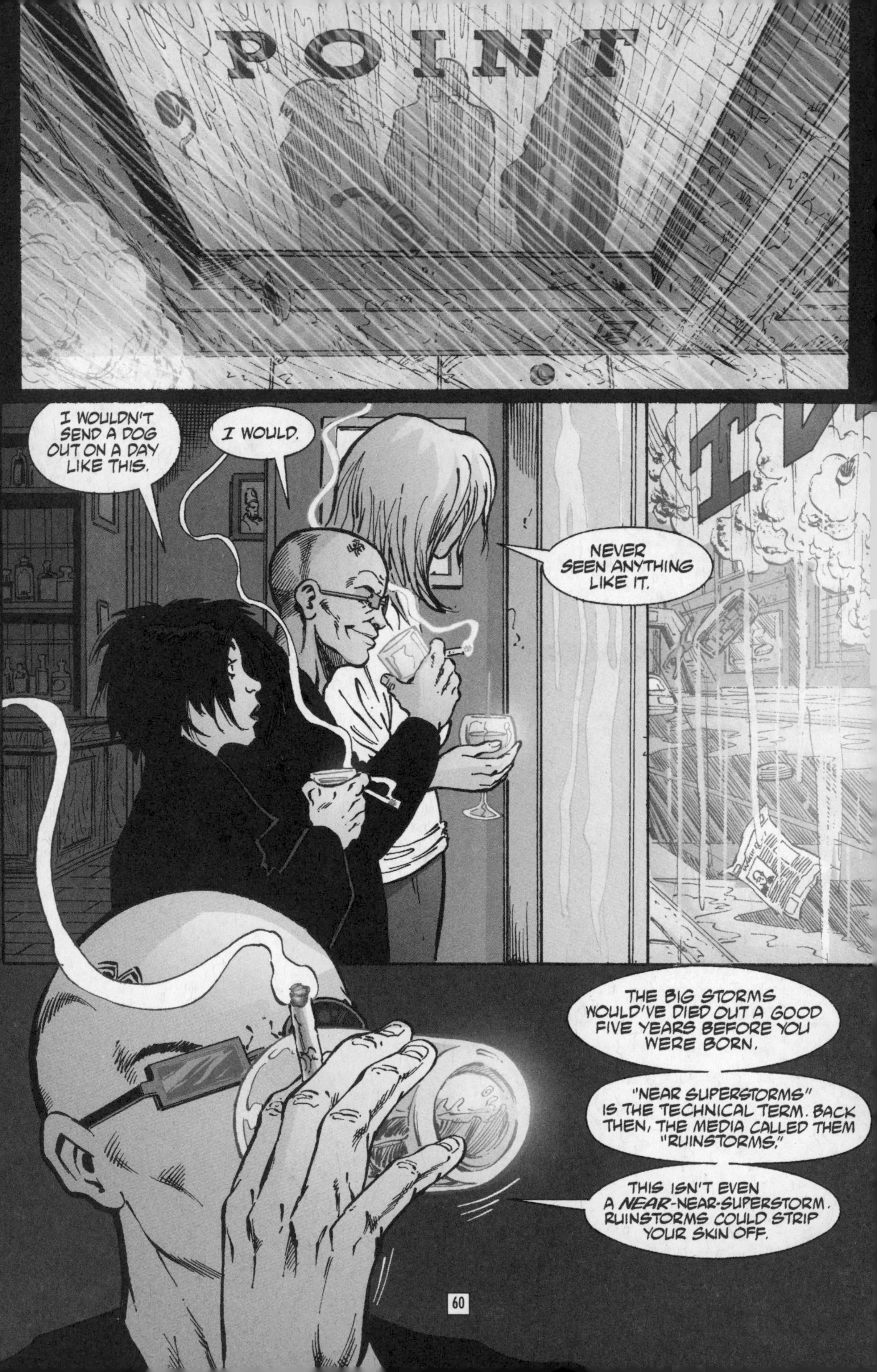
POINT
I WOULDN'T SEND A DOG OUT ON A DAY LIKE THIS.
I WOULD.
NEVER SEEN ANYTHING LIKE IT.
THE BIG STORMS WOULD'VE DIED OUT A GOOD FIVE YEARS BEFORE YOU WERE BORN.
"NEAR SUPERSTORMS" IS THE TECHNICAL TERM. BACK THEN, THE MEDIA CALLED THEM "RUINSTORMS."
THIS ISN'T EVEN A *NEAR*-NEAR-SUPERSTORM. RUINSTORMS COULD STRIP YOUR SKIN OFF.

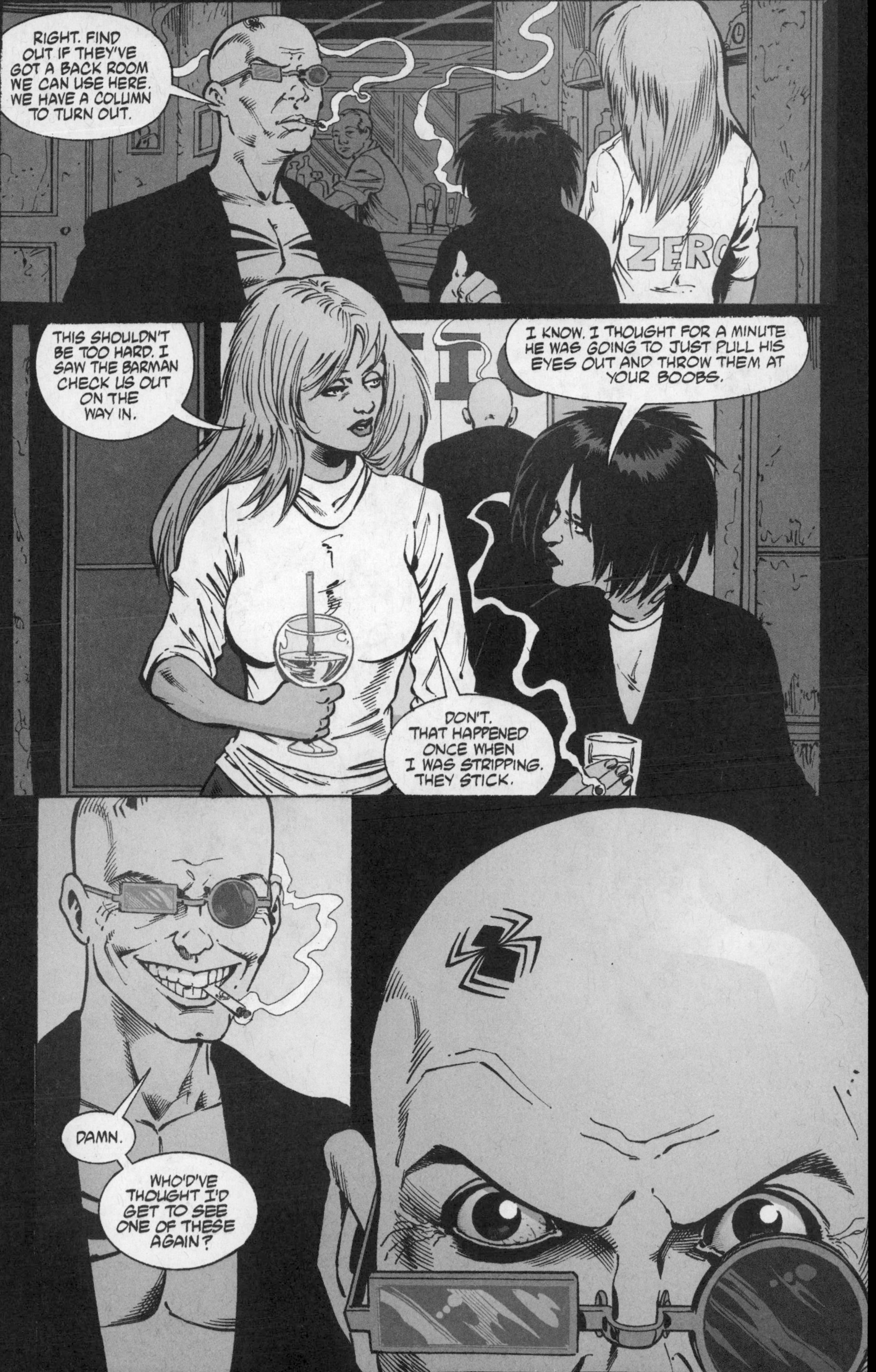

RIGHT. FIND OUT IF THEY'VE GOT A BACK ROOM WE CAN USE HERE. WE HAVE A COLUMN TO TURN OUT.
ZERO
THIS SHOULDN'T BE TOO HARD. I SAW THE BARMAN CHECK US OUT ON THE WAY IN.
I KNOW. I THOUGHT FOR A MINUTE HE WAS GOING TO JUST PULL HIS EYES OUT AND THROW THEM AT YOUR BOOBS.
DON'T. THAT HAPPENED ONCE WHEN I WAS STRIPPING. THEY STICK.
DAMN.
WHO'D'VE THOUGHT I'D GET TO SEE ONE OF THESE AGAIN?

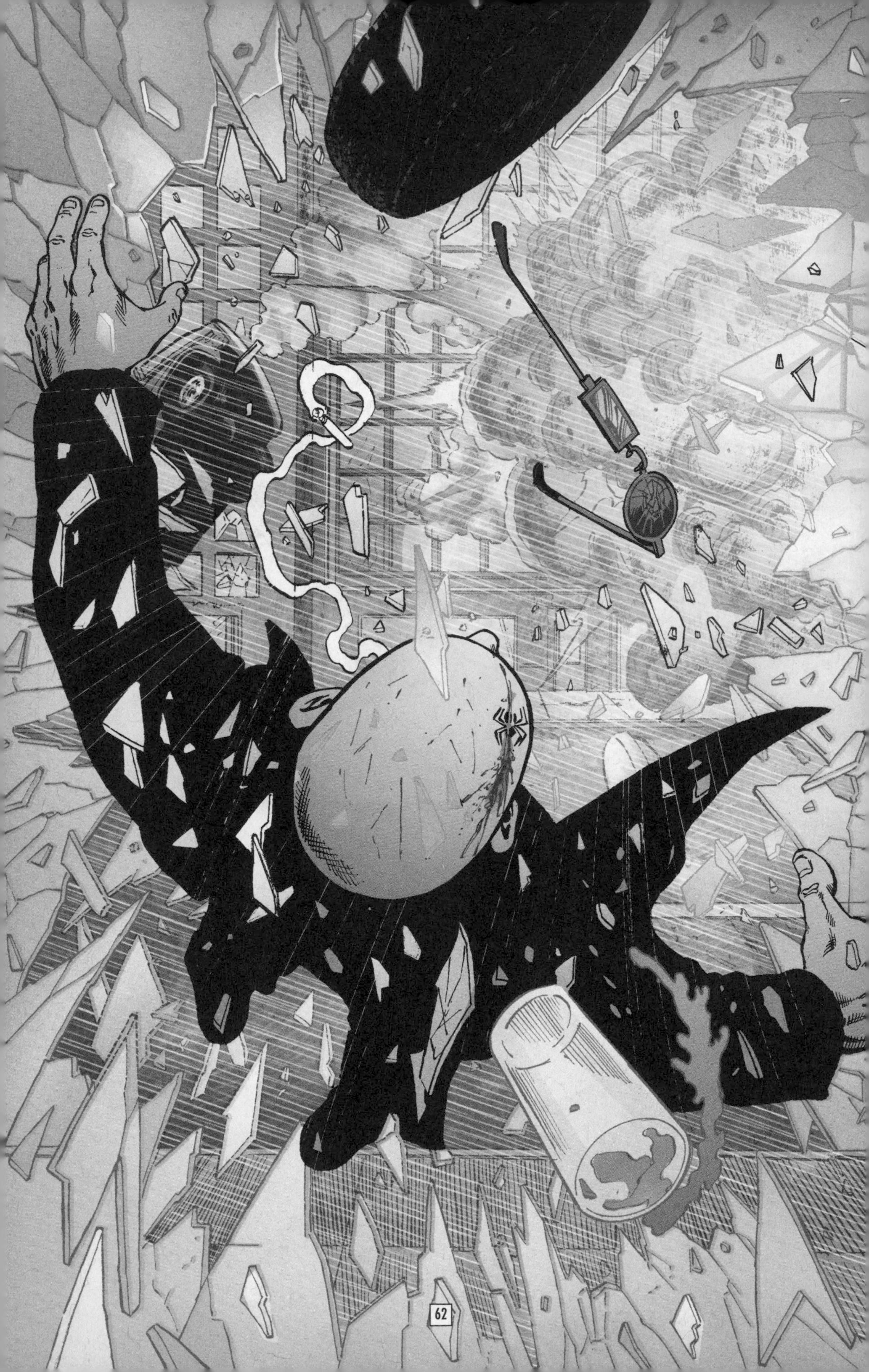

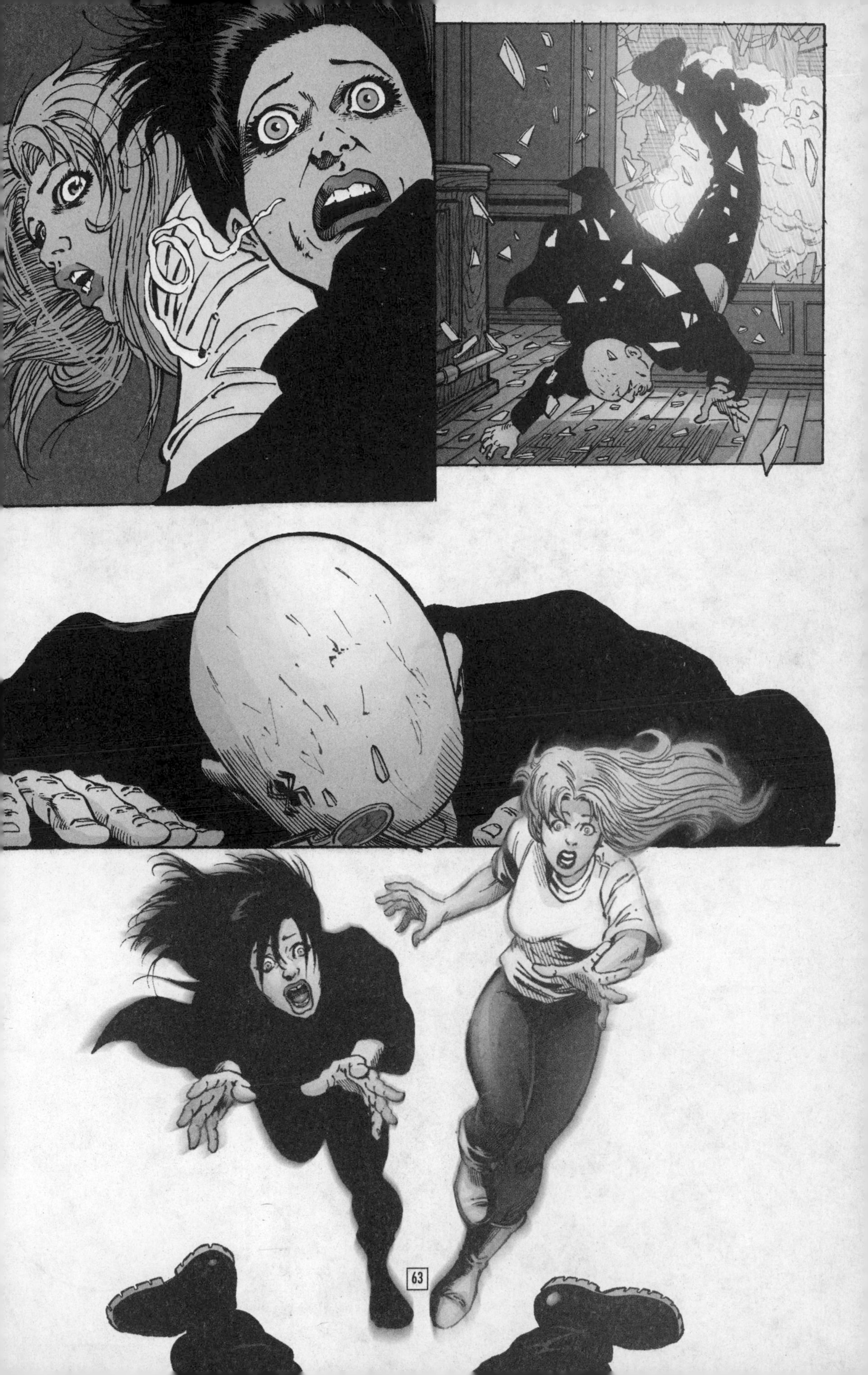

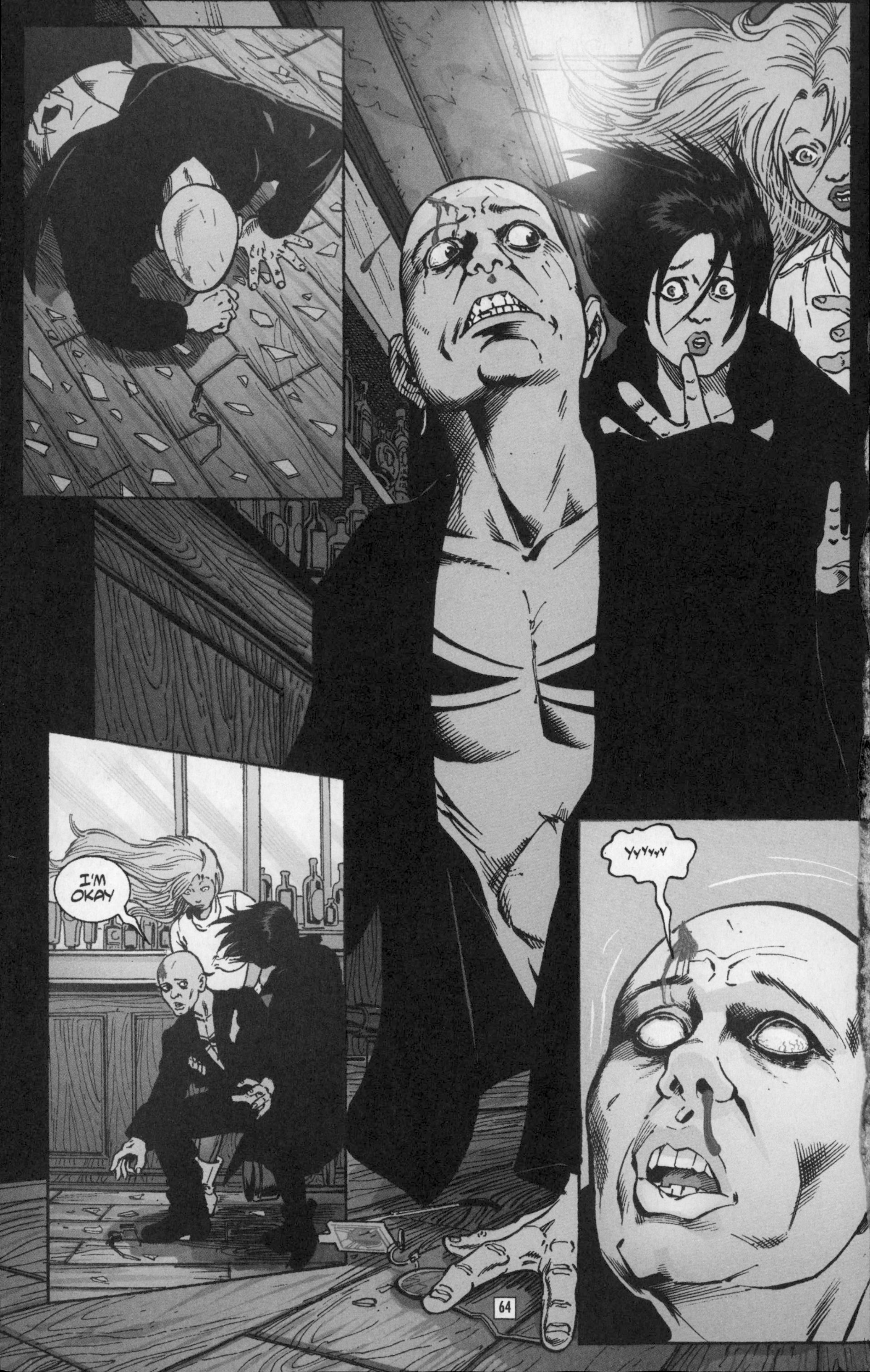

I'M OKAY
YYYYYY

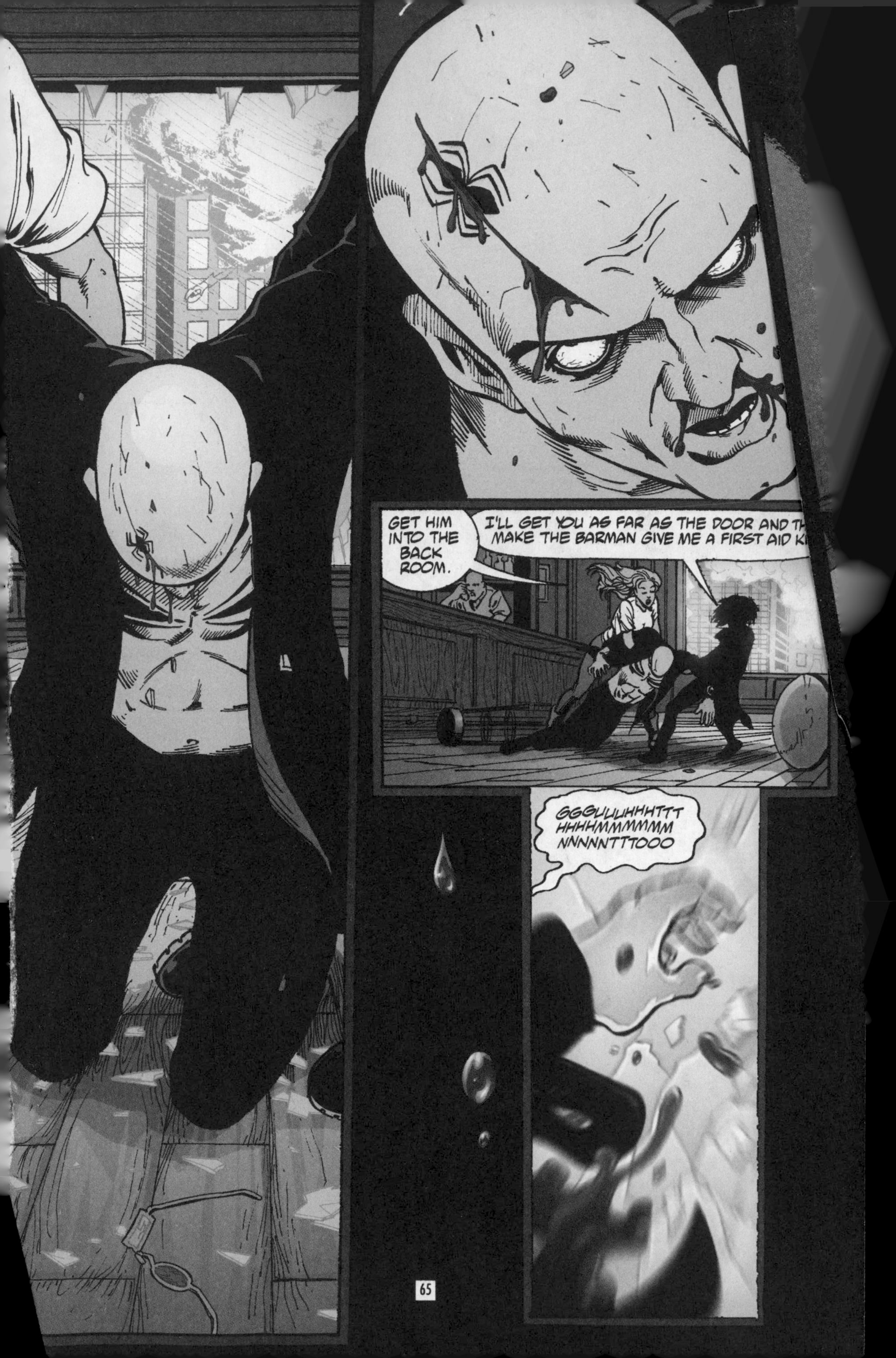
GET HIM INTO THE BACK ROOM.
I'LL GET YOU AS FAR AS THE DOOR AND TH MAKE THE BARMAN GIVE ME A FIRST AID KI
GGGUUUHHHTTT HHHHMMMMMM NNNNNTTTOOO

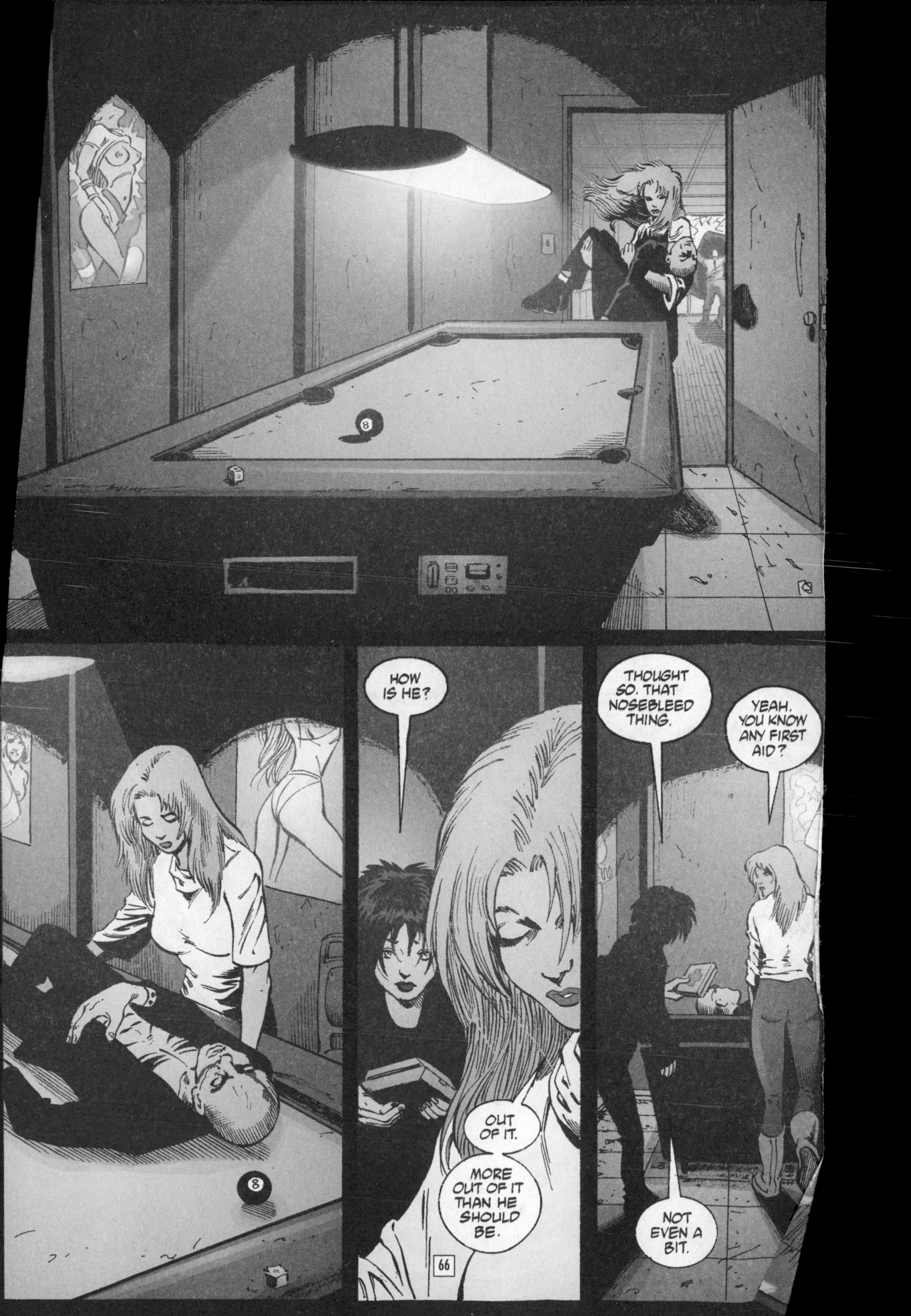
HOW IS HE?
OUT OF IT.
MORE OUT OF IT THAN HE SHOULD BE.
THOUGHT SO. THAT NOSEBLEED THING.
YEAH. YOU KNOW ANY FIRST AID?
NOT EVEN A BIT.

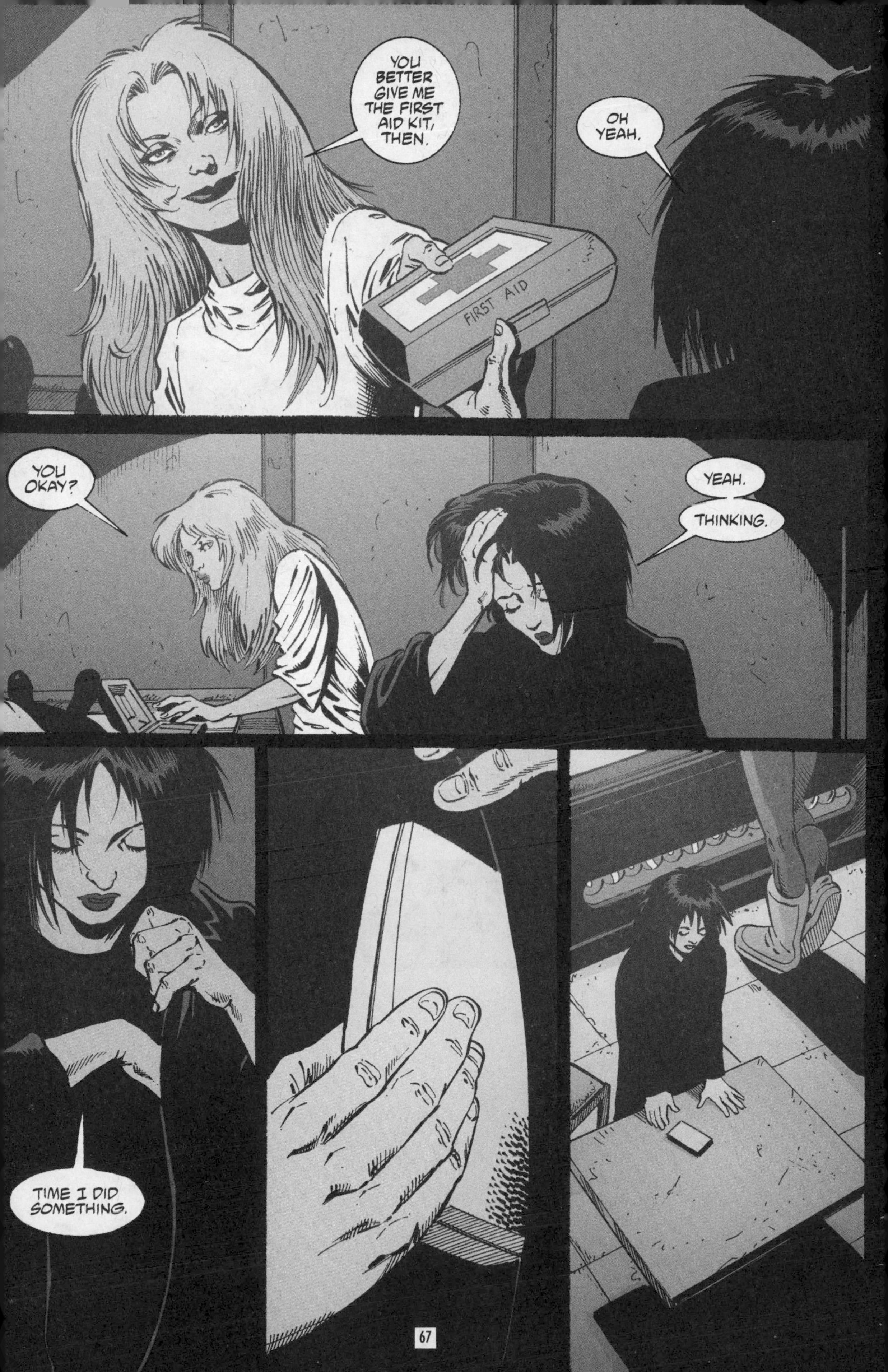

YOU BETTER GIVE ME THE FIRST AID KIT, THEN.
OH YEAH.
FIRST AID
YOU OKAY?
YEAH.
THINKING.
TIME I DID SOMETHING.

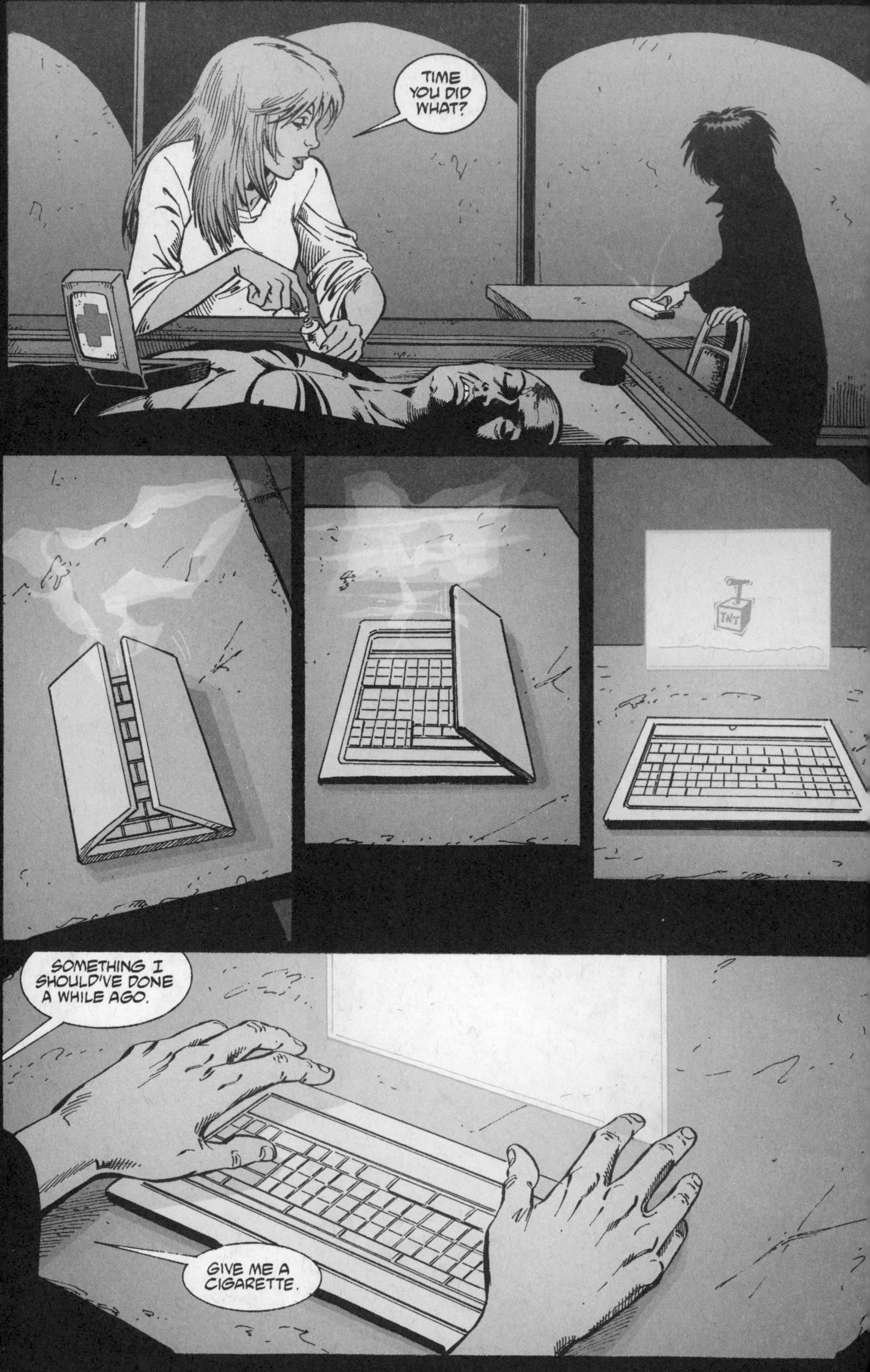
TIME YOU DID WHAT?
TNT
SOMETHING I SHOULD'VE DONE A WHILE AGO.
GIVE ME A CIGARETTE.

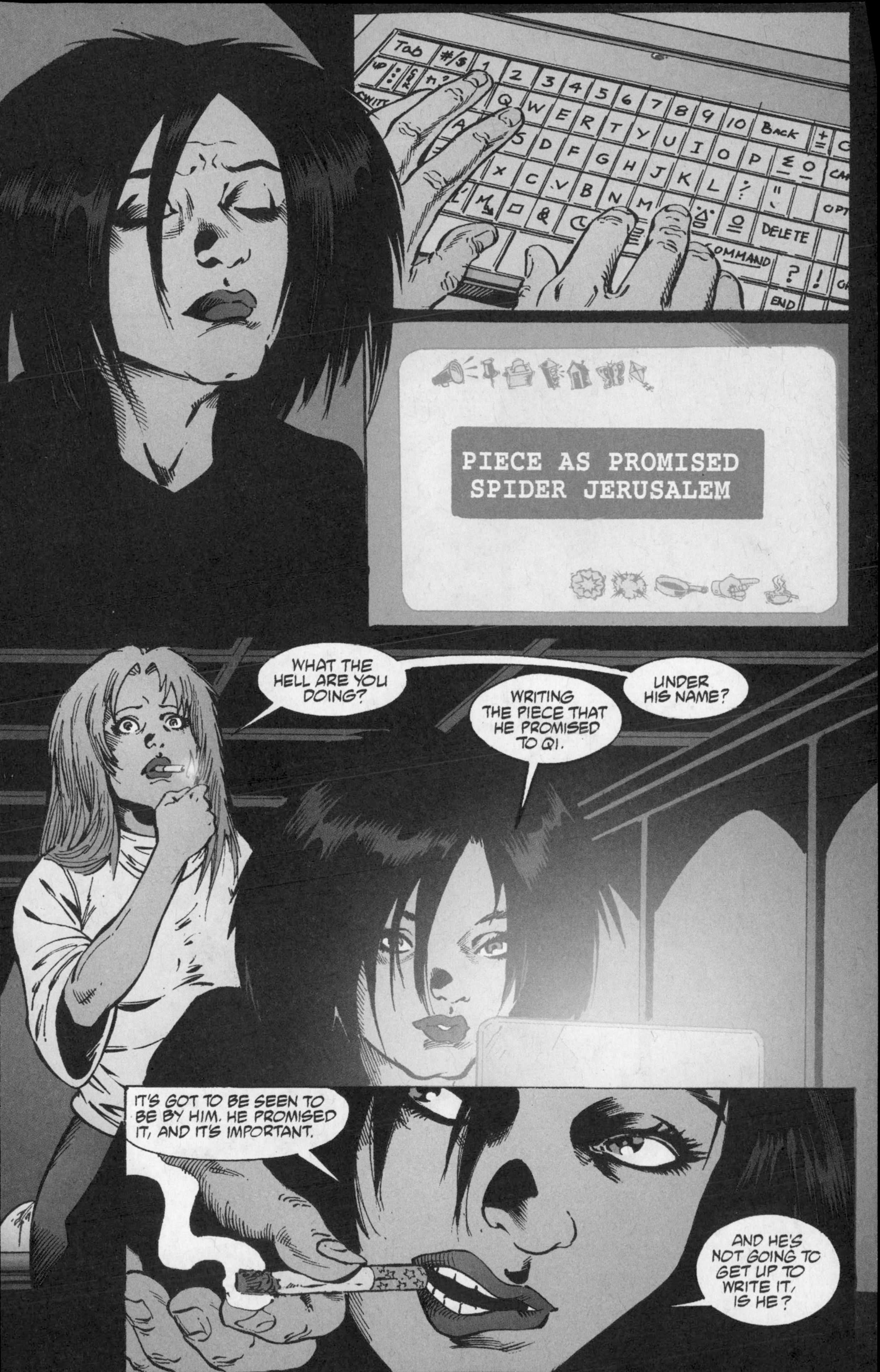
PIECE AS PROMISED
SPIDER JERUSALEM
WHAT THE HELL ARE YOU DOING?
UNDER HIS NAME?
WRITING THE PIECE THAT HE PROMISED TO QI.
IT'S GOT TO BE SEEN TO BE BY HIM. HE PROMISED IT, AND IT'S IMPORTANT.
AND HE'S NOT GOING TO GET UP TO WRITE IT, IS HE?

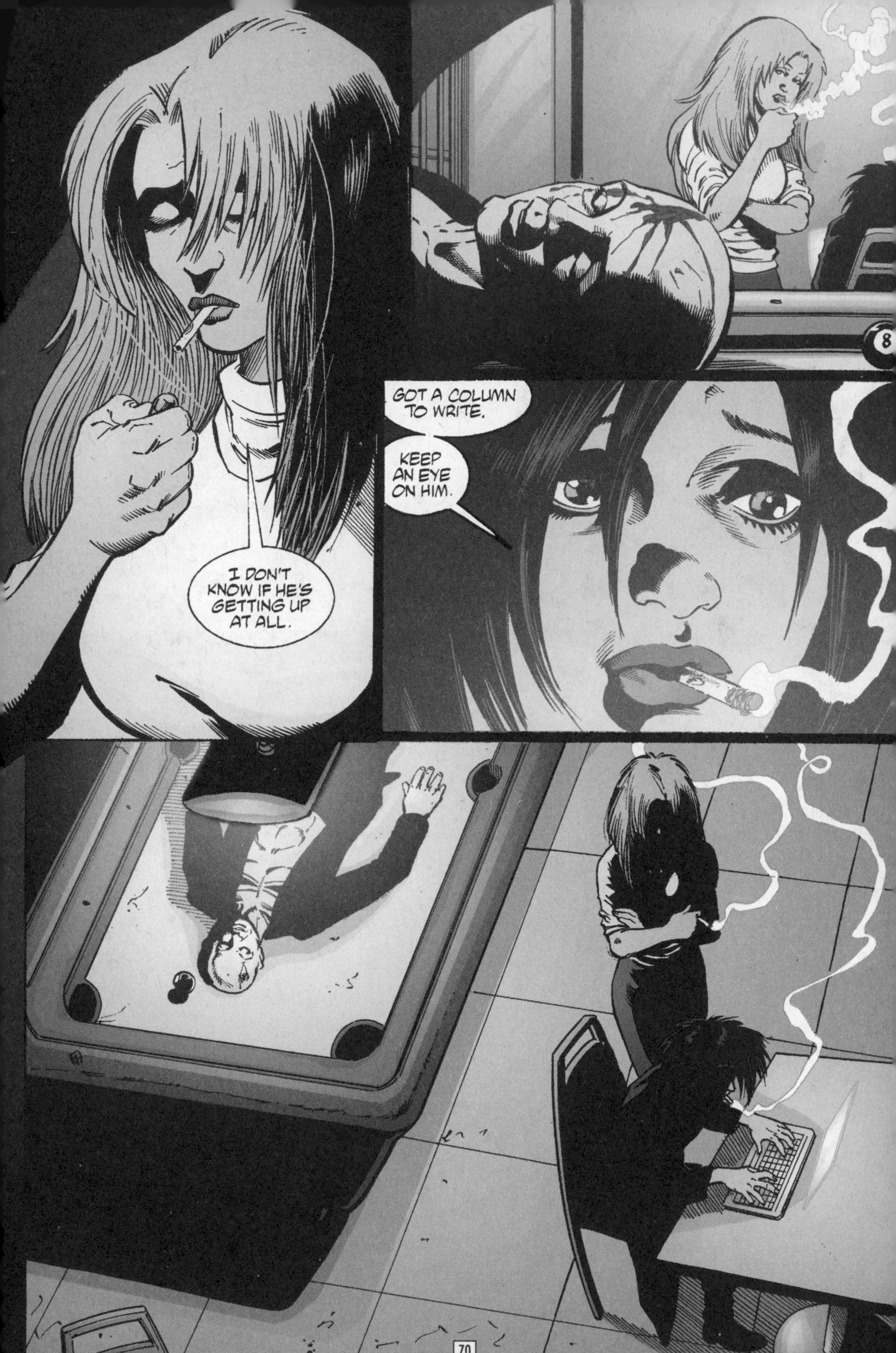
I DON'T KNOW IF HE'S GETTING UP AT ALL.
GOT A COLUMN TO WRITE.
KEEP AN EYE ON HIM.

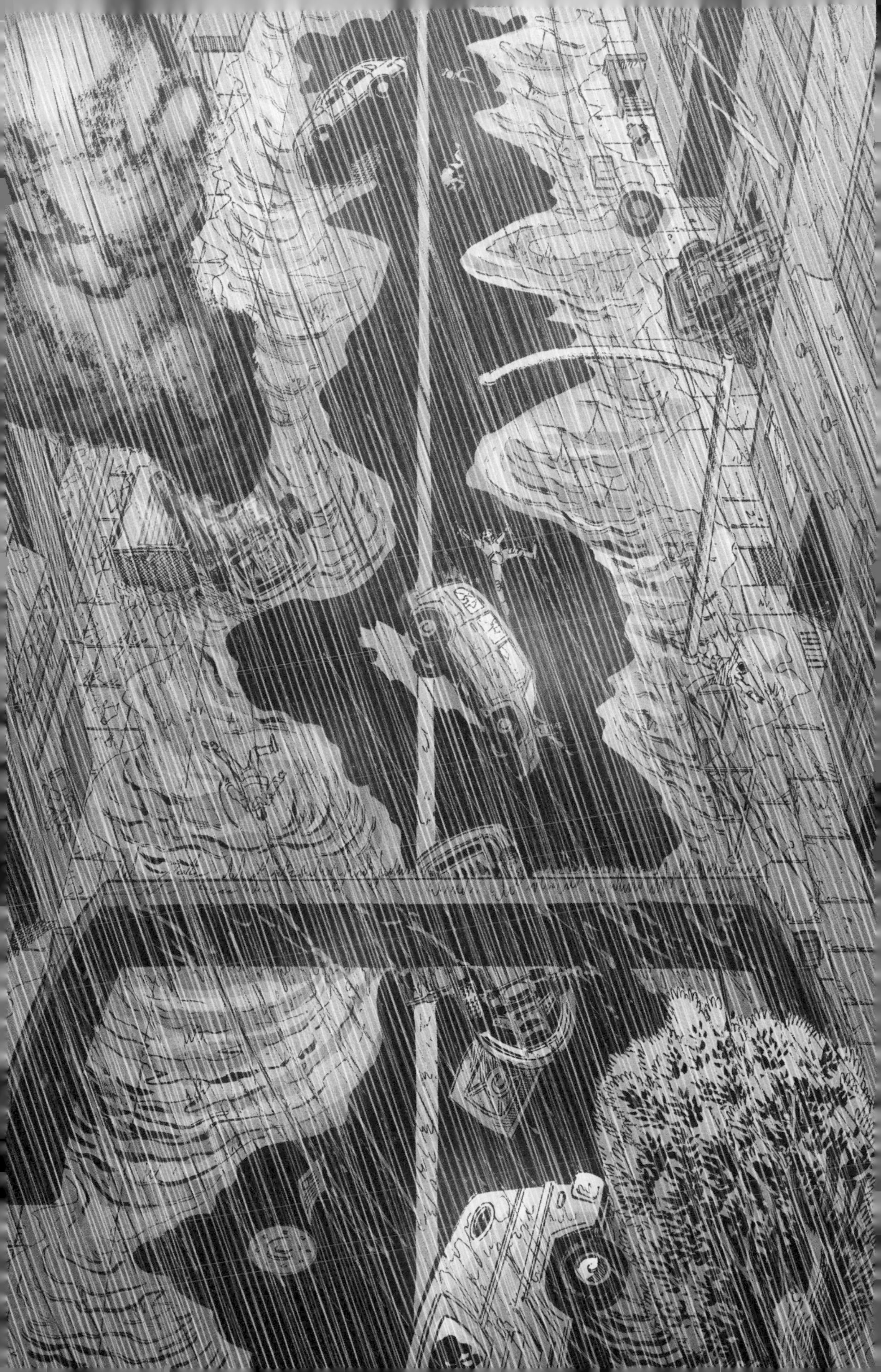

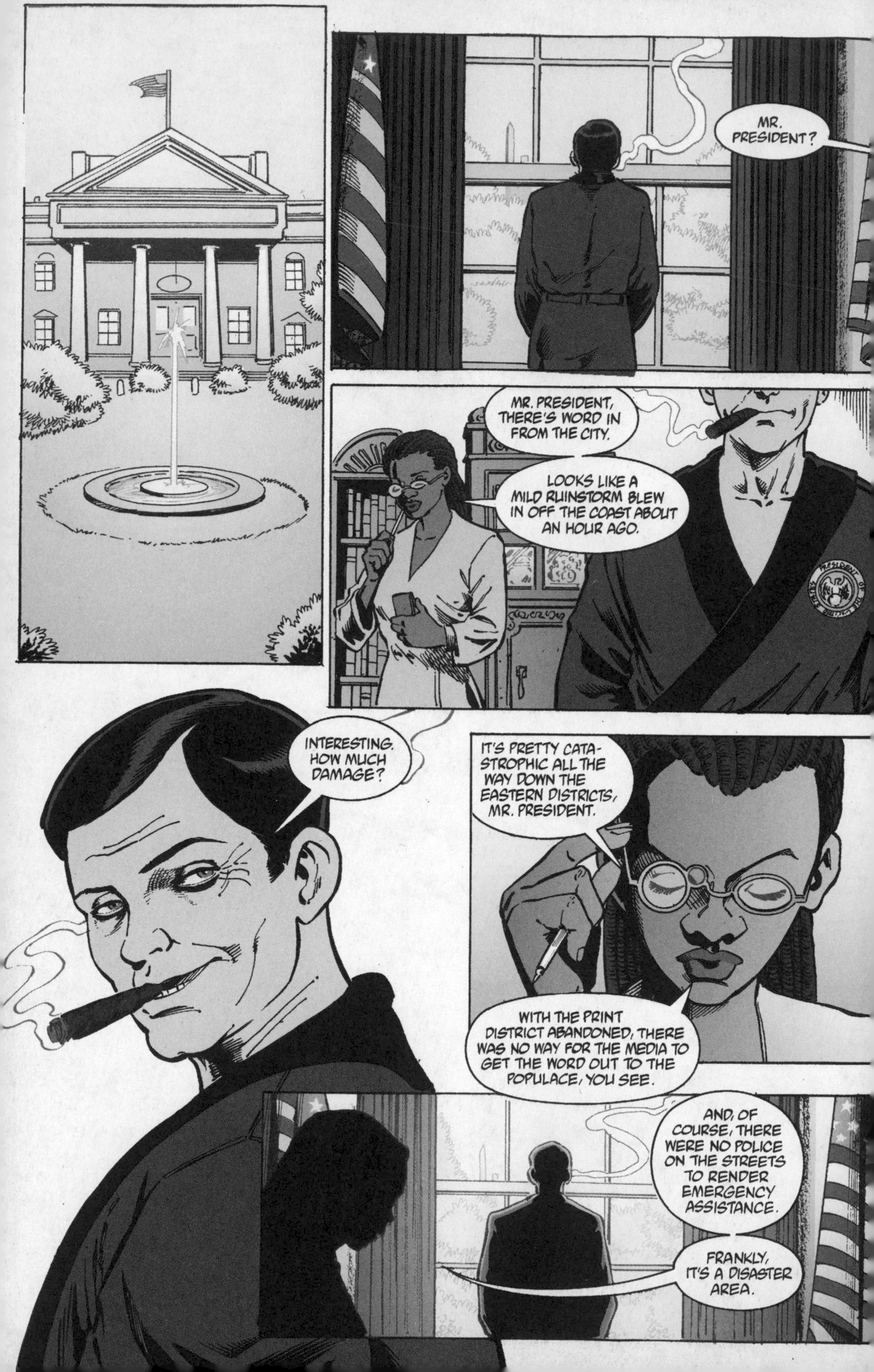
MR. PRESIDENT?
MR. PRESIDENT, THERE'S WORD IN FROM THE CITY.
LOOKS LIKE A MILD RUINSTORM BLEW IN OFF THE COAST ABOUT AN HOUR AGO.
PRESIDENT OF THE UNITED STATES
INTERESTING. HOW MUCH DAMAGE?
IT'S PRETTY CATA-STROPHIC ALL THE WAY DOWN THE EASTERN DISTRICTS, MR. PRESIDENT.
WITH THE PRINT DISTRICT ABANDONED, THERE WAS NO WAY FOR THE MEDIA TO GET THE WORD OUT TO THE POPULACE, YOU SEE.
AND, OF COURSE, THERE WERE NO POLICE ON THE STREETS TO RENDER EMERGENCY ASSISTANCE.
FRANKLY, IT'S A DISASTER AREA.

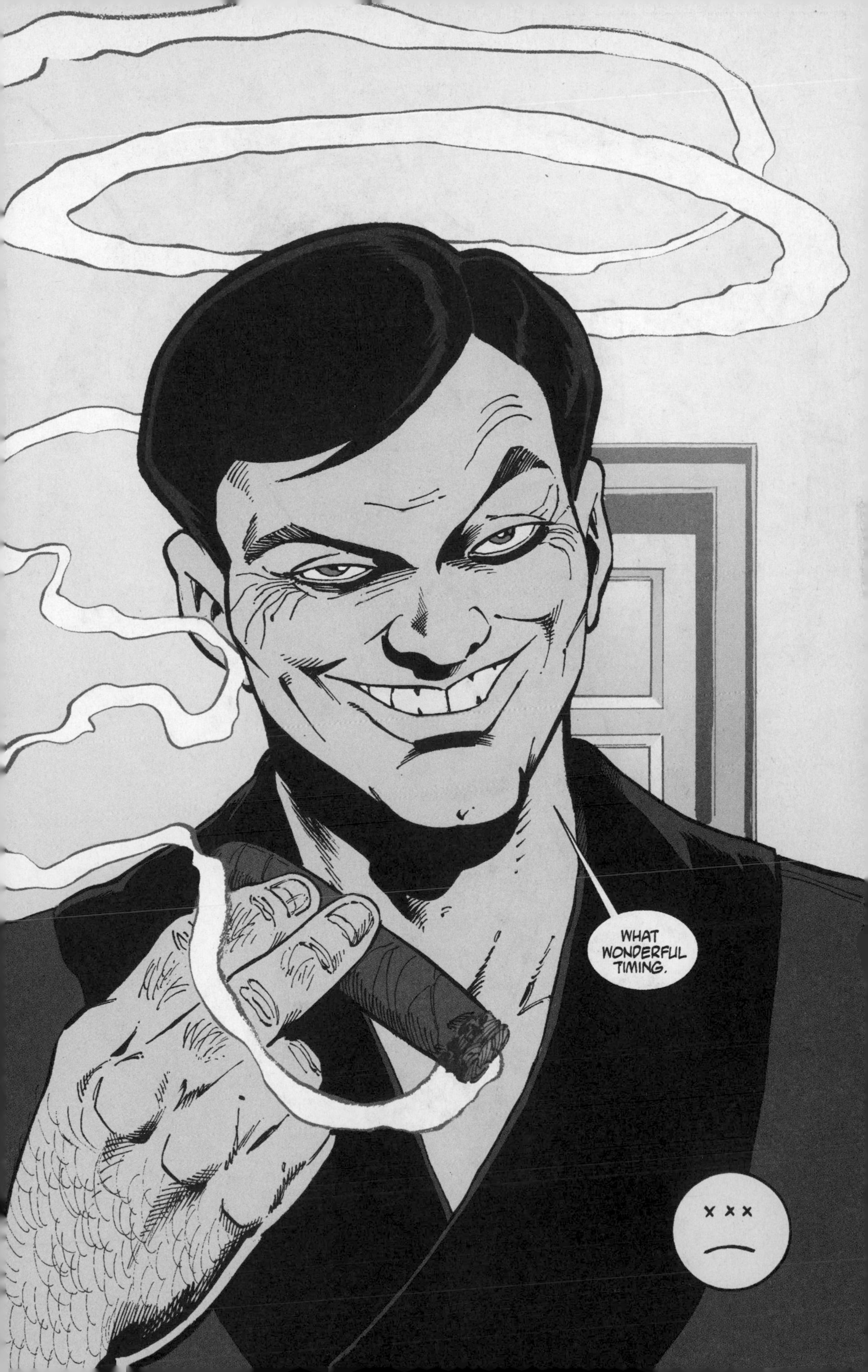
WHAT WONDERFUL TIMING.

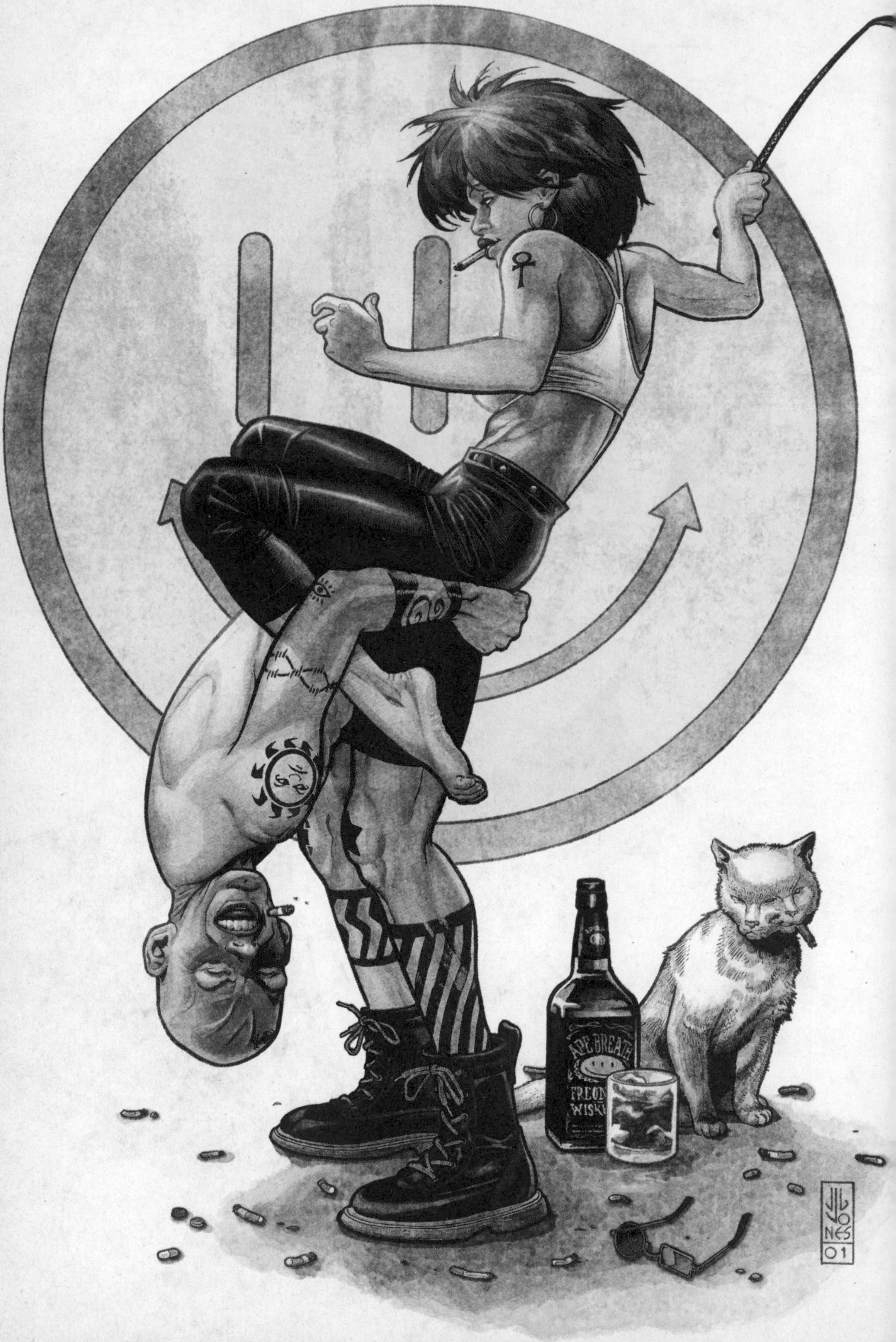
APE BREATH
JG JONES 01

★ ★ ★ ★ LATE EDITION ★ ★ ★ ★

TRANSMETROPOLITAN

WHAT I KNOW

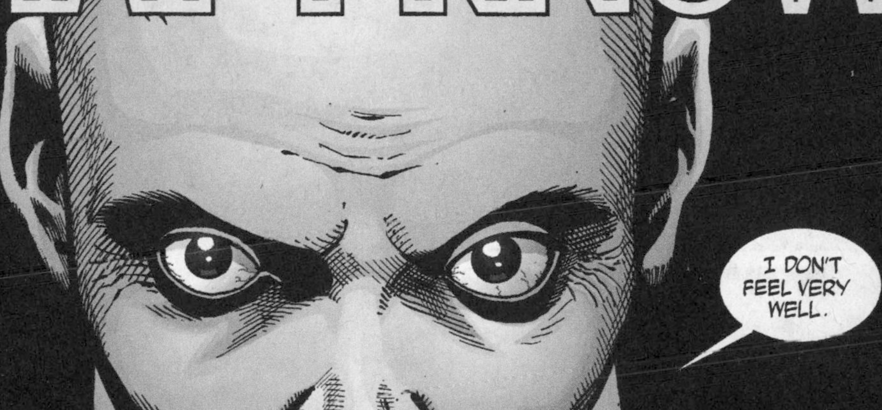
I DON'T FEEL VERY WELL.

WARREN ELLIS writes and
DARICK ROBERTSON and **RODNEY RAMOS** draw

Clem Robins letterer

Nathan Eyring color & separations

J.G. Jones cover

Tammy Beatty assistant editor

Tony Bedard editor

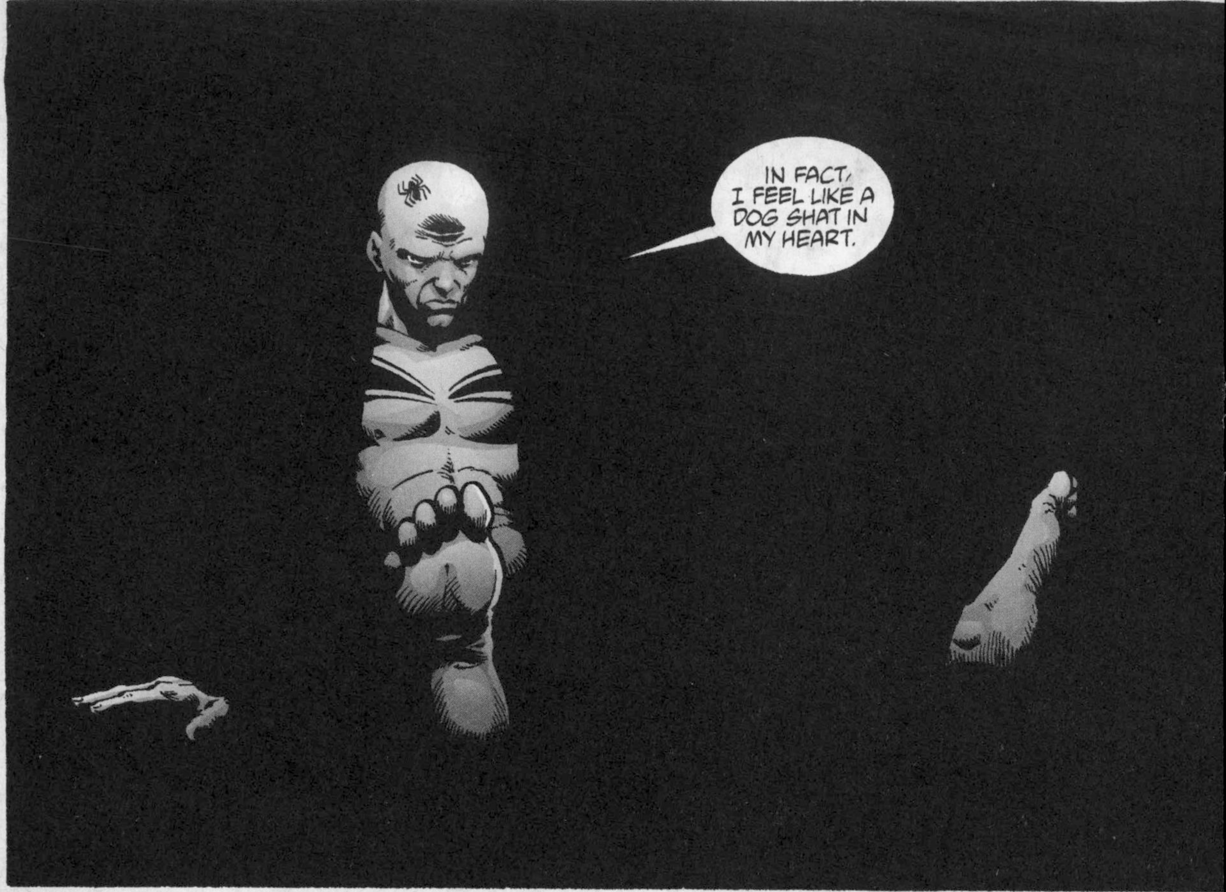
IN FACT, I FEEL LIKE A DOG SHAT IN MY HEART.

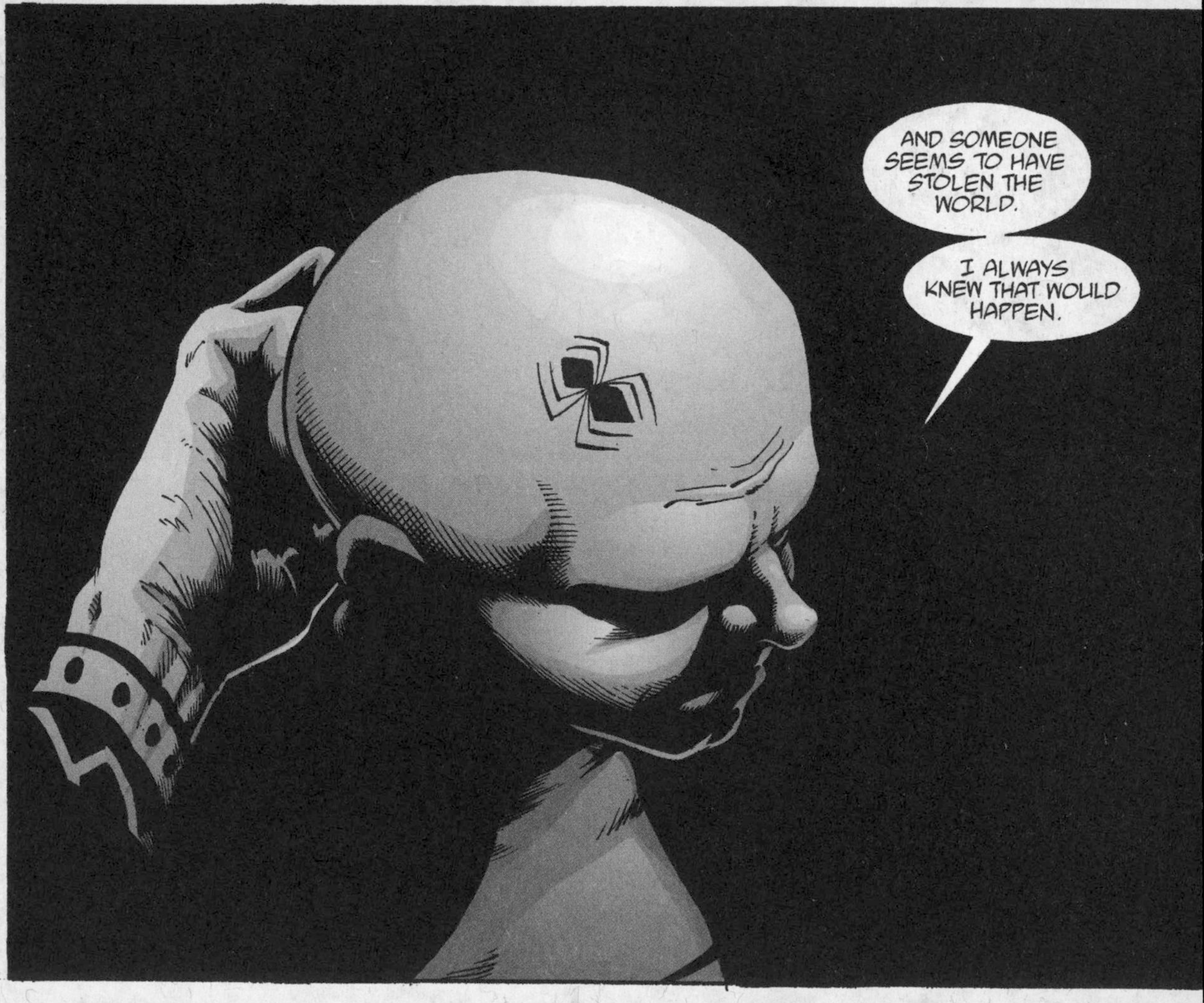
AND SOMEONE SEEMS TO HAVE STOLEN THE WORLD.
I ALWAYS KNEW THAT WOULD HAPPEN.

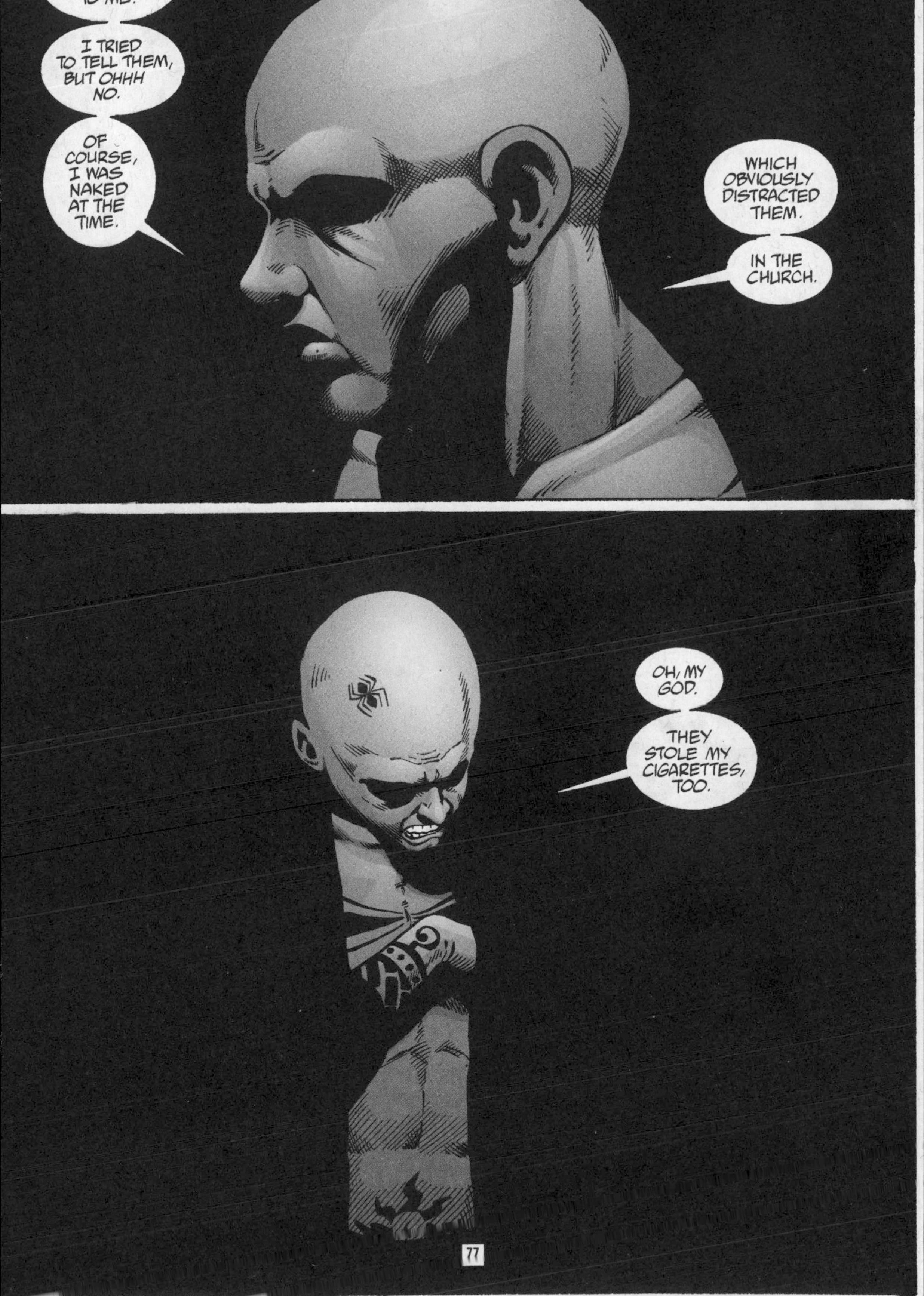
I TRIED TO TELL THEM, BUT OHHH NO.
OF COURSE, I WAS NAKED AT THE TIME.
WHICH OBVIOUSLY DISTRACTED THEM.
IN THE CHURCH.
OH, MY GOD.
THEY STOLE MY CIGARETTES, TOO.

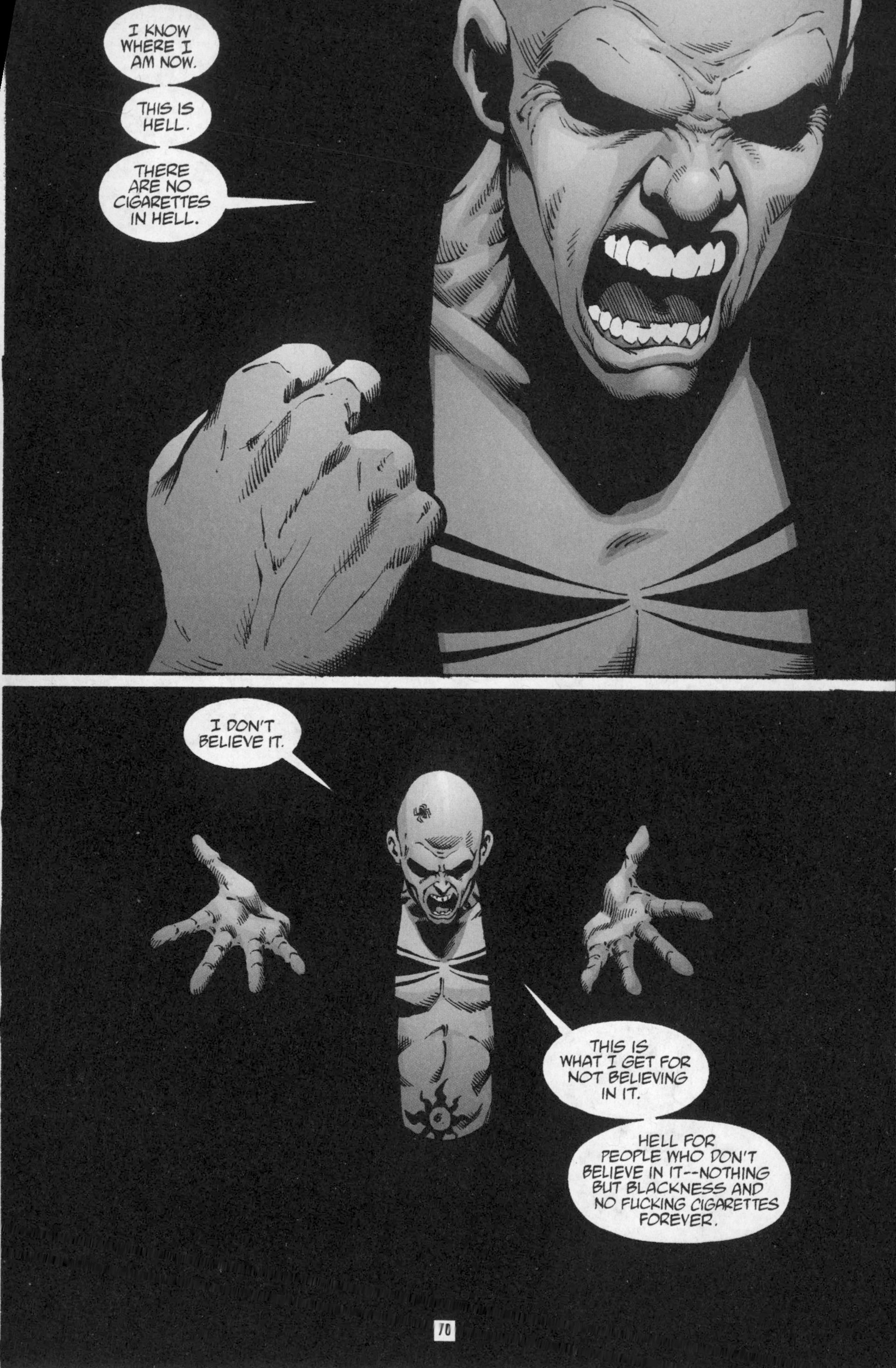
I KNOW WHERE I AM NOW.
THIS IS HELL.
THERE ARE NO CIGARETTES IN HELL.
I DON'T BELIEVE IT.
THIS IS WHAT I GET FOR NOT BELIEVING IN IT.
HELL FOR PEOPLE WHO DON'T BELIEVE IN IT--NOTHING BUT BLACKNESS AND NO FUCKING CIGARETTES FOREVER.

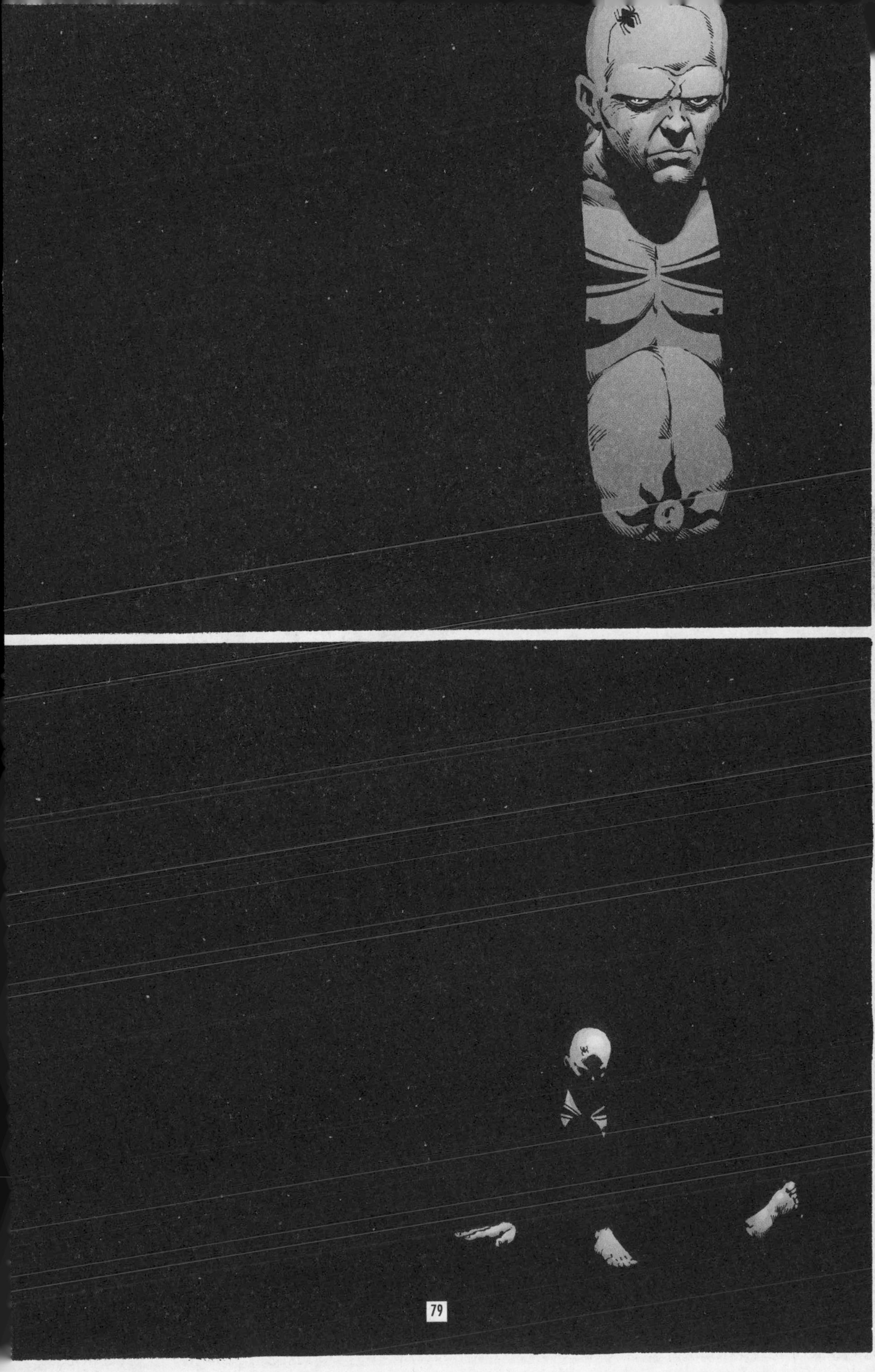

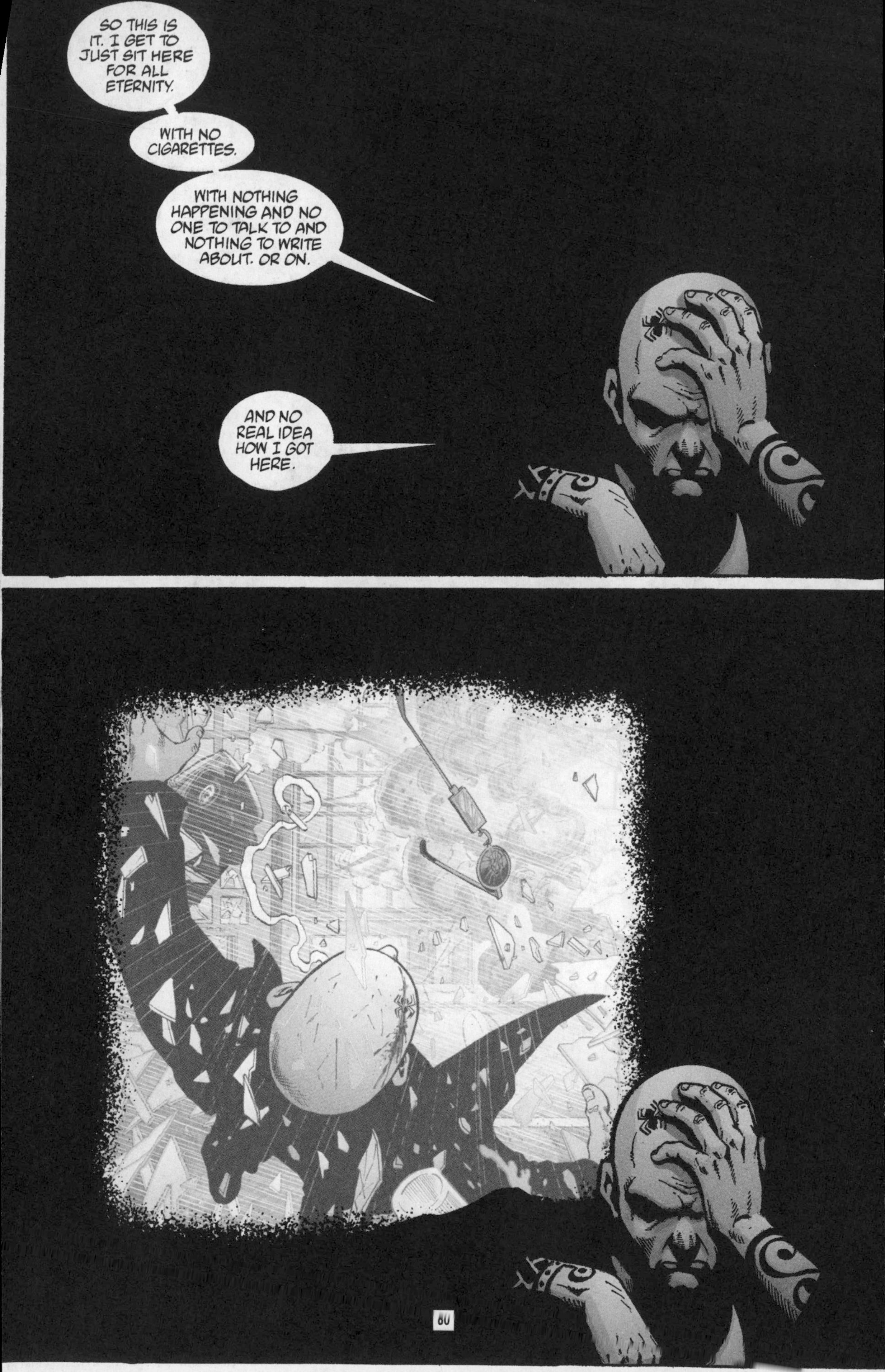
SO THIS IS IT. I GET TO JUST SIT HERE FOR ALL ETERNITY.
WITH NO CIGARETTES.
WITH NOTHING HAPPENING AND NO ONE TO TALK TO AND NOTHING TO WRITE ABOUT. OR ON.
AND NO REAL IDEA HOW I GOT HERE.

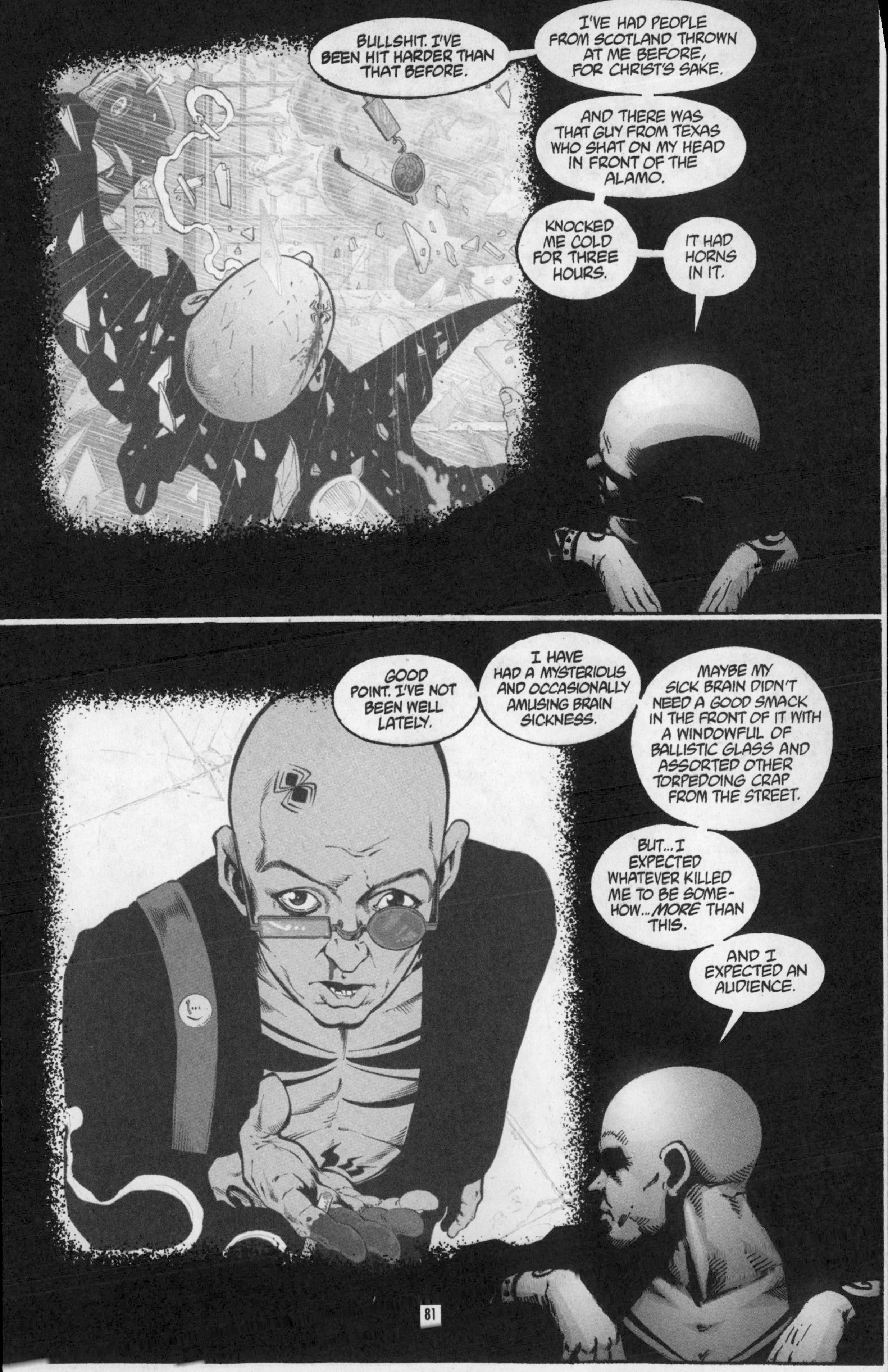
BULLSHIT. I'VE BEEN HIT HARDER THAN THAT BEFORE.
I'VE HAD PEOPLE FROM SCOTLAND THROWN AT ME BEFORE, FOR CHRIST'S SAKE.
AND THERE WAS THAT GUY FROM TEXAS WHO SHAT ON MY HEAD IN FRONT OF THE ALAMO.
KNOCKED ME COLD FOR THREE HOURS.
IT HAD HORNS IN IT.
GOOD POINT. I'VE NOT BEEN WELL LATELY.
I HAVE HAD A MYSTERIOUS AND OCCASIONALLY AMUSING BRAIN SICKNESS.
MAYBE MY SICK BRAIN DIDN'T NEED A GOOD SMACK IN THE FRONT OF IT WITH A WINDOWFUL OF BALLISTIC GLASS AND ASSORTED OTHER TORPEDOING CRAP FROM THE STREET.
BUT... I EXPECTED WHATEVER KILLED ME TO BE SOME-HOW... *MORE* THAN THIS.
AND I EXPECTED AN AUDIENCE.

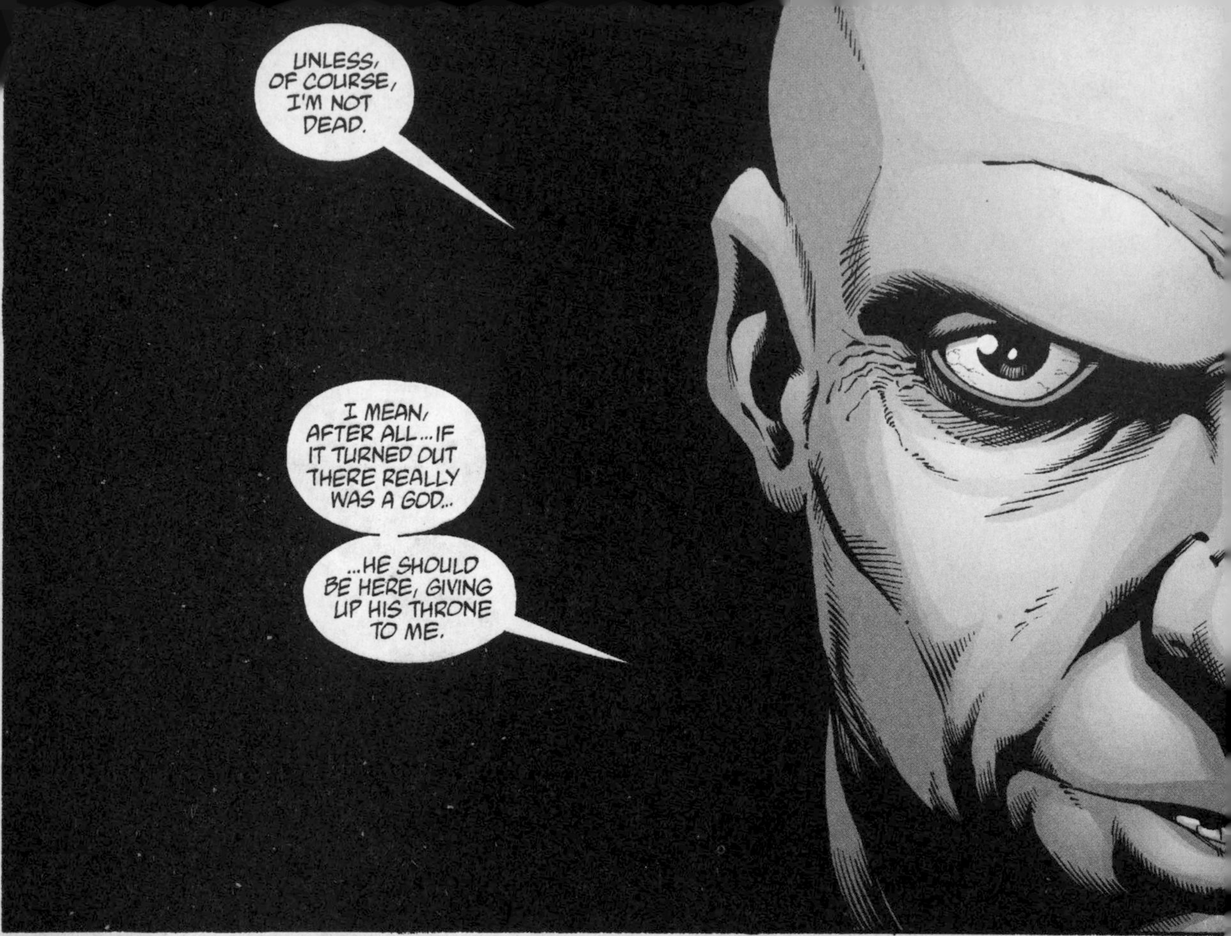
UNLESS, OF COURSE, I'M NOT DEAD.
I MEAN, AFTER ALL...IF IT TURNED OUT THERE REALLY WAS A GOD..
...HE SHOULD BE HERE, GIVING UP HIS THRONE TO ME.

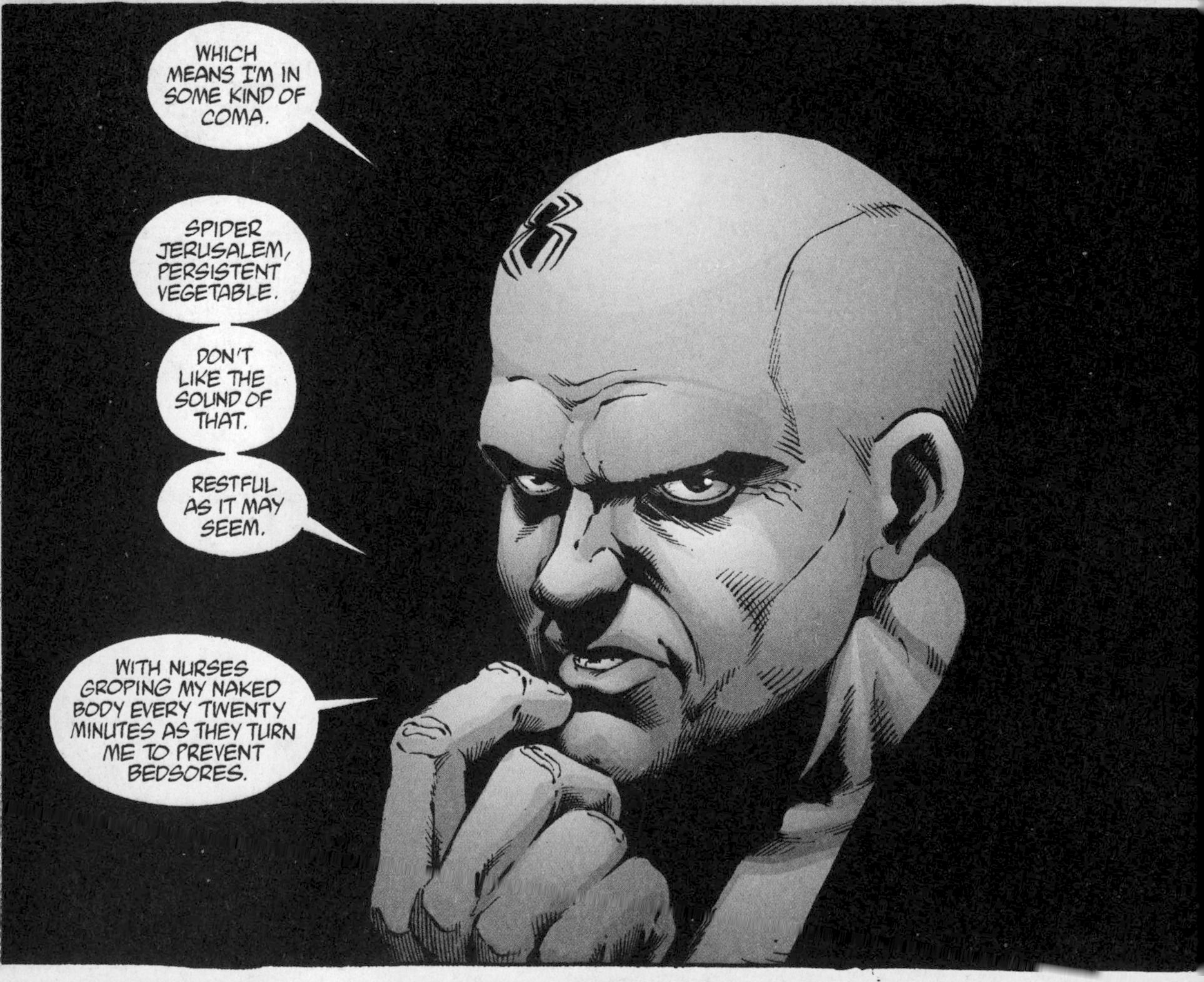
WHICH MEANS I'M IN SOME KIND OF COMA.
SPIDER JERUSALEM, PERSISTENT VEGETABLE.
DON'T LIKE THE SOUND OF THAT.
RESTFUL AS IT MAY SEEM.
WITH NURSES GROPING MY NAKED BODY EVERY TWENTY MINUTES AS THEY TURN ME TO PREVENT BEDSORES.

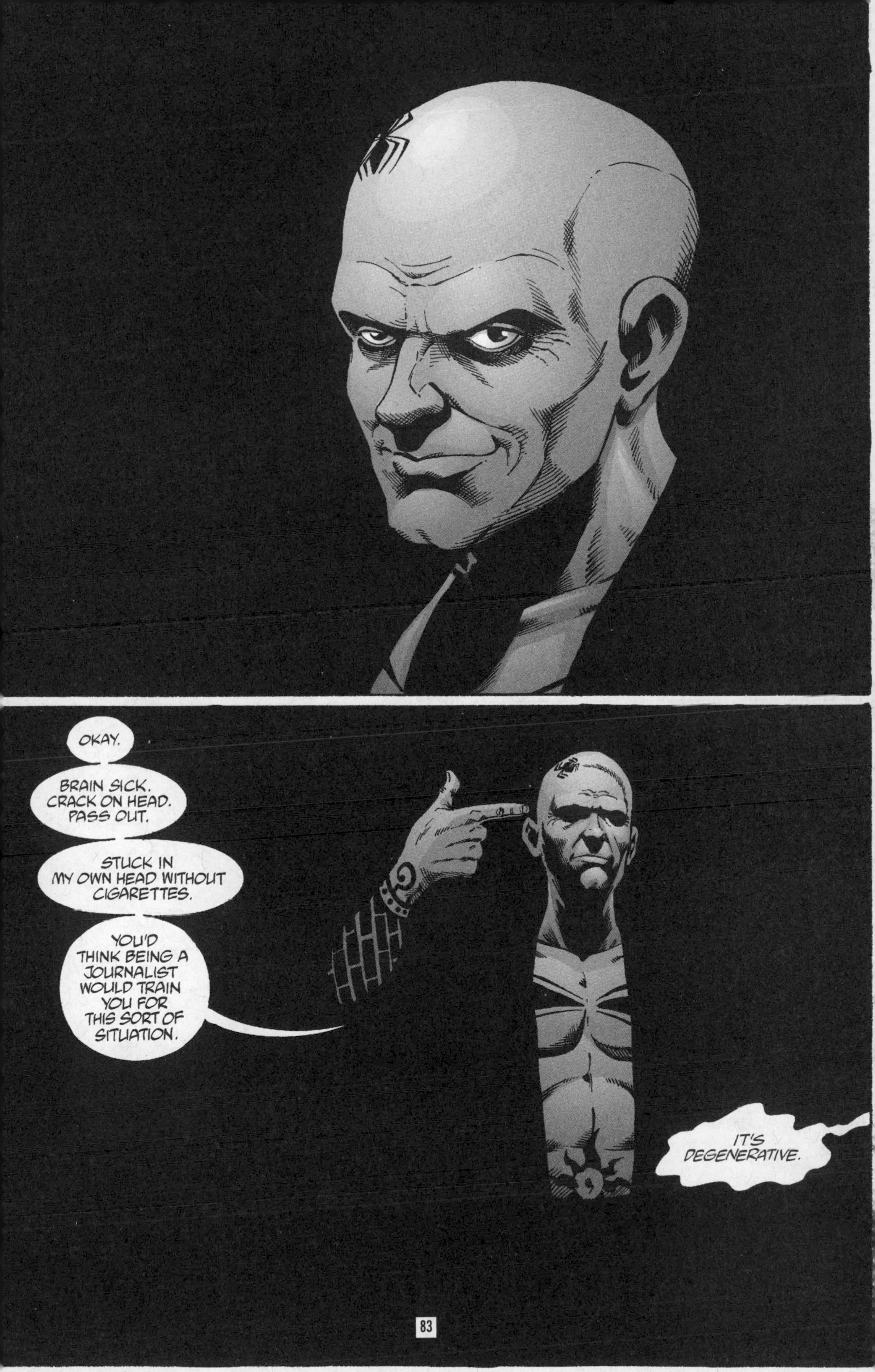
OKAY.
BRAIN SICK. CRACK ON HEAD. PASS OUT.
STUCK IN MY OWN HEAD WITHOUT CIGARETTES.
YOU'D THINK BEING A JOURNALIST WOULD TRAIN YOU FOR THIS SORT OF SITUATION.
IT'S DEGENERATIVE.

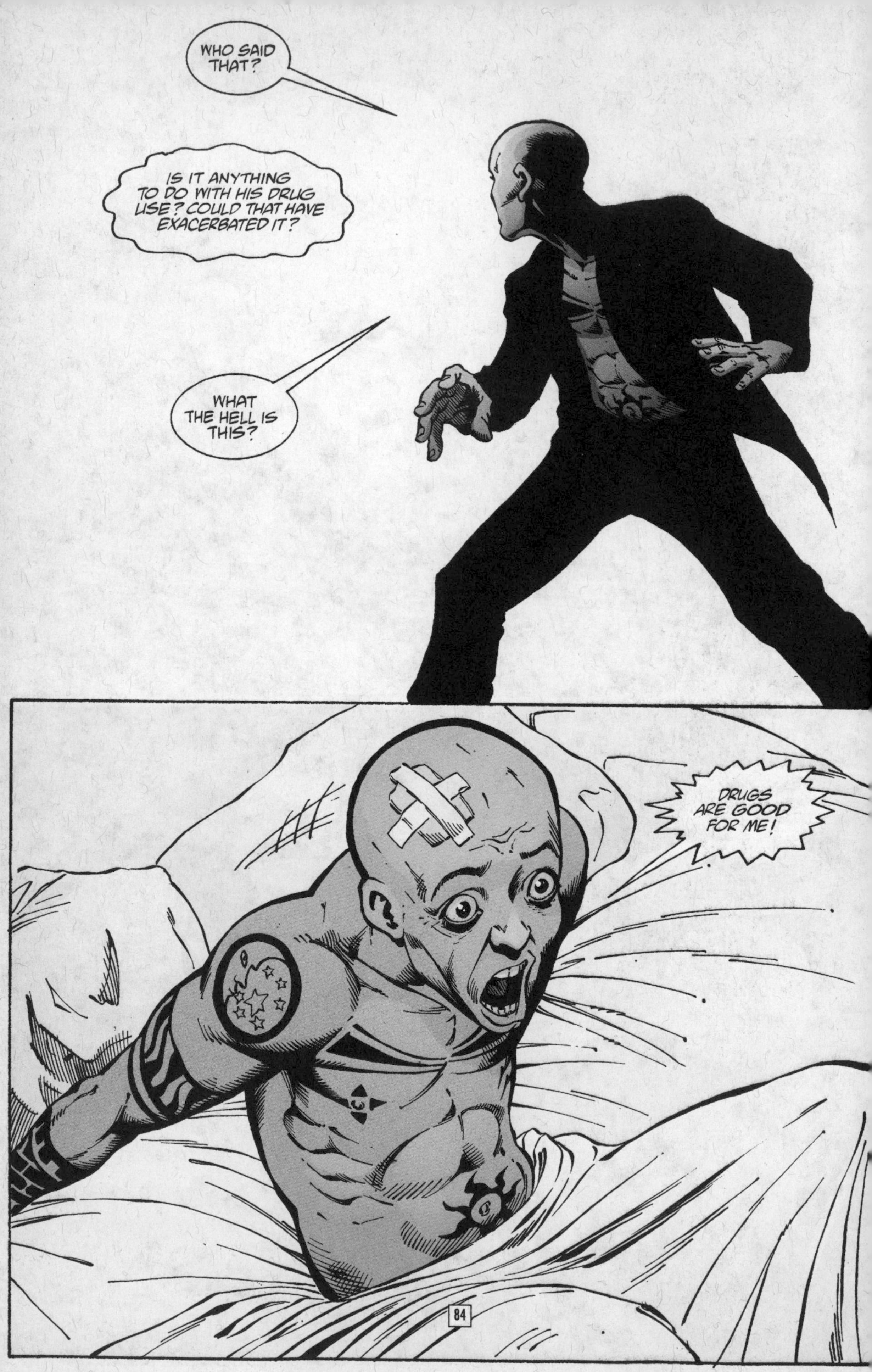
WHO SAID THAT?
IS IT ANYTHING TO DO WITH HIS DRUG USE? COULD THAT HAVE EXACERBATED IT?
WHAT THE HELL IS THIS?
DRUGS ARE GOOD FOR ME!

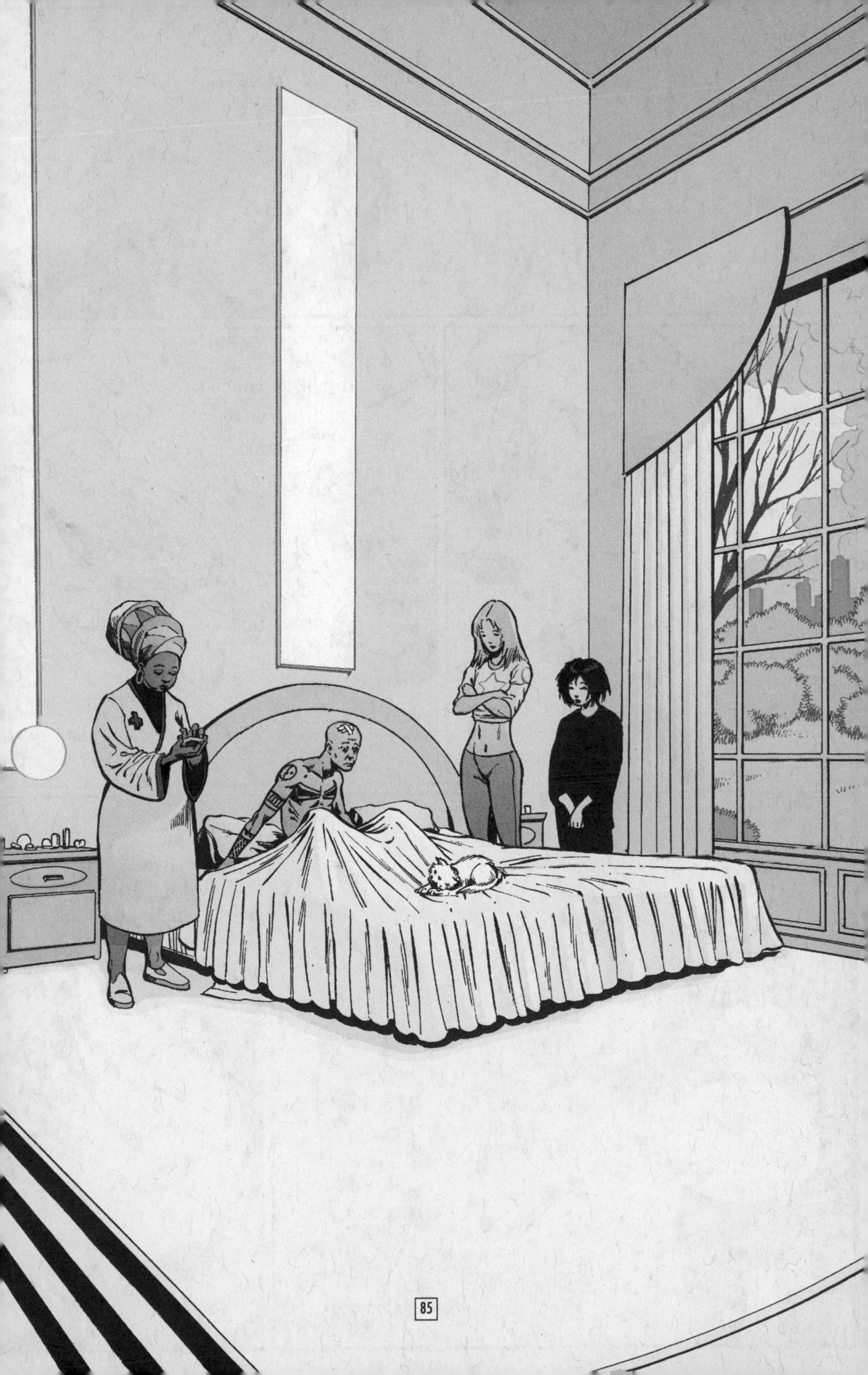

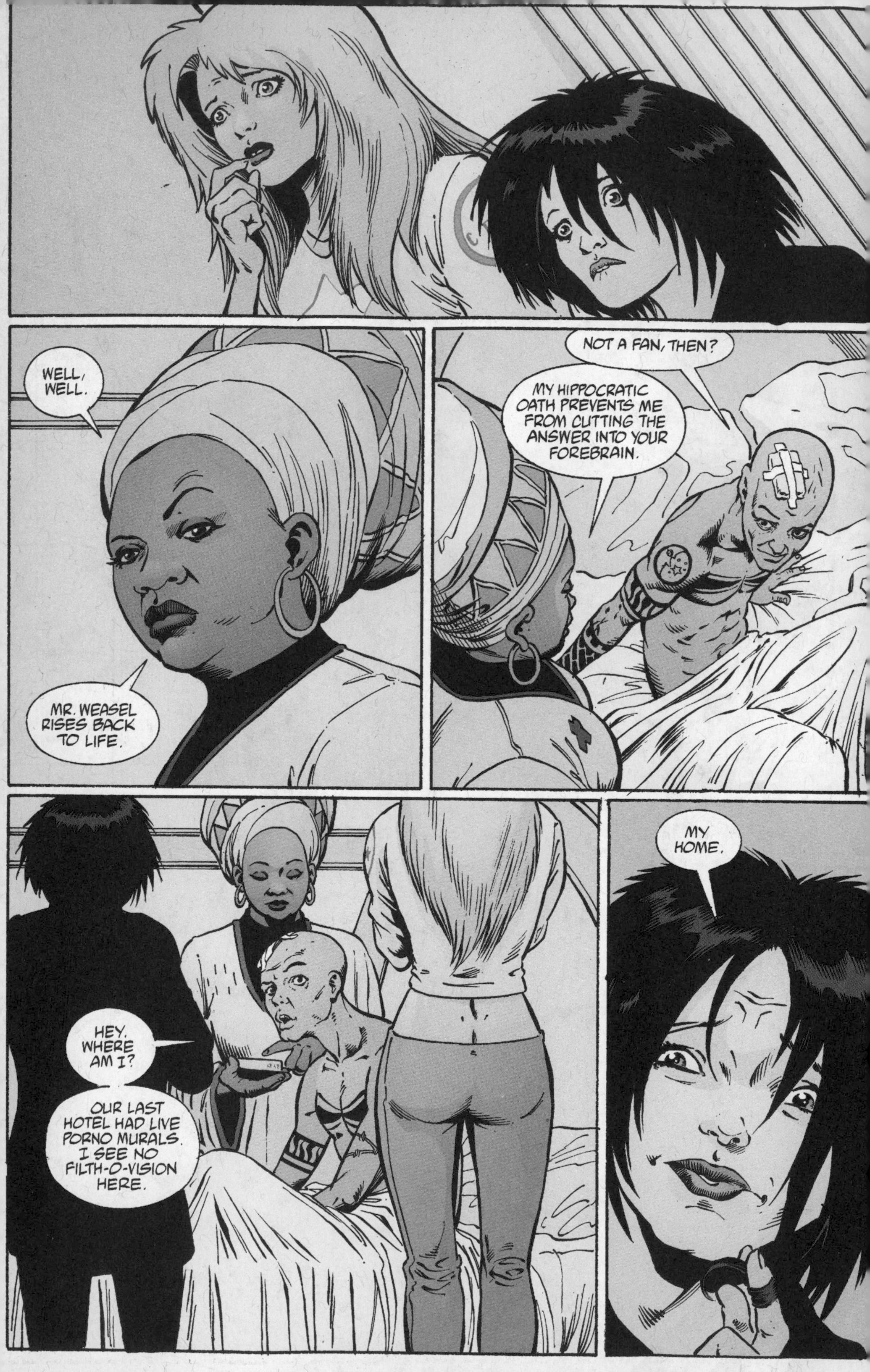
WELL, WELL.
MR. WEASEL RISES BACK TO LIFE.
NOT A FAN, THEN?
MY HIPPOCRATIC OATH PREVENTS ME FROM CUTTING THE ANSWER INTO YOUR FOREBRAIN.
HEY. WHERE AM I?
OUR LAST HOTEL HAD LIVE PORNO MURALS. I SEE NO FILTH-O-VISION HERE.
MY HOME.

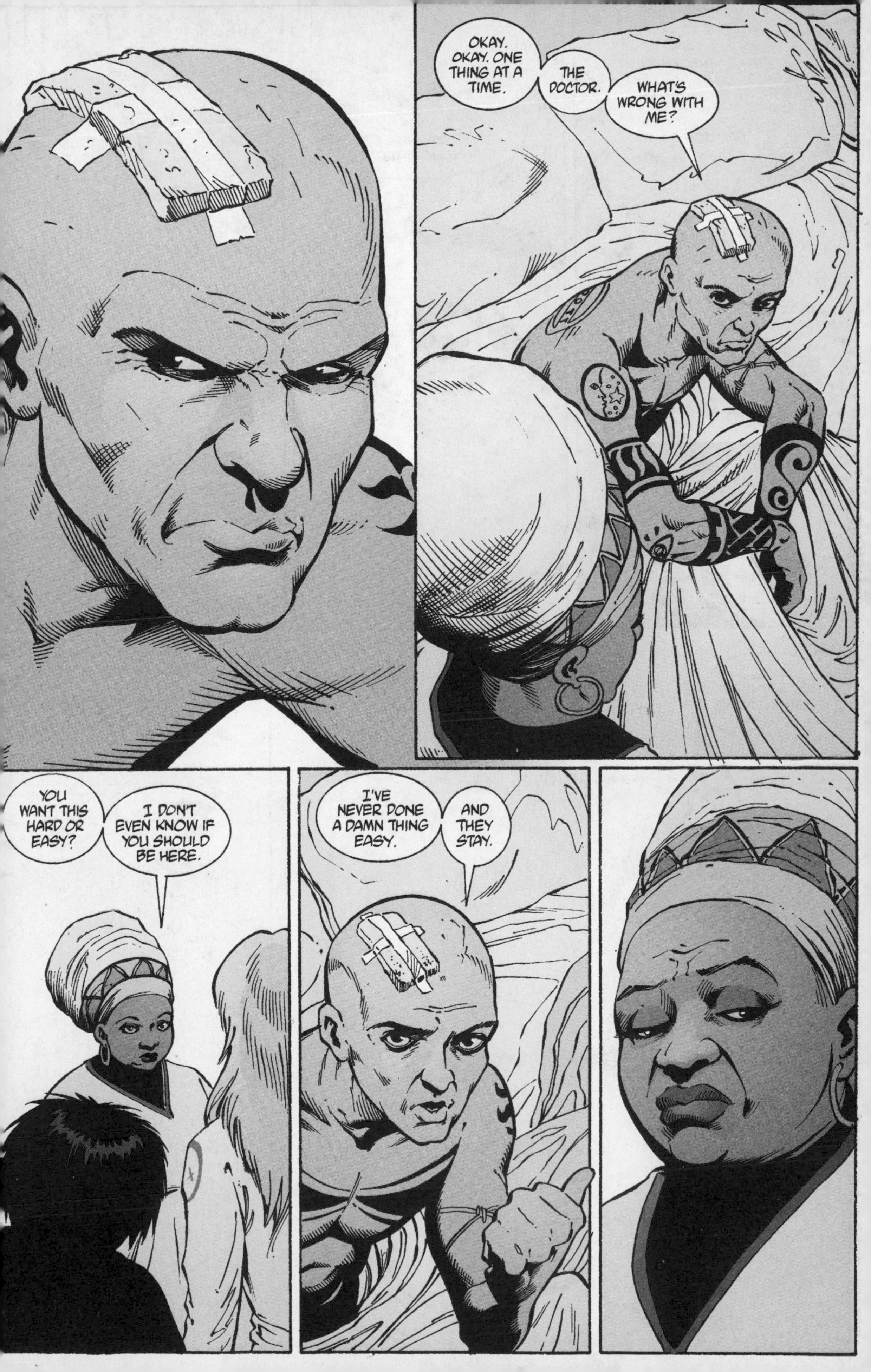

OKAY. OKAY. ONE THING AT A TIME.
THE DOCTOR.
WHAT'S WRONG WITH ME?
YOU WANT THIS HARD OR EASY?
I DON'T EVEN KNOW IF YOU SHOULD BE HERE.
I'VE NEVER DONE A DAMN THING EASY.
AND THEY STAY.

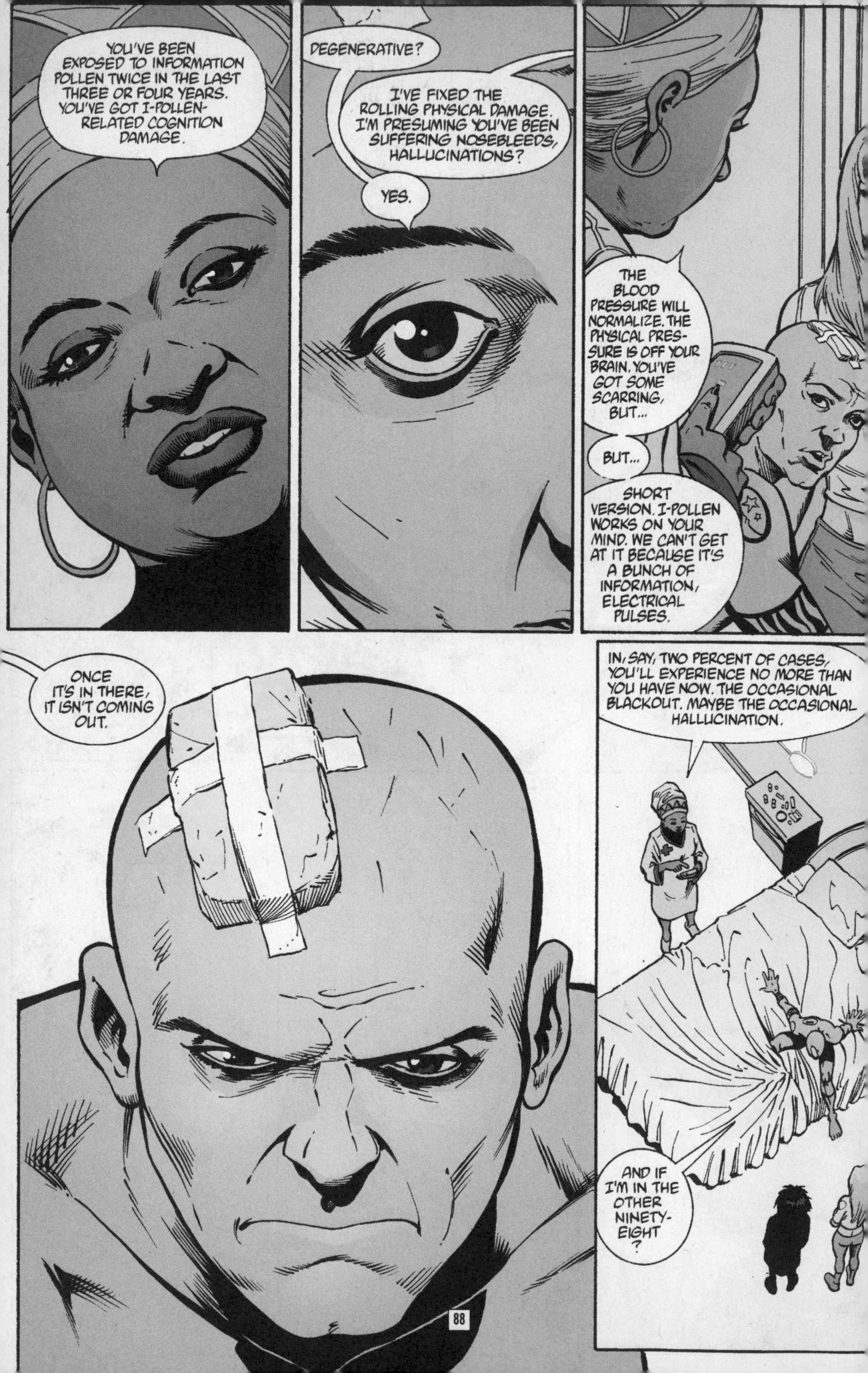
YOU'VE BEEN EXPOSED TO INFORMATION POLLEN TWICE IN THE LAST THREE OR FOUR YEARS. YOU'VE GOT I-POLLEN-RELATED COGNITION DAMAGE.
DEGENERATIVE?
I'VE FIXED THE ROLLING PHYSICAL DAMAGE. I'M PRESUMING YOU'VE BEEN SUFFERING NOSEBLEEDS, HALLUCINATIONS?
YES.
THE BLOOD PRESSURE WILL NORMALIZE. THE PHYSICAL PRESSURE IS OFF YOUR BRAIN. YOU'VE GOT SOME SCARRING, BUT...
BUT...
SHORT VERSION. I-POLLEN WORKS ON YOUR MIND. WE CAN'T GET AT IT BECAUSE IT'S A BUNCH OF INFORMATION, ELECTRICAL PULSES.
ONCE IT'S IN THERE, IT ISN'T COMING OUT.
IN, SAY, TWO PERCENT OF CASES, YOU'LL EXPERIENCE NO MORE THAN YOU HAVE NOW. THE OCCASIONAL BLACKOUT. MAYBE THE OCCASIONAL HALLUCINATION.
AND IF I'M IN THE OTHER NINETY-EIGHT?

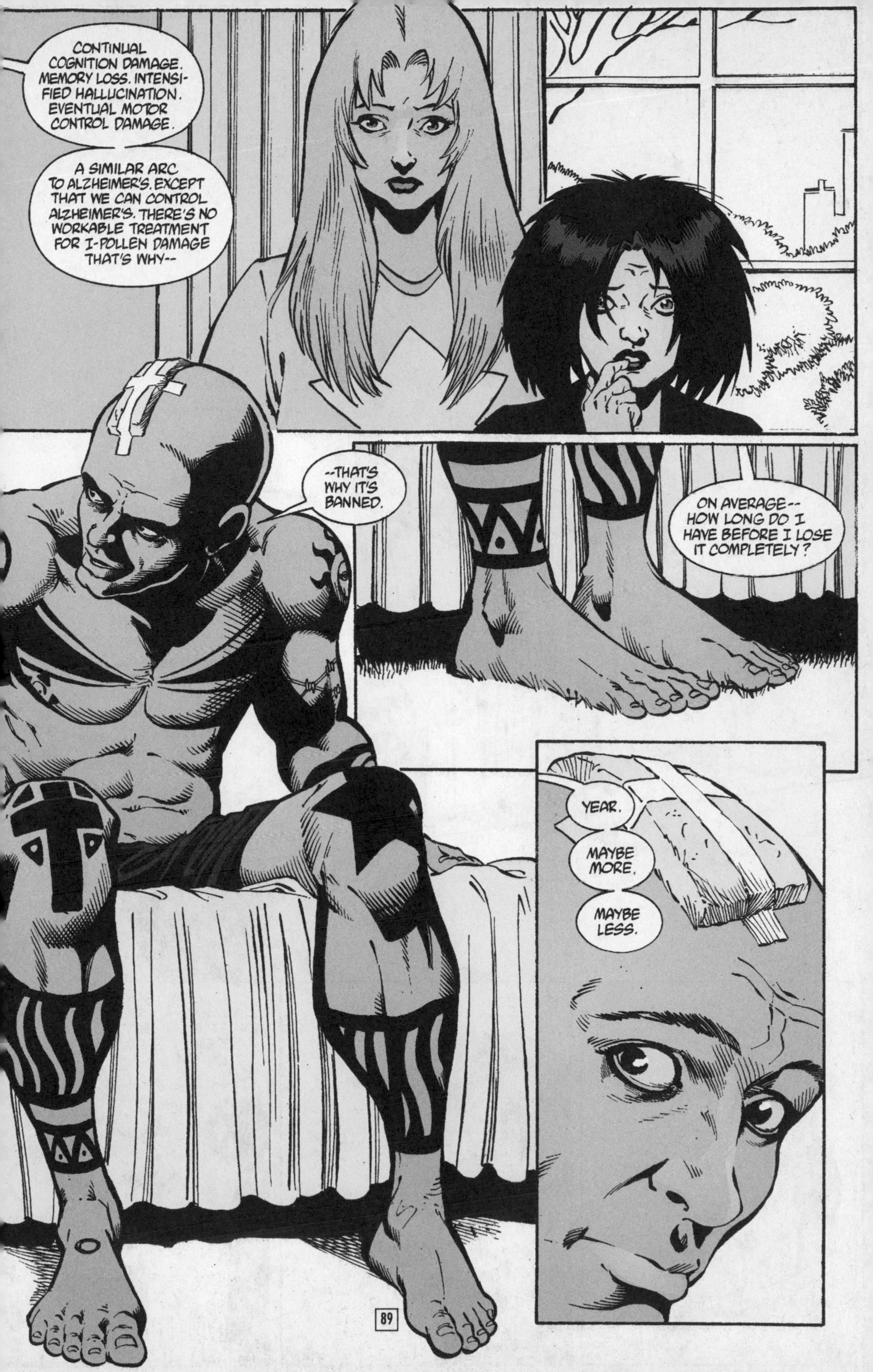
CONTINUAL COGNITION DAMAGE. MEMORY LOSS. INTENSIFIED HALLUCINATION. EVENTUAL MOTOR CONTROL DAMAGE.
A SIMILAR ARC TO ALZHEIMER'S. EXCEPT THAT WE CAN CONTROL ALZHEIMER'S. THERE'S NO WORKABLE TREATMENT FOR I-POLLEN DAMAGE THAT'S WHY--
--THAT'S WHY IT'S BANNED.
ON AVERAGE-- HOW LONG DO I HAVE BEFORE I LOSE IT COMPLETELY?
YEAR.
MAYBE MORE.
MAYBE LESS.

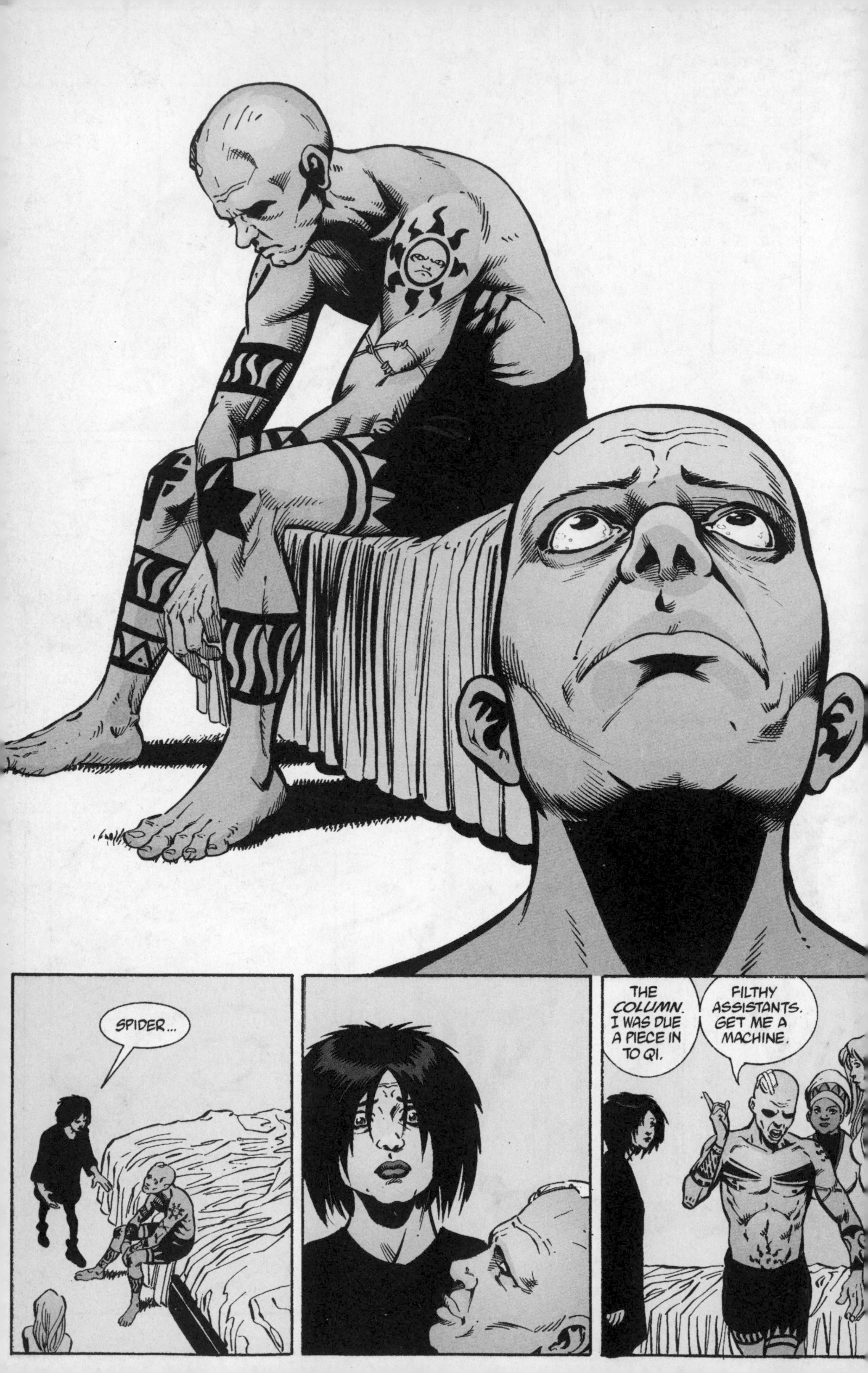

SPIDER...
THE *COLUMN*. I WAS DUE A PIECE IN TO QI.
FILTHY ASSISTANTS. GET ME A MACHINE.

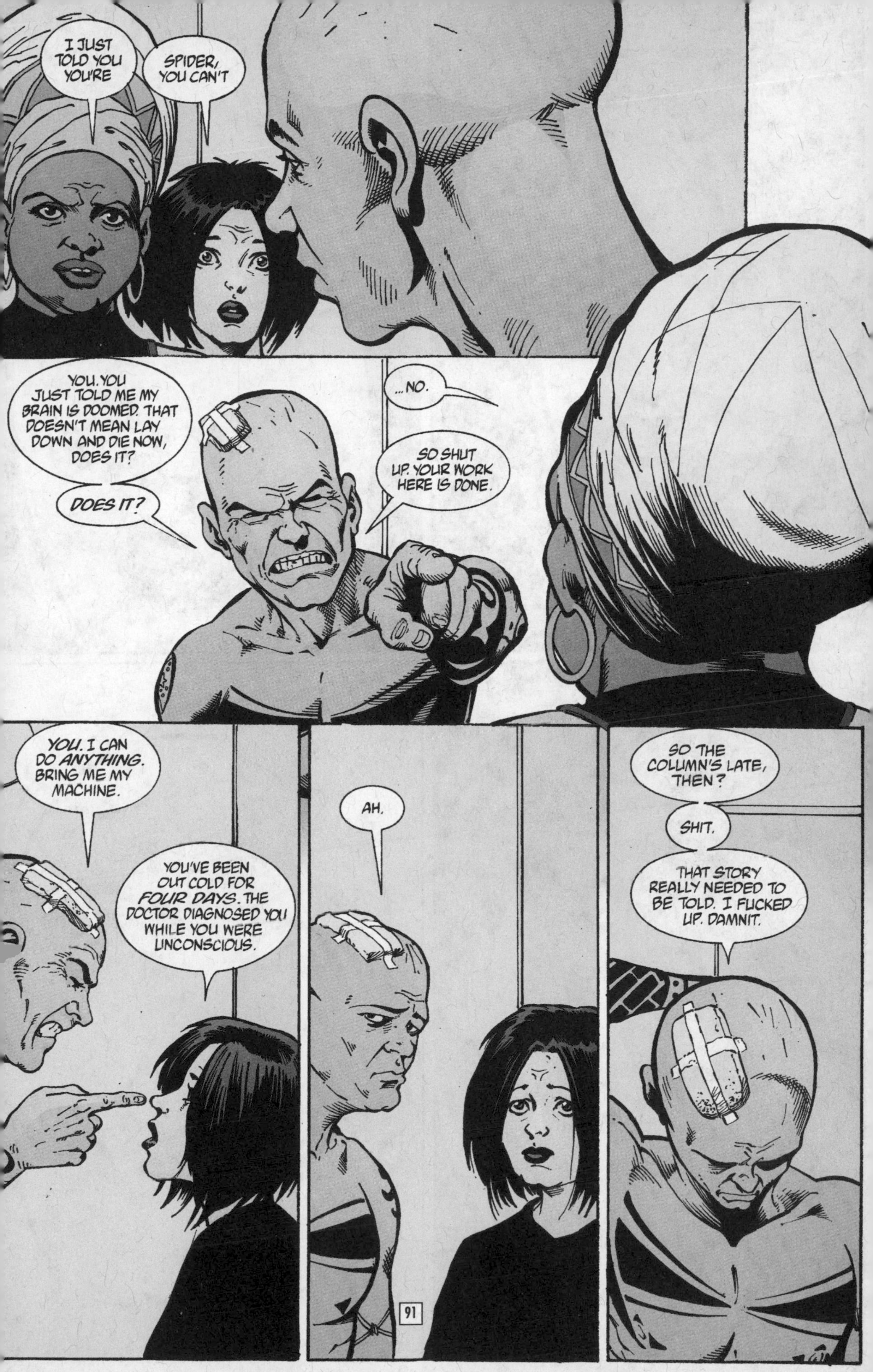
I JUST TOLD YOU YOU'RE
SPIDER, YOU CAN'T
YOU. YOU JUST TOLD ME MY BRAIN IS DOOMED. THAT DOESN'T MEAN LAY DOWN AND DIE NOW, DOES IT?
DOES IT?
...NO.
SO SHUT UP. YOUR WORK HERE IS DONE.
YOU. I CAN DO ANYTHING. BRING ME MY MACHINE.
YOU'VE BEEN OUT COLD FOR FOUR DAYS. THE DOCTOR DIAGNOSED YOU WHILE YOU WERE UNCONSCIOUS.
AH.
SO THE COLUMN'S LATE, THEN?
SHIT.
THAT STORY REALLY NEEDED TO BE TOLD. I FUCKED UP. DAMNIT.

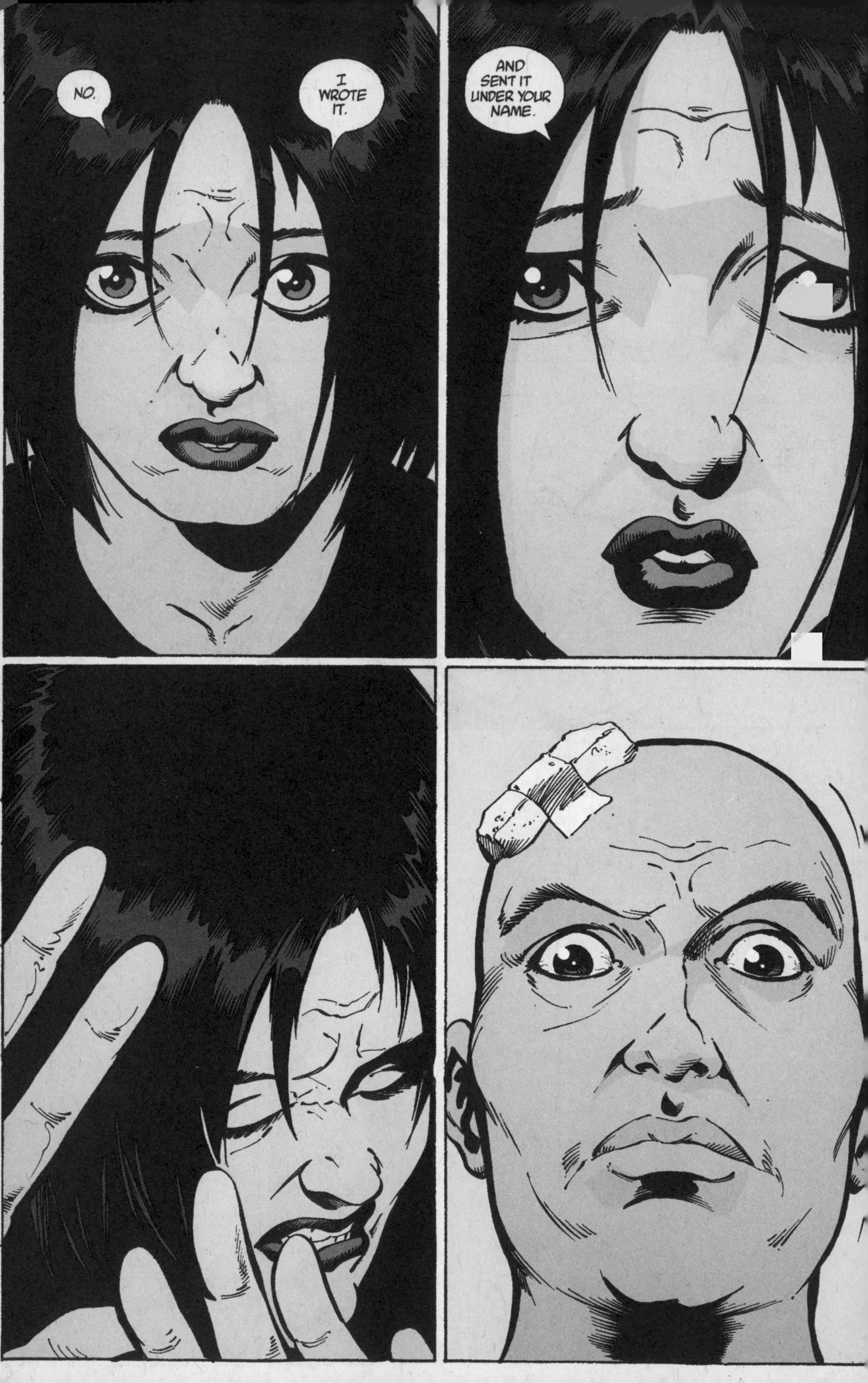
NO.
I WROTE IT.
AND SENT IT UNDER YOUR NAME.

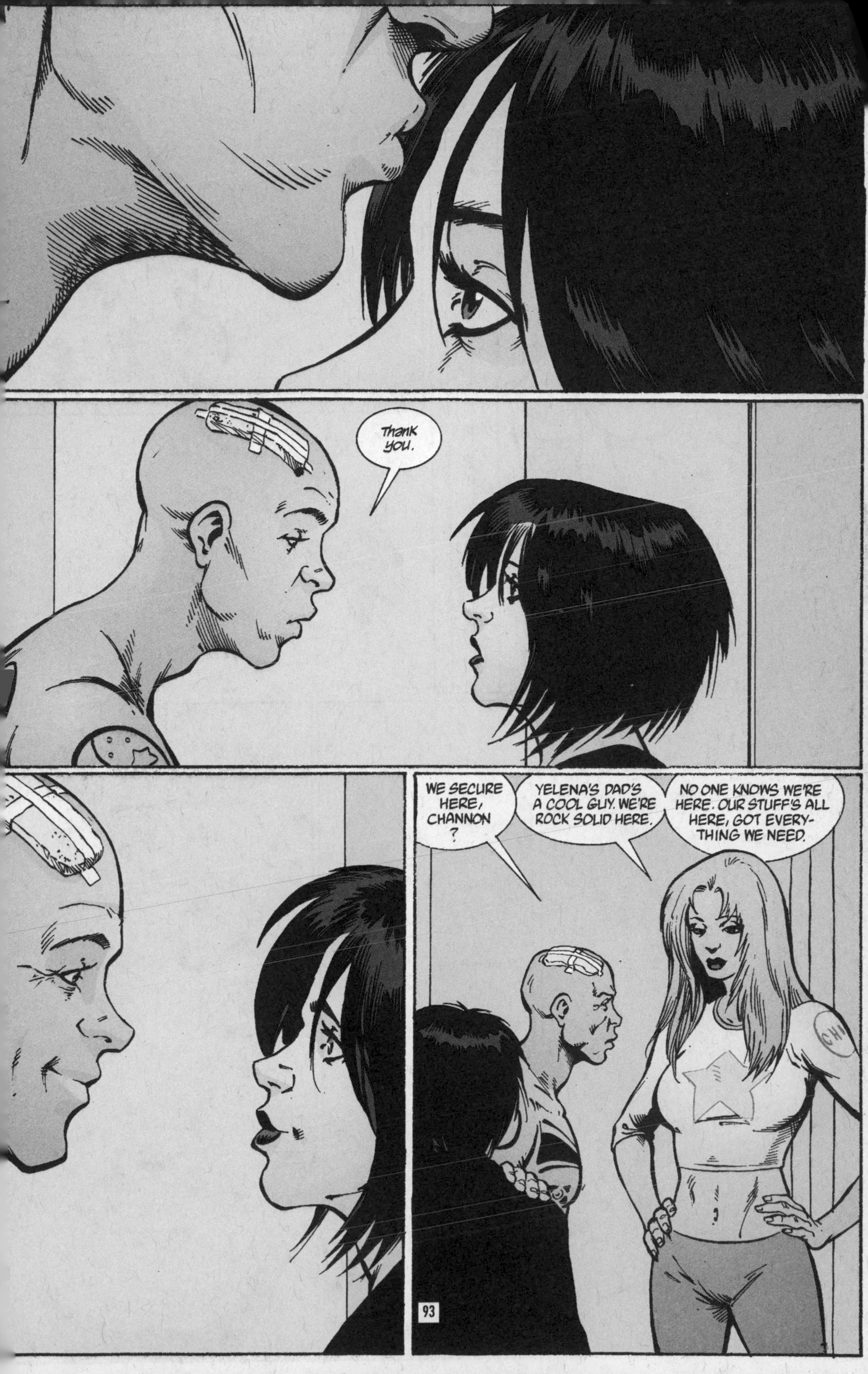
Thank you.
WE SECURE HERE, CHANNON ?
YELENA'S DAD'S A COOL GUY. WE'RE ROCK SOLID HERE.
NO ONE KNOWS WE'RE HERE. OUR STUFF'S ALL HERE, GOT EVERY-THING WE NEED.
CHI

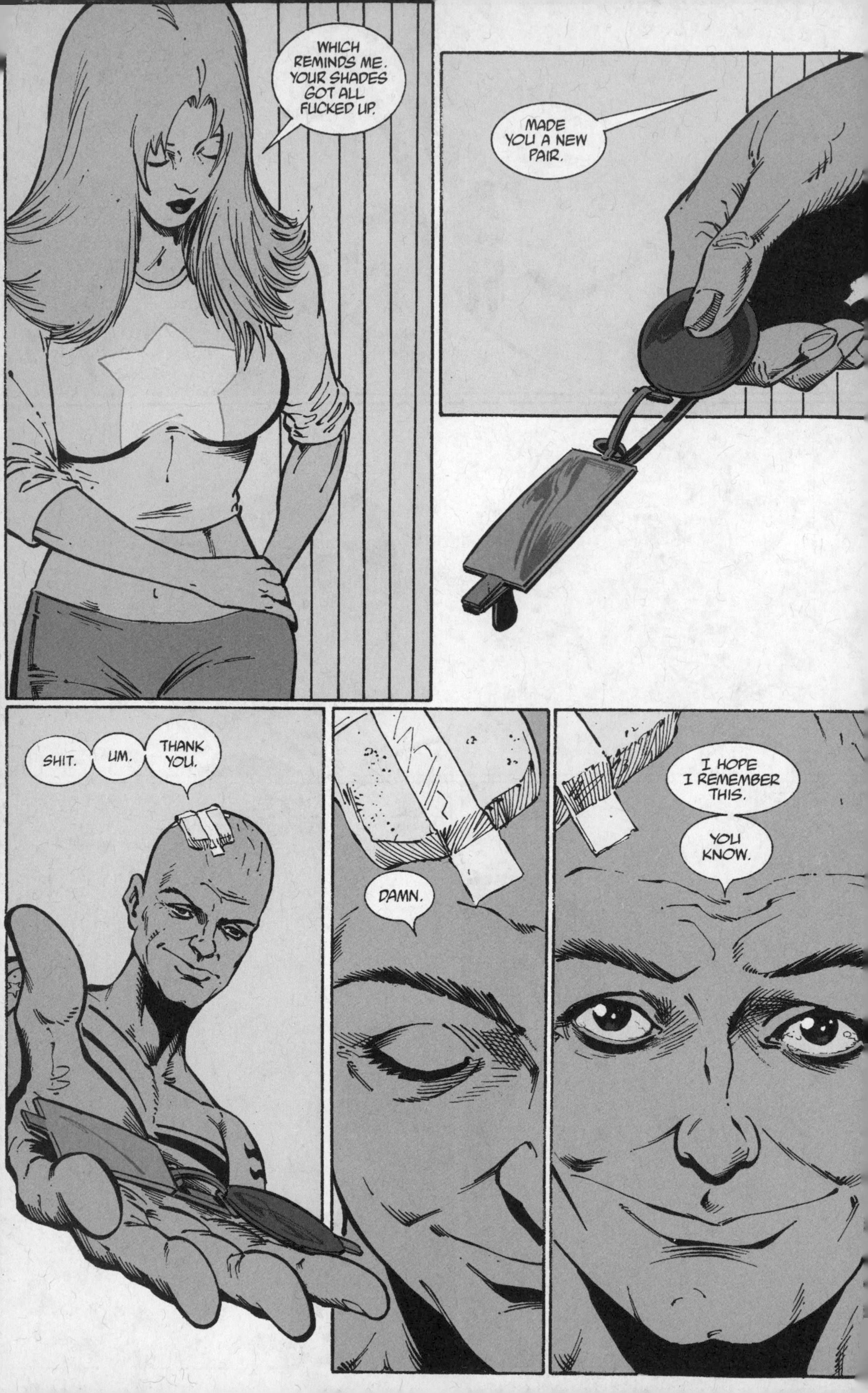
WHICH REMINDS ME. YOUR SHADES GOT ALL FUCKED UP.
MADE YOU A NEW PAIR.
SHIT.
UM.
THANK YOU.
DAMN.
I HOPE I REMEMBER THIS.
YOU KNOW.

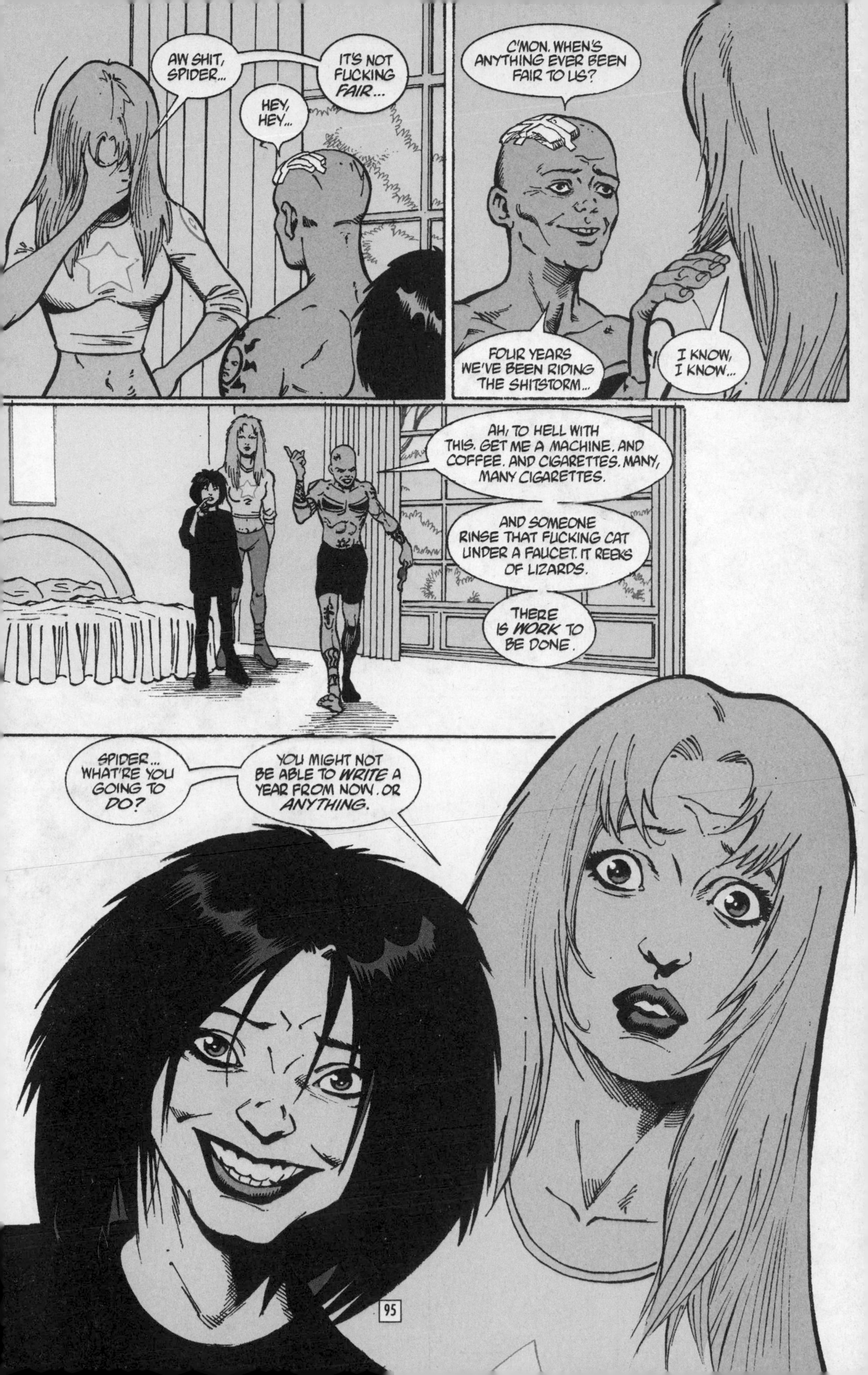
AW SHIT, SPIDER...
IT'S NOT FUCKING FAIR...
HEY, HEY...
C'MON. WHEN'S ANYTHING EVER BEEN FAIR TO US?
FOUR YEARS WE'VE BEEN RIDING THE SHITSTORM...
I KNOW, I KNOW...
AH, TO HELL WITH THIS. GET ME A MACHINE. AND COFFEE. AND CIGARETTES. MANY, MANY CIGARETTES.
AND SOMEONE RINSE THAT FUCKING CAT UNDER A FAUCET. IT REEKS OF LIZARDS.
THERE IS WORK TO BE DONE.
SPIDER... WHAT'RE YOU GOING TO DO?
YOU MIGHT NOT BE ABLE TO WRITE A YEAR FROM NOW. OR ANYTHING.

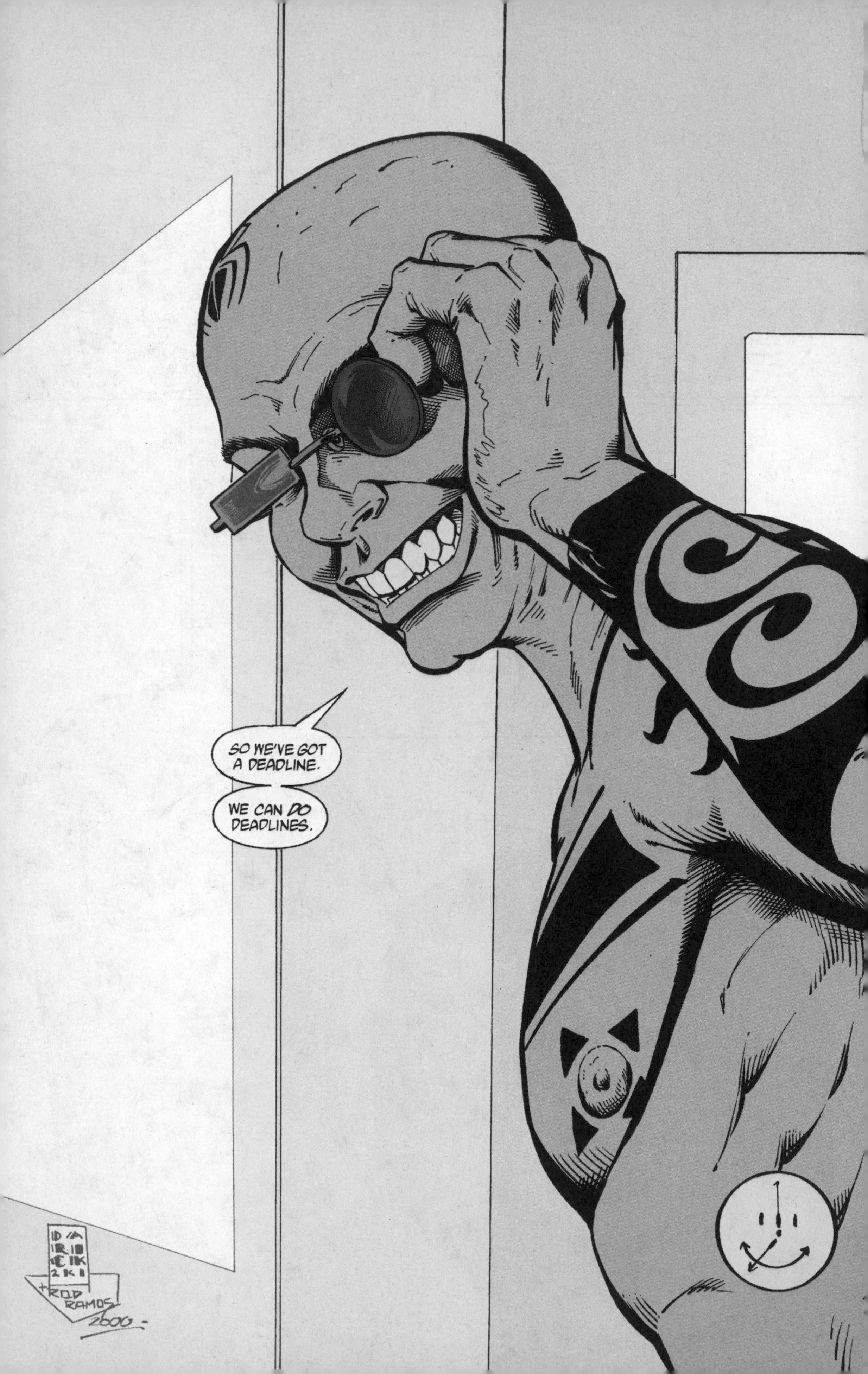
SO WE'VE GOT A DEADLINE.
WE CAN DO DEADLINES.
+ROD RAMOS 2000

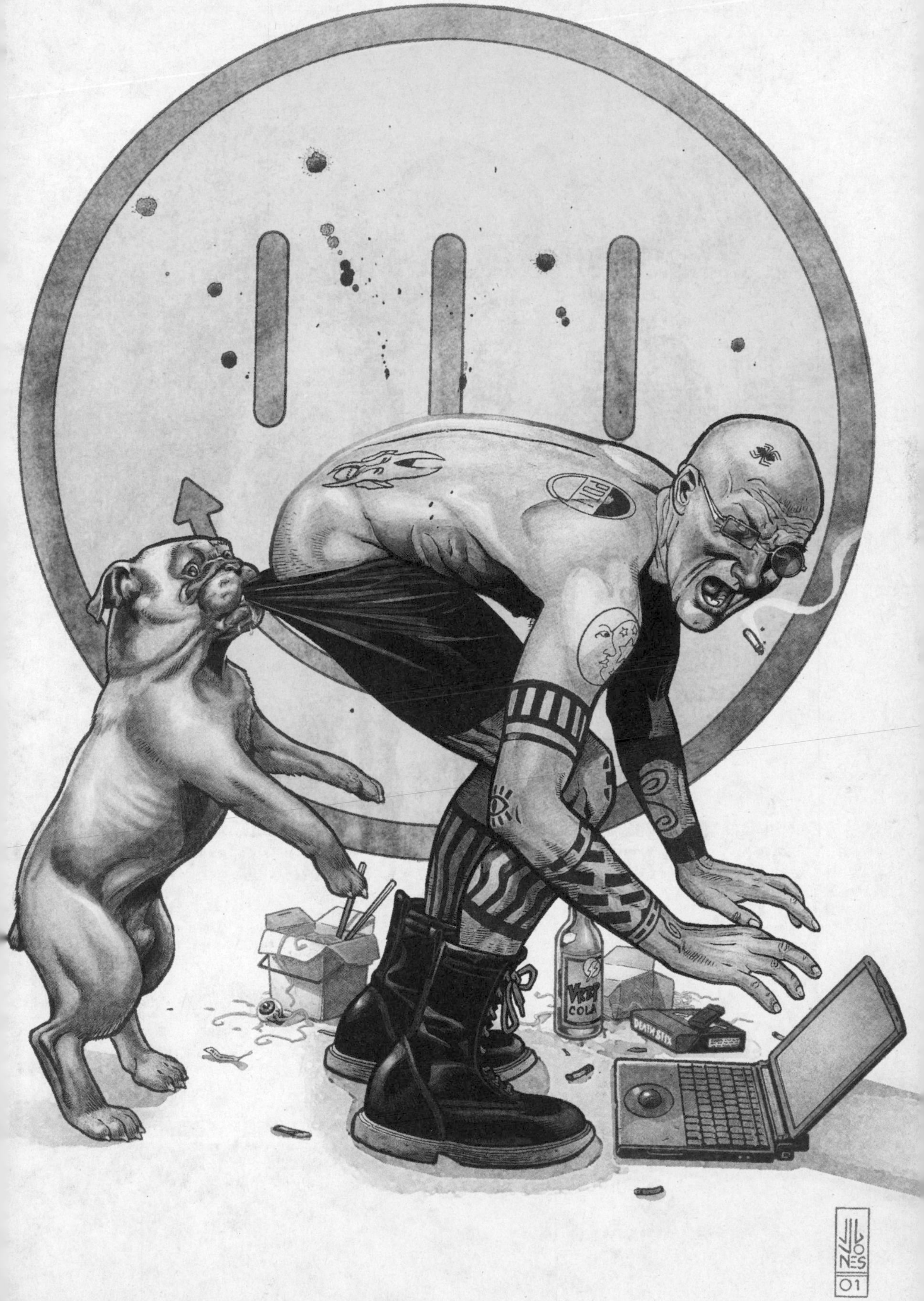
COLA
DEATH STIX
JG JONES 01

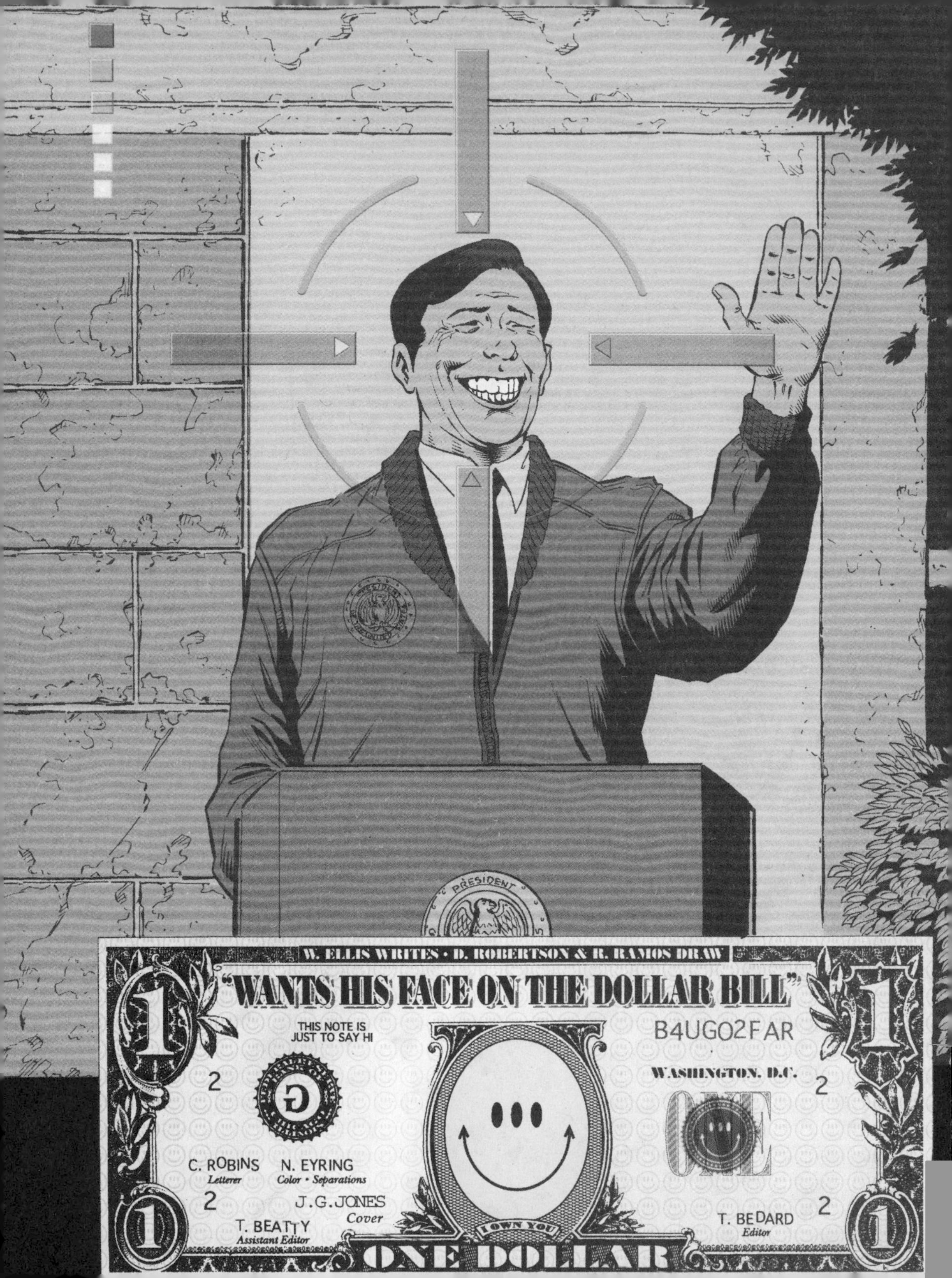

W. ELLIS WRITES • D. ROBERTSON & R. RAMOS DRAW
"WANTS HIS FACE ON THE DOLLAR BILL"
THIS NOTE IS JUST TO SAY HI
B4UGO2FAR
WASHINGTON, D.C.
C. ROBINS Letterer
N. EYRING Color • Separations
J.G. JONES Cover
T. BEATTY Assistant Editor
T. BEDARD Editor
I OWN YOU
ONE
ONE DOLLAR

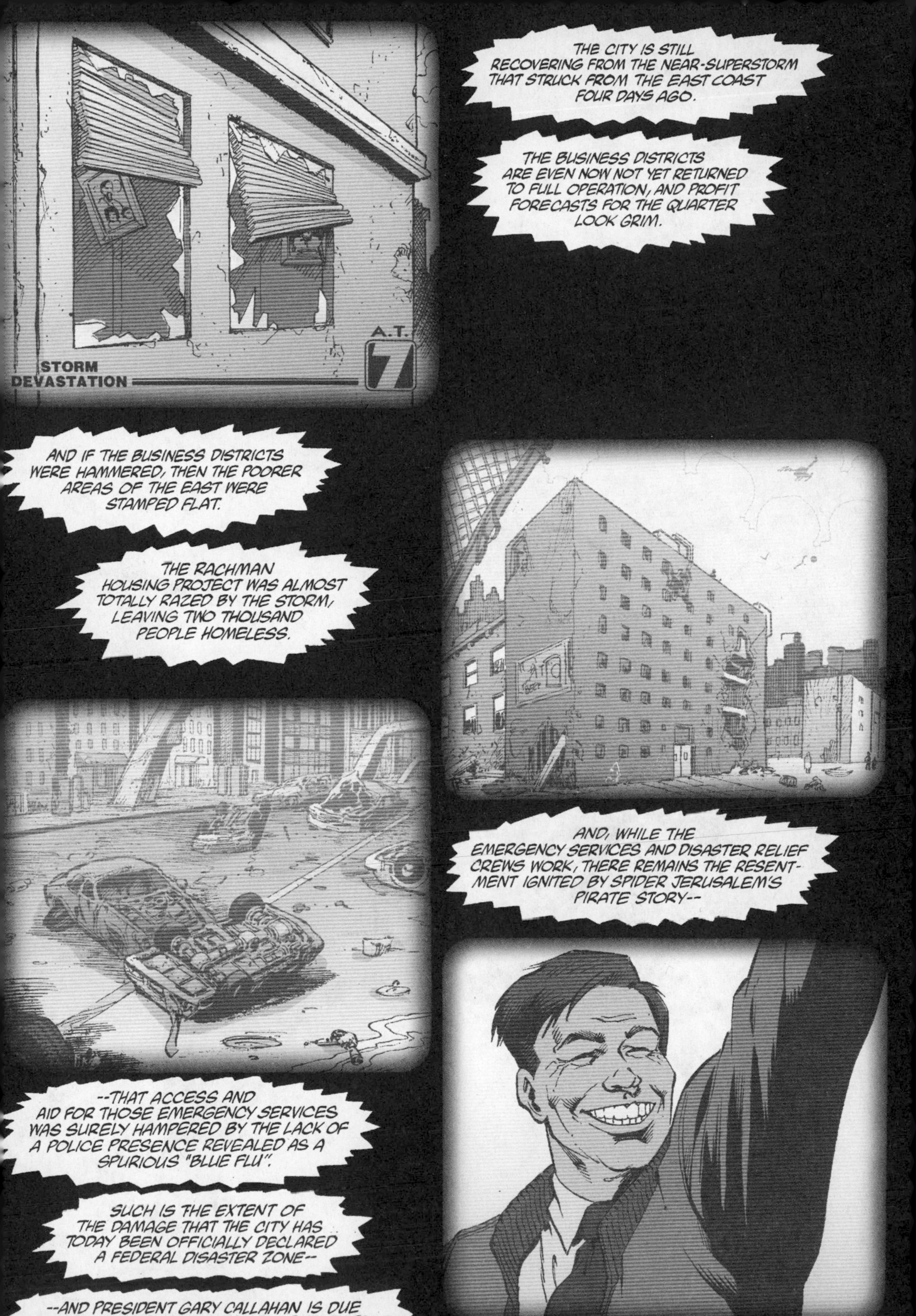
A.T.
7
STORM
DEVASTATION
THE CITY IS STILL RECOVERING FROM THE NEAR-SUPERSTORM THAT STRUCK FROM THE EAST COAST FOUR DAYS AGO.
THE BUSINESS DISTRICTS ARE EVEN NOW NOT YET RETURNED TO FULL OPERATION, AND PROFIT FORECASTS FOR THE QUARTER LOOK GRIM.
AND IF THE BUSINESS DISTRICTS WERE HAMMERED, THEN THE POORER AREAS OF THE EAST WERE STAMPED FLAT.
THE RACHMAN HOUSING PROJECT WAS ALMOST TOTALLY RAZED BY THE STORM, LEAVING TWO THOUSAND PEOPLE HOMELESS.
AND, WHILE THE EMERGENCY SERVICES AND DISASTER RELIEF CREWS WORK, THERE REMAINS THE RESENT-MENT IGNITED BY SPIDER JERUSALEM'S PIRATE STORY--
--THAT ACCESS AND AID FOR THOSE EMERGENCY SERVICES WAS SURELY HAMPERED BY THE LACK OF A POLICE PRESENCE REVEALED AS A SPURIOUS "BLUE FLU".
SUCH IS THE EXTENT OF THE DAMAGE THAT THE CITY HAS TODAY BEEN OFFICIALLY DECLARED A FEDERAL DISASTER ZONE--
--AND PRESIDENT GARY CALLAHAN IS DUE TO VISIT THERE WITHIN THE NEXT TWENTY-FOUR HOURS TO PERSONALLY ASSESS THE SITUATION.

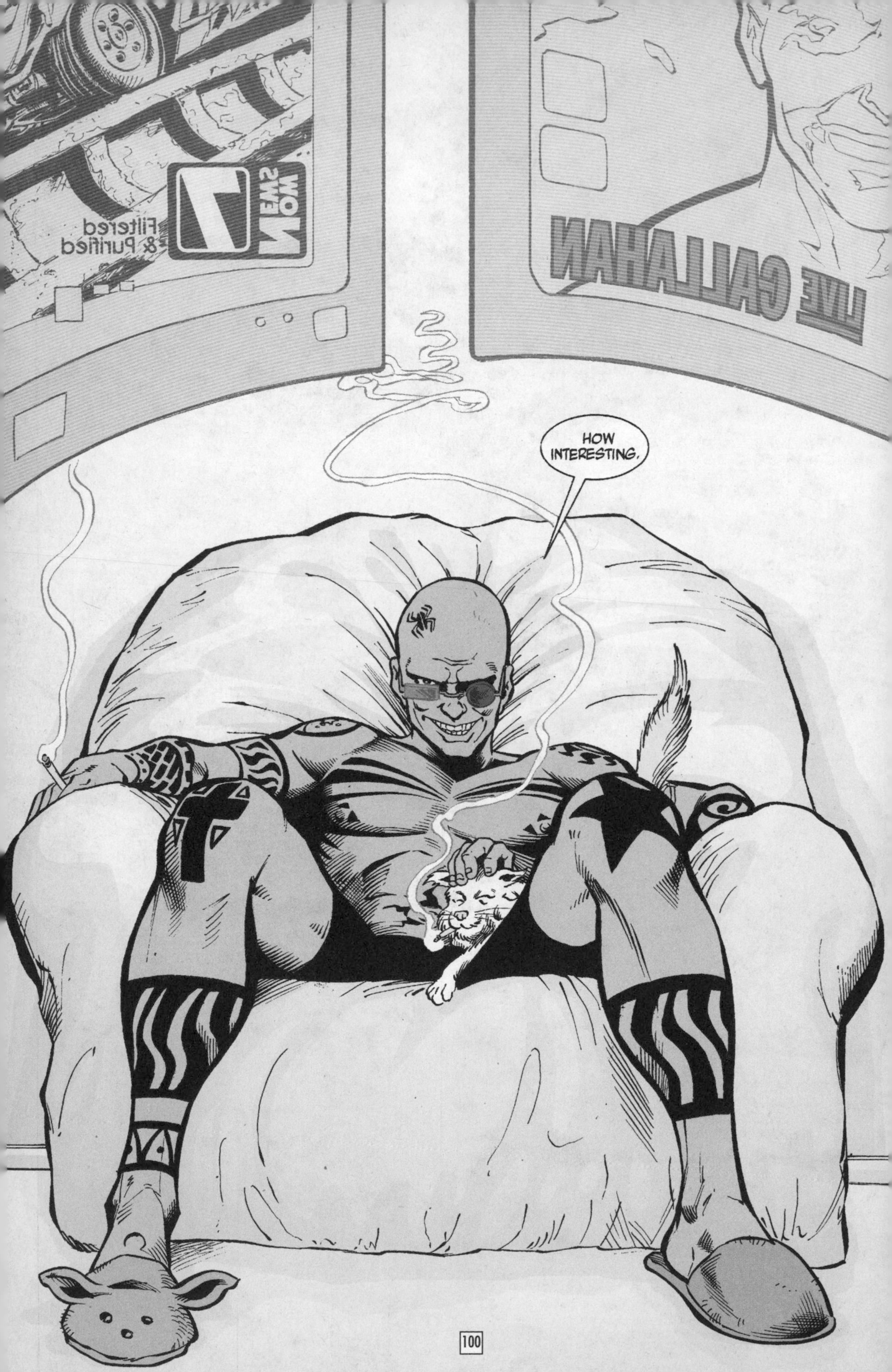
HOW INTERESTING.

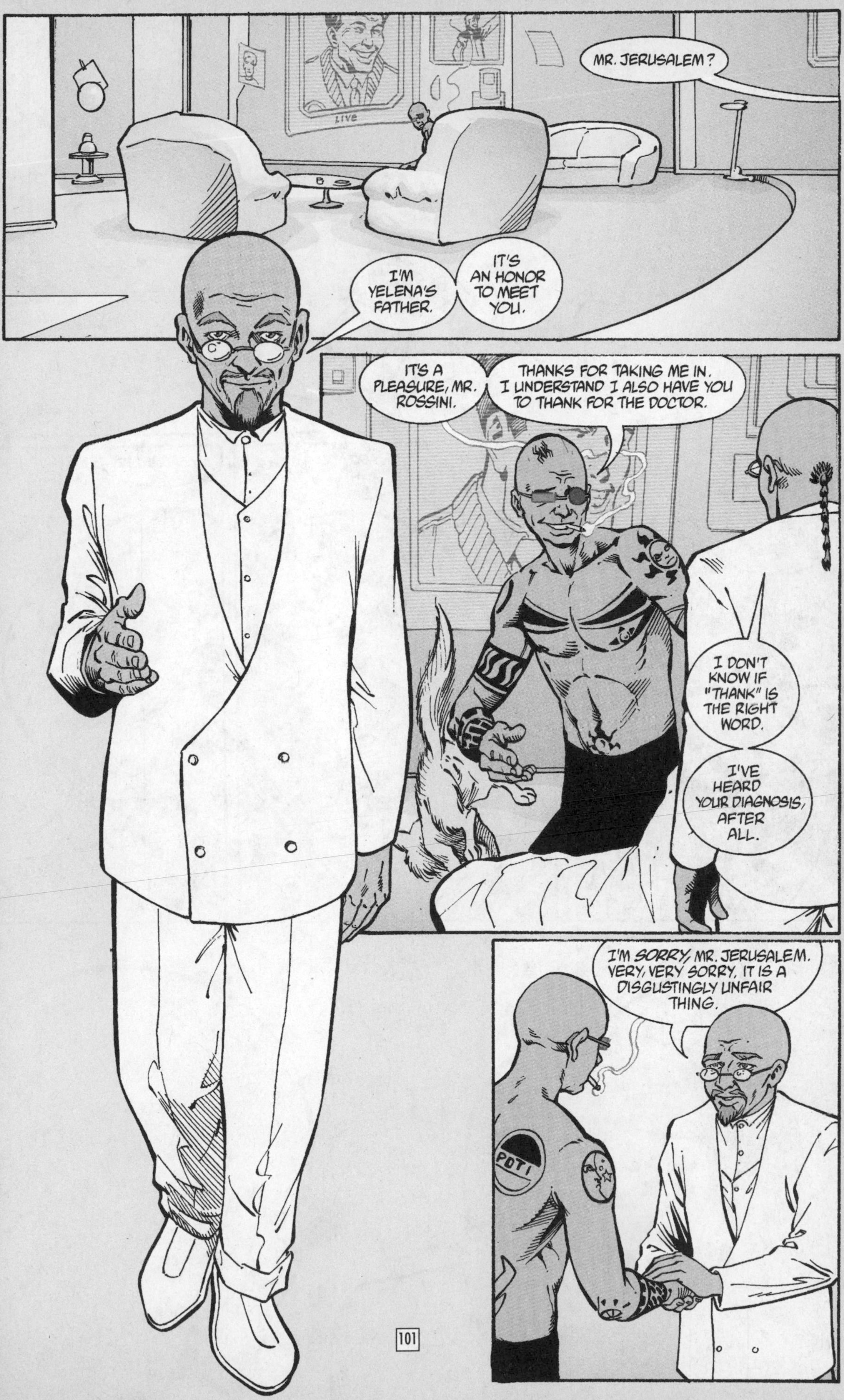

MR. JERUSALEM?
I'M YELENA'S FATHER.
IT'S AN HONOR TO MEET YOU.
IT'S A PLEASURE, MR. ROSSINI.
THANKS FOR TAKING ME IN. I UNDERSTAND I ALSO HAVE YOU TO THANK FOR THE DOCTOR.
I DON'T KNOW IF "THANK" IS THE RIGHT WORD.
I'VE HEARD YOUR DIAGNOSIS, AFTER ALL.
I'M *SORRY*, MR. JERUSALEM. VERY, VERY SORRY, IT IS A DISGUSTINGLY UNFAIR THING.

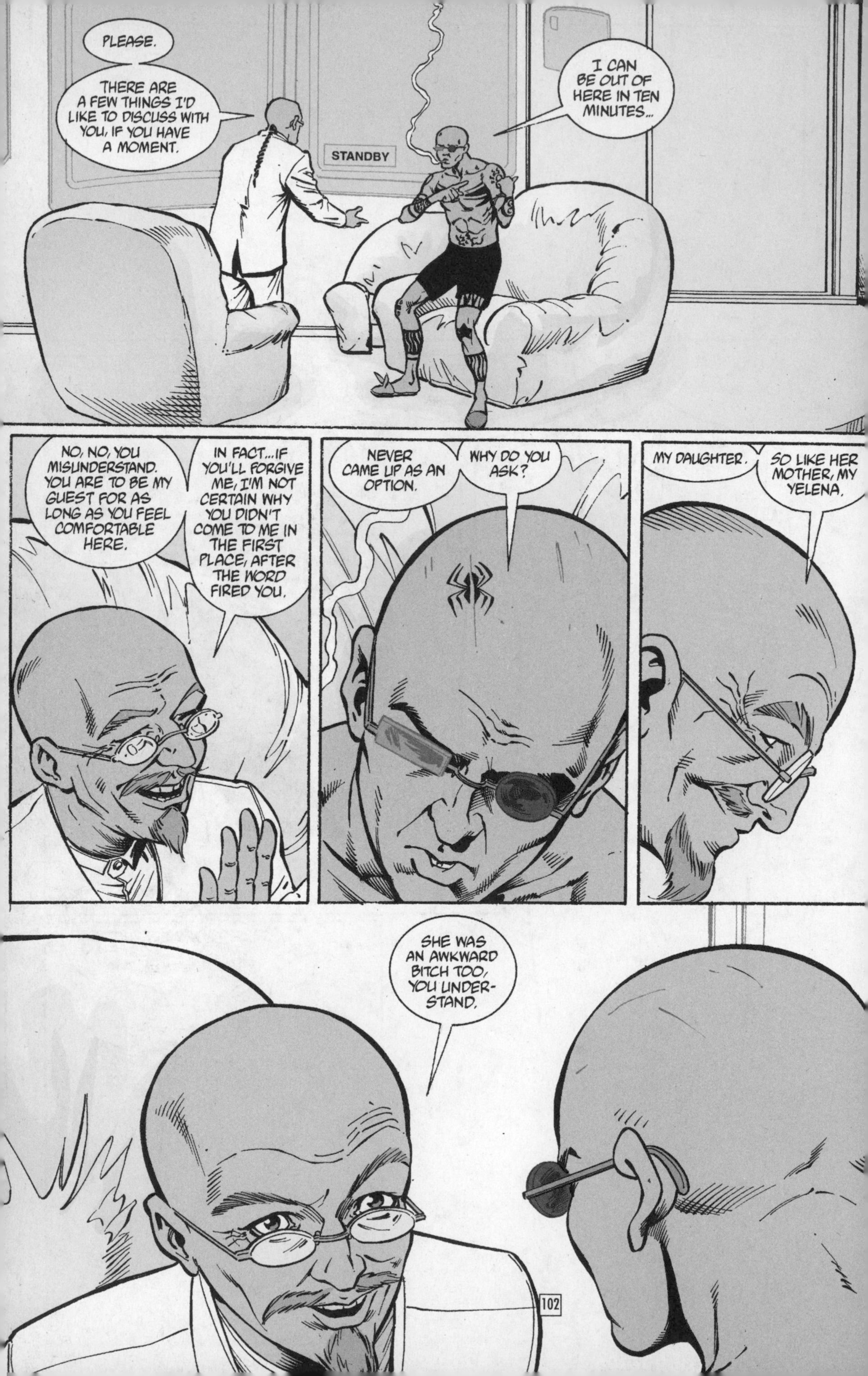
PLEASE.
THERE ARE A FEW THINGS I'D LIKE TO DISCUSS WITH YOU, IF YOU HAVE A MOMENT.
I CAN BE OUT OF HERE IN TEN MINUTES...
STANDBY
NO, NO, YOU MISUNDERSTAND. YOU ARE TO BE MY GUEST FOR AS LONG AS YOU FEEL COMFORTABLE HERE.
IN FACT...IF YOU'LL FORGIVE ME, I'M NOT CERTAIN WHY YOU DIDN'T COME TO ME IN THE FIRST PLACE, AFTER THE WORD FIRED YOU.
NEVER CAME UP AS AN OPTION.
WHY DO YOU ASK?
MY DAUGHTER.
SO LIKE HER MOTHER, MY YELENA.
SHE WAS AN AWKWARD BITCH TOO, YOU UNDER-STAND.

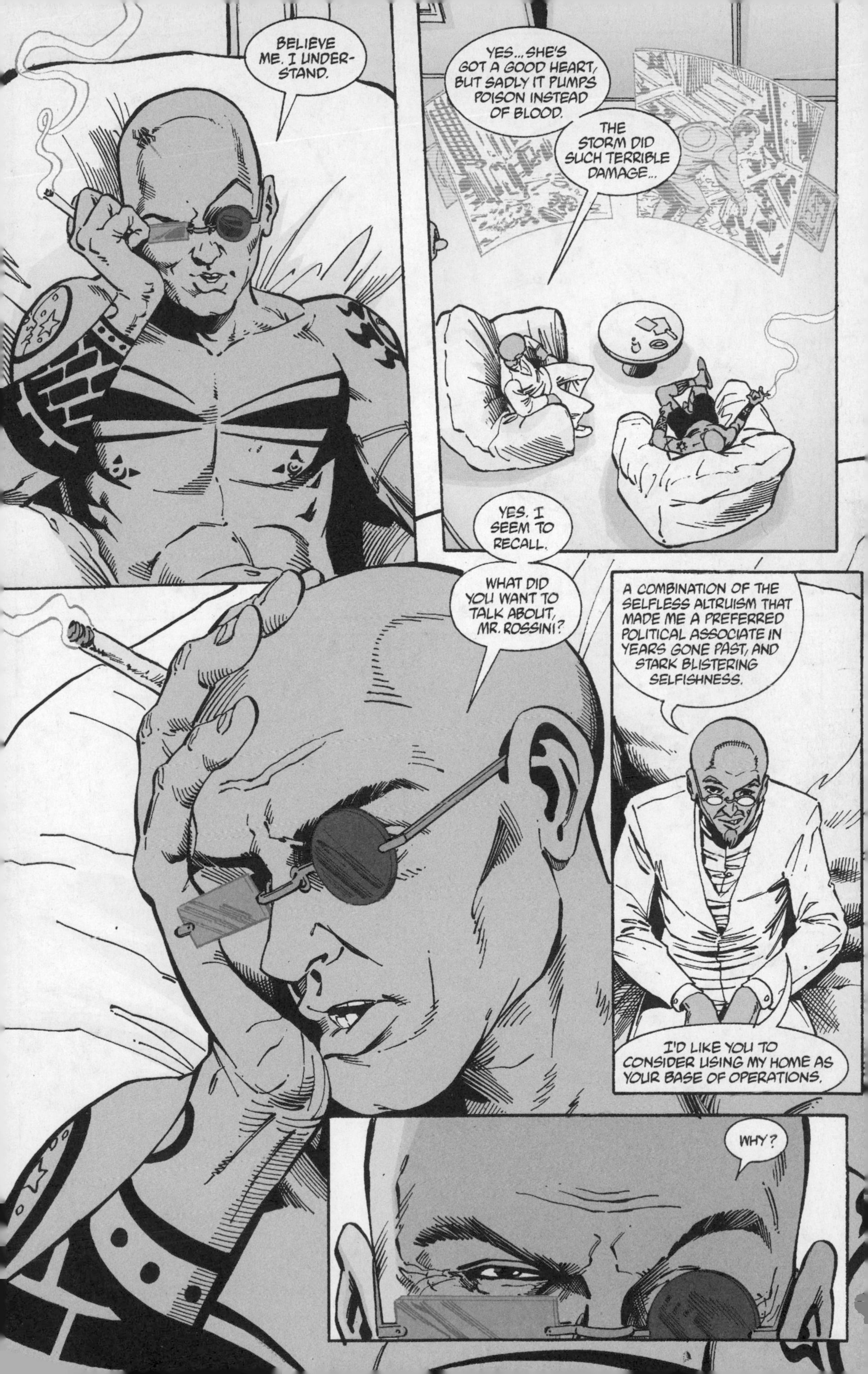
BELIEVE ME. I UNDER-STAND.
YES... SHE'S GOT A GOOD HEART, BUT SADLY IT PUMPS POISON INSTEAD OF BLOOD.
THE STORM DID SUCH TERRIBLE DAMAGE...
YES. I SEEM TO RECALL.
WHAT DID YOU WANT TO TALK ABOUT, MR. ROSSINI?
A COMBINATION OF THE SELFLESS ALTRUISM THAT MADE ME A PREFERRED POLITICAL ASSOCIATE IN YEARS GONE PAST, AND STARK BLISTERING SELFISHNESS.
I'D LIKE YOU TO CONSIDER USING MY HOME AS YOUR BASE OF OPERATIONS.
WHY?

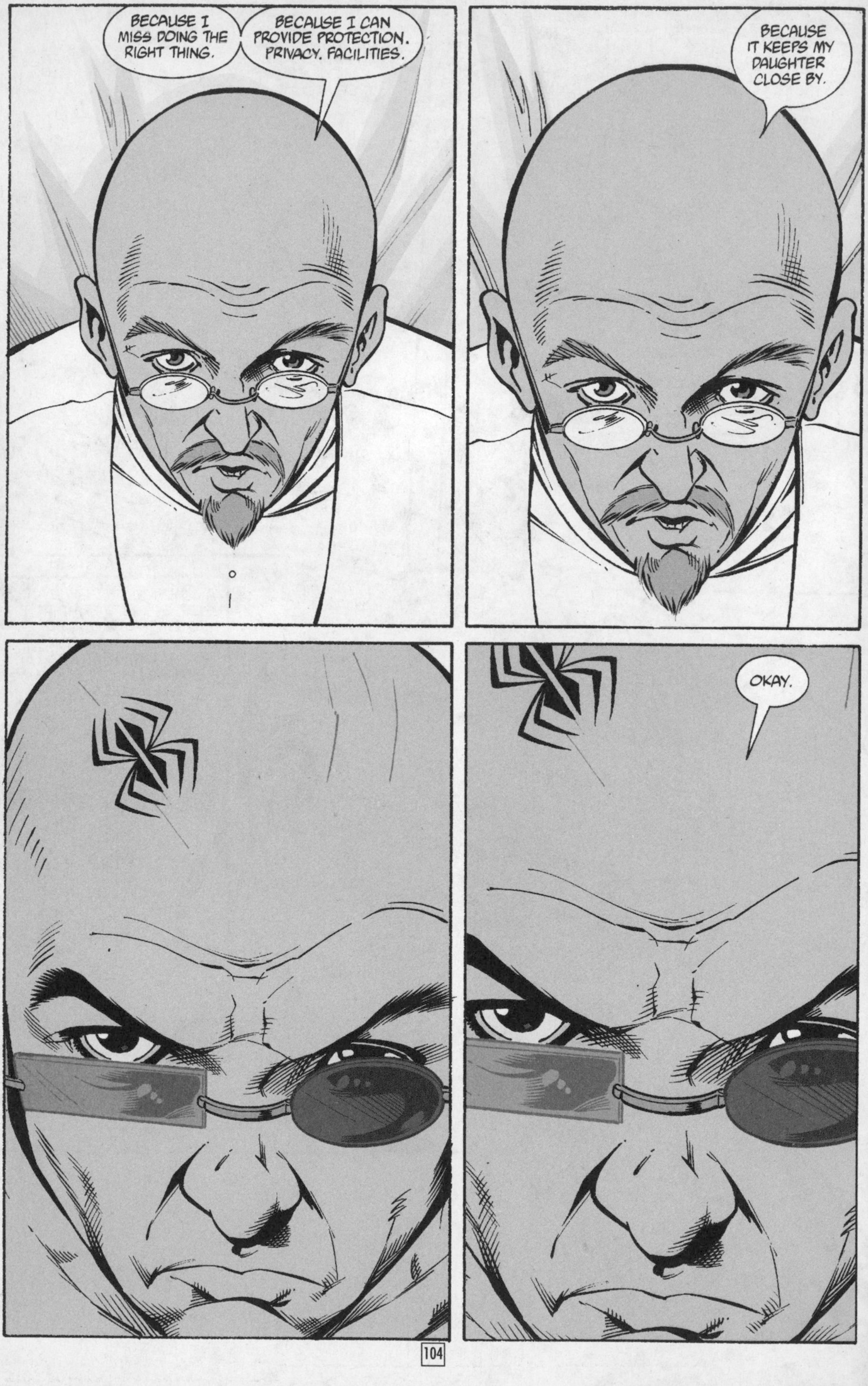
BECAUSE I MISS DOING THE RIGHT THING.
BECAUSE I CAN PROVIDE PROTECTION. PRIVACY. FACILITIES.
BECAUSE IT KEEPS MY DAUGHTER CLOSE BY.
OKAY.

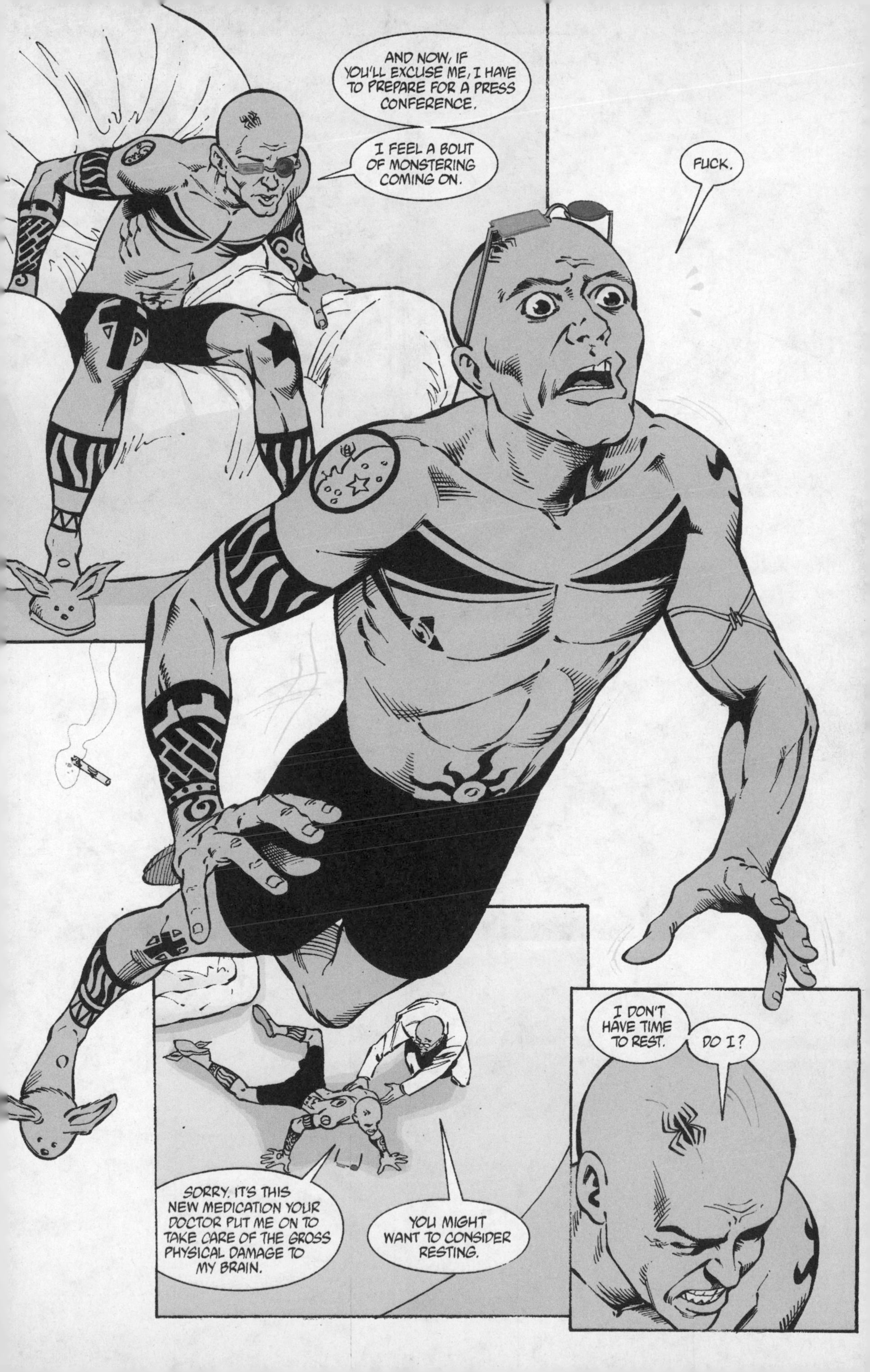
AND NOW, IF YOU'LL EXCUSE ME, I HAVE TO PREPARE FOR A PRESS CONFERENCE.
I FEEL A BOUT OF MONSTERING COMING ON.
FUCK.
SORRY. IT'S THIS NEW MEDICATION YOUR DOCTOR PUT ME ON TO TAKE CARE OF THE GROSS PHYSICAL DAMAGE TO MY BRAIN.
YOU MIGHT WANT TO CONSIDER RESTING.
I DON'T HAVE TIME TO REST.
DO I?

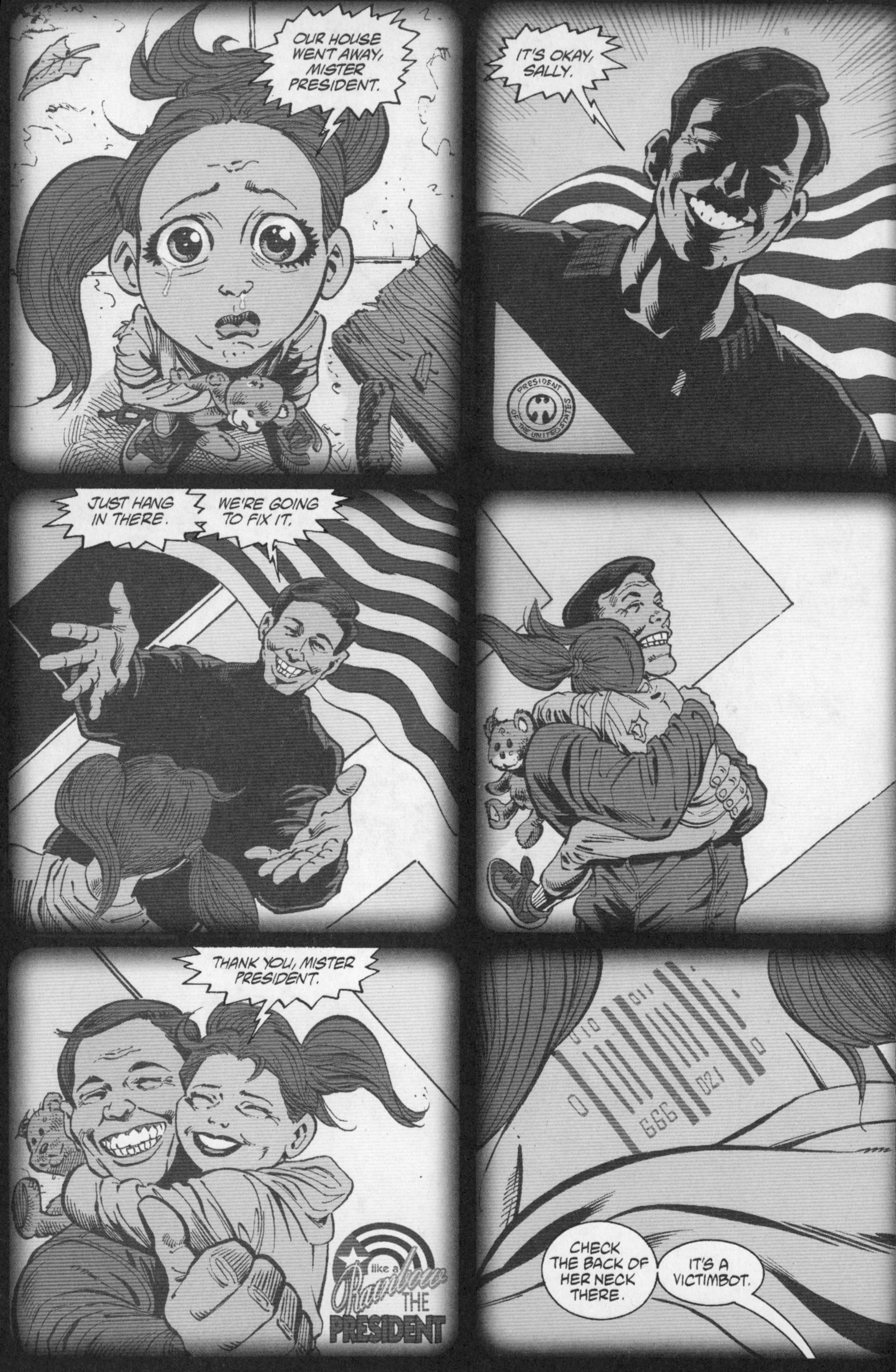
OUR HOUSE WENT AWAY, MISTER PRESIDENT.
IT'S OKAY, SALLY.
PRESIDENT OF THE UNITED STATES
JUST HANG IN THERE.
WE'RE GOING TO FIX IT.
THANK YOU, MISTER PRESIDENT.
like a Rainbow THE PRESIDENT
CHECK THE BACK OF HER NECK THERE.
IT'S A VICTIMBOT.

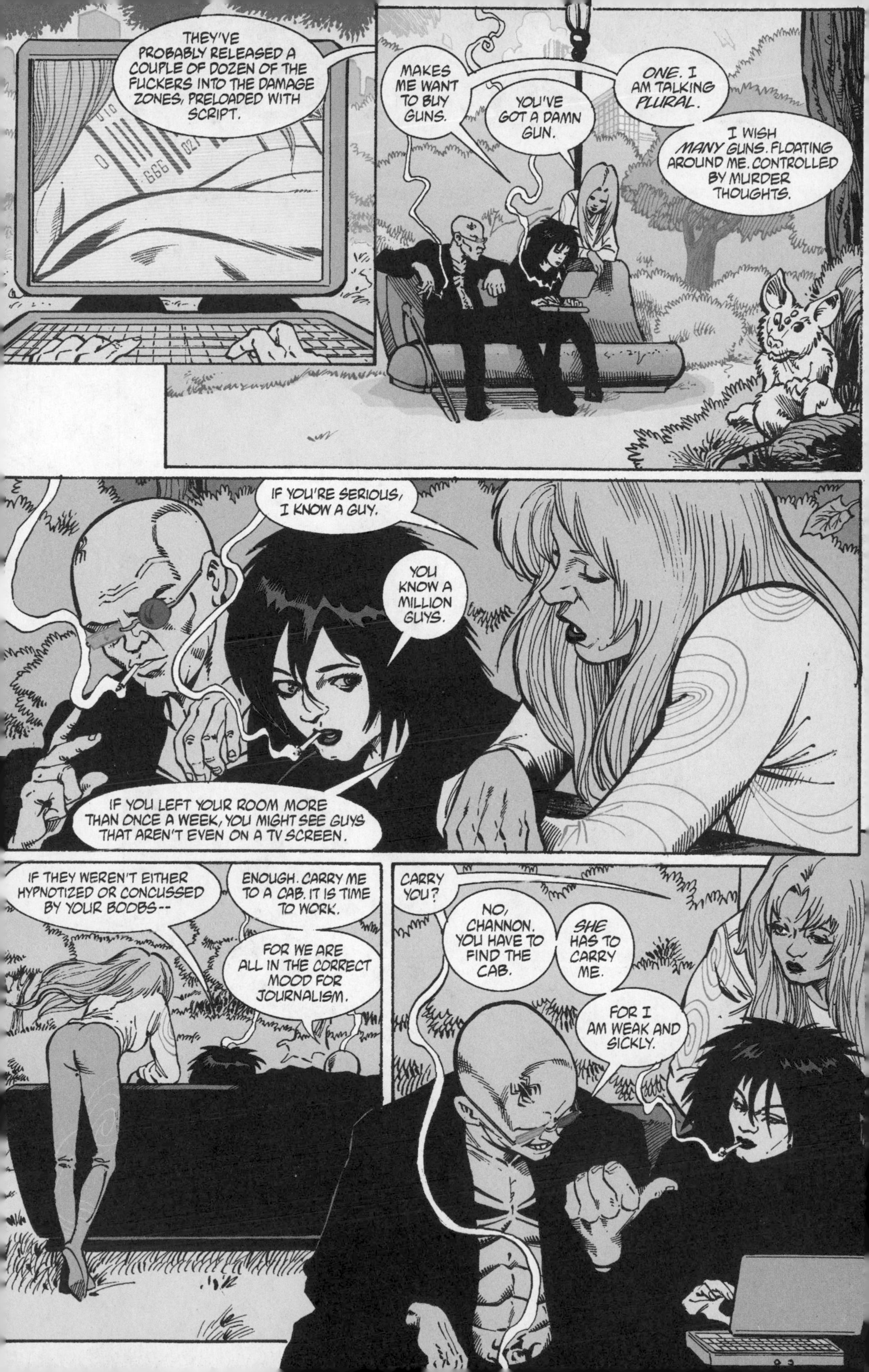
THEY'VE PROBABLY RELEASED A COUPLE OF DOZEN OF THE FUCKERS INTO THE DAMAGE ZONES, PRELOADED WITH SCRIPT.
MAKES ME WANT TO BUY GUNS.
YOU'VE GOT A DAMN GUN.
ONE. I AM TALKING PLURAL.
I WISH MANY GUNS. FLOATING AROUND ME. CONTROLLED BY MURDER THOUGHTS.
IF YOU'RE SERIOUS, I KNOW A GUY.
YOU KNOW A MILLION GUYS.
IF YOU LEFT YOUR ROOM MORE THAN ONCE A WEEK, YOU MIGHT SEE GUYS THAT AREN'T EVEN ON A TV SCREEN.
IF THEY WEREN'T EITHER HYPNOTIZED OR CONCUSSED BY YOUR BOOBS--
ENOUGH. CARRY ME TO A CAB. IT IS TIME TO WORK.
FOR WE ARE ALL IN THE CORRECT MOOD FOR JOURNALISM.
CARRY YOU?
NO, CHANNON. YOU HAVE TO FIND THE CAB.
SHE HAS TO CARRY ME.
FOR I AM WEAK AND SICKLY.

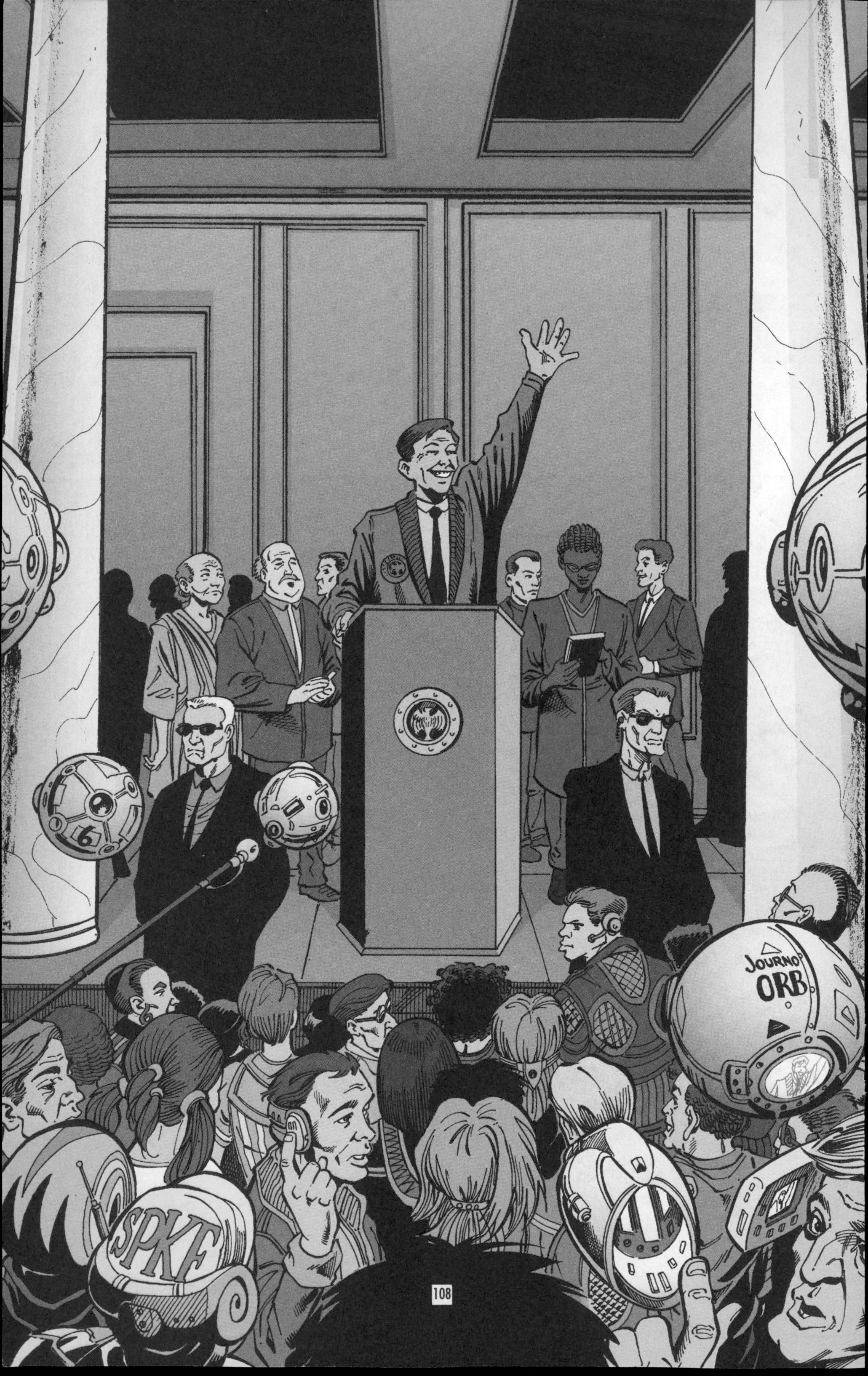
JOURNO ORB
SPKF

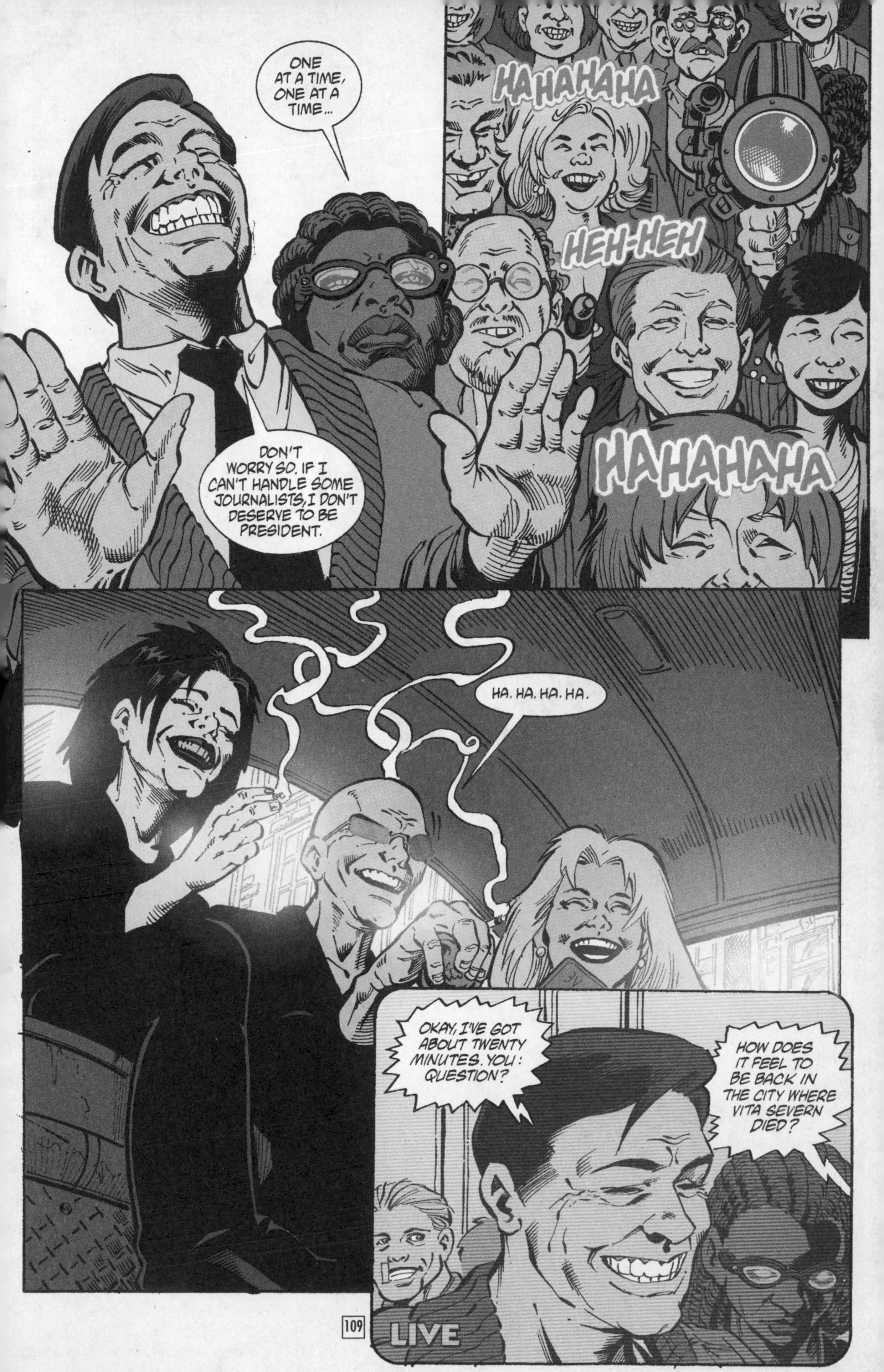
ONE AT A TIME, ONE AT A TIME...
HAHAHAHA
HEH-HEH
HAHAHAHA
DON'T WORRY SO. IF I CAN'T HANDLE SOME JOURNALISTS, I DON'T DESERVE TO BE PRESIDENT.
HA. HA. HA. HA.
OKAY, I'VE GOT ABOUT TWENTY MINUTES. YOU: QUESTION?
HOW DOES IT FEEL TO BE BACK IN THE CITY WHERE VITA SEVERN DIED?
LIVE

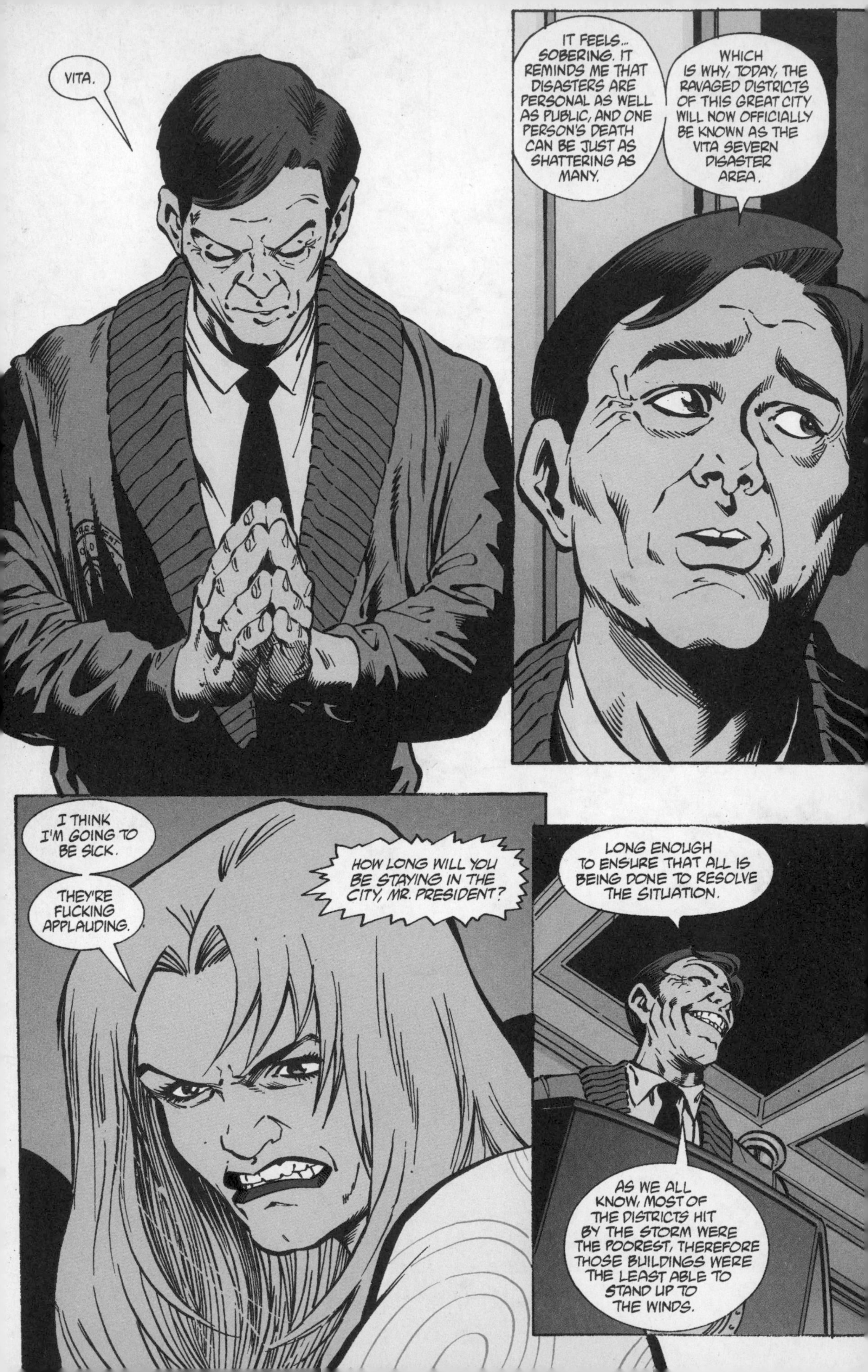
VITA.
IT FEELS... SOBERING. IT REMINDS ME THAT DISASTERS ARE PERSONAL AS WELL AS PUBLIC, AND ONE PERSON'S DEATH CAN BE JUST AS SHATTERING AS MANY.
WHICH IS WHY, TODAY, THE RAVAGED DISTRICTS OF THIS GREAT CITY WILL NOW OFFICIALLY BE KNOWN AS THE VITA SEVERN DISASTER AREA.
I THINK I'M GOING TO BE SICK.
THEY'RE FUCKING APPLAUDING.
HOW LONG WILL YOU BE STAYING IN THE CITY, MR. PRESIDENT?
LONG ENOUGH TO ENSURE THAT ALL IS BEING DONE TO RESOLVE THE SITUATION.
AS WE ALL KNOW, MOST OF THE DISTRICTS HIT BY THE STORM WERE THE POOREST, THEREFORE THOSE BUILDINGS WERE THE LEAST ABLE TO STAND UP TO THE WINDS.

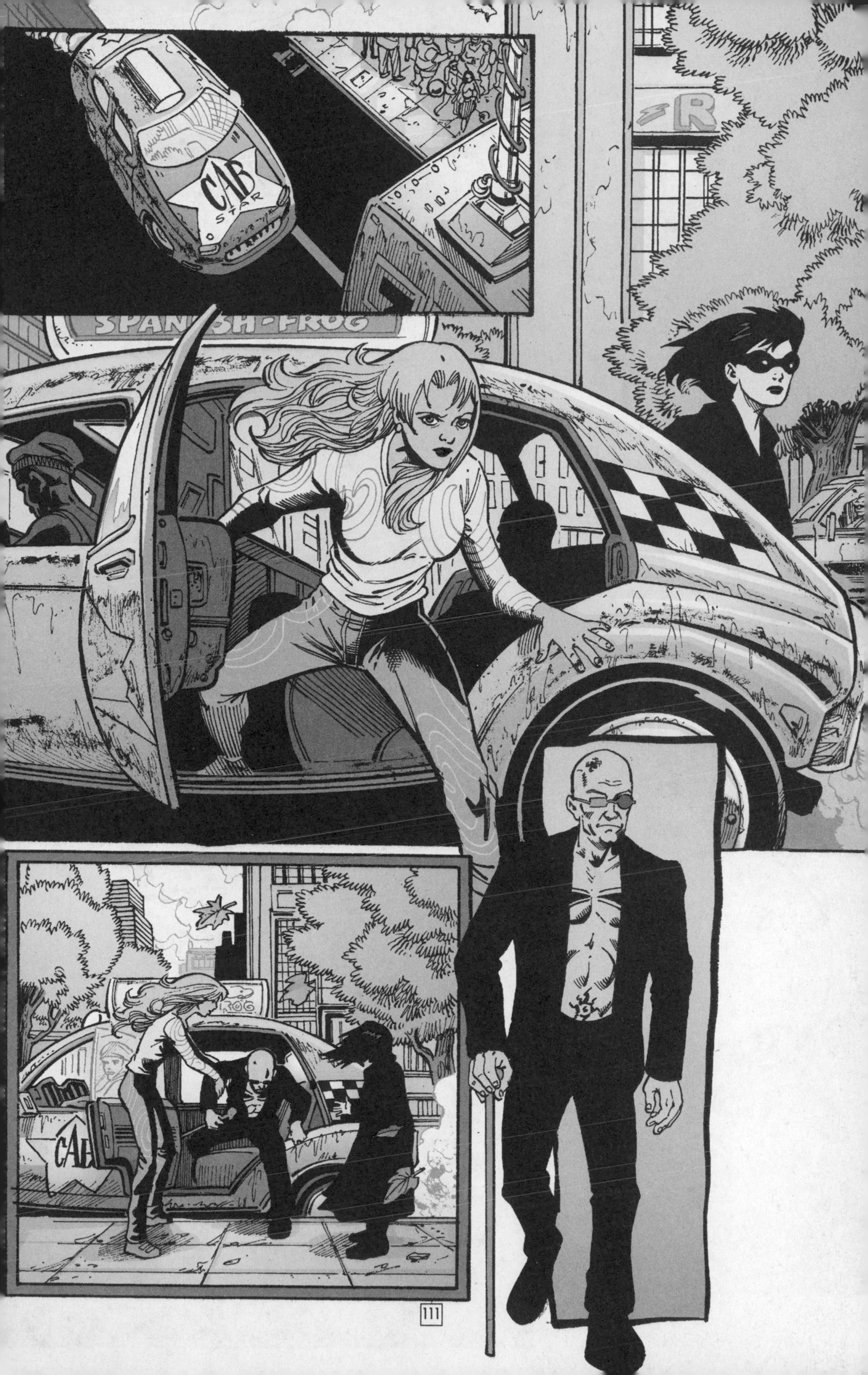
CAB STAR
SPANISH-FROG
R

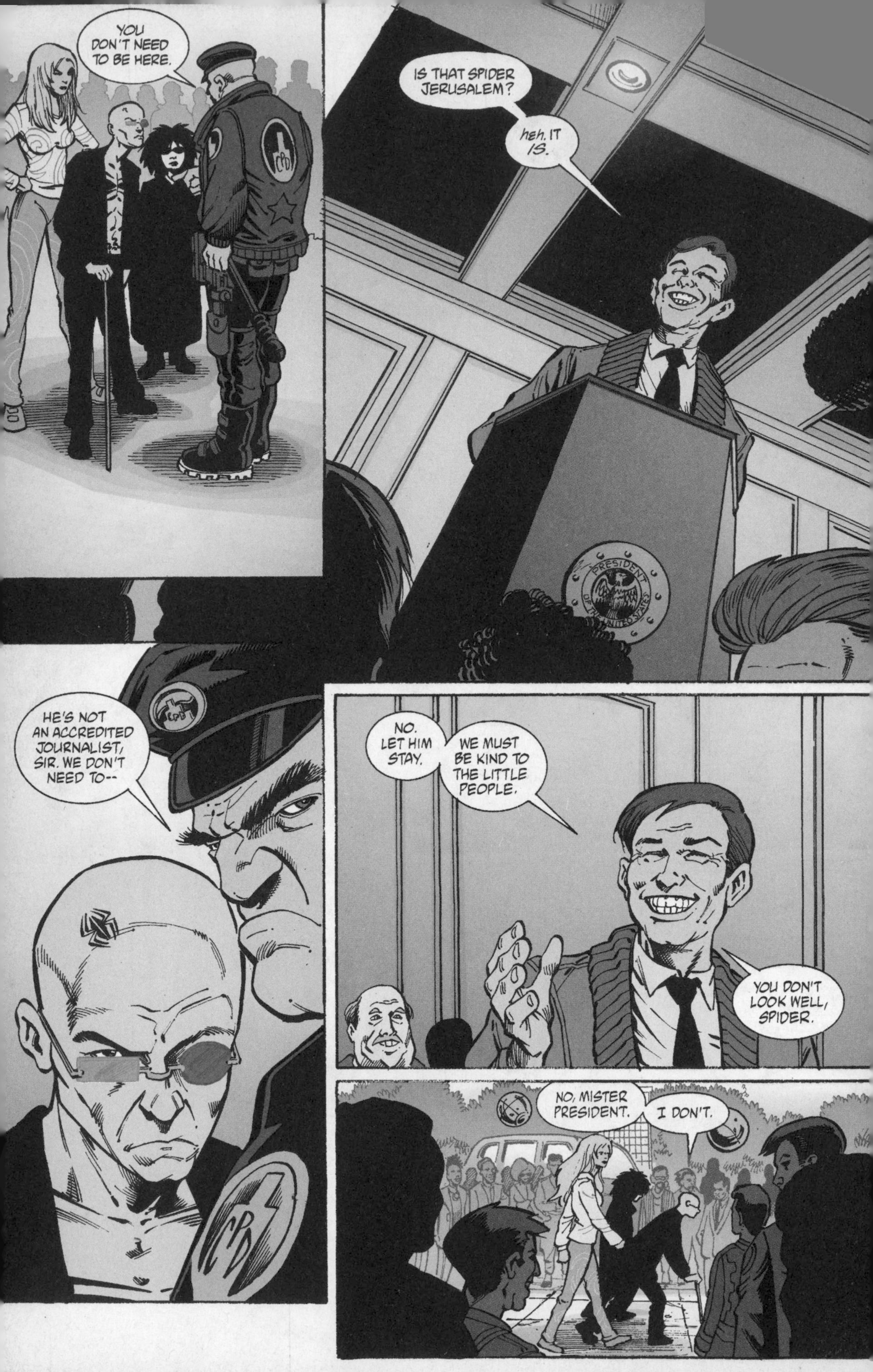
YOU DON'T NEED TO BE HERE.
IS THAT SPIDER JERUSALEM?
heh. IT IS.
HE'S NOT AN ACCREDITED JOURNALIST, SIR. WE DON'T NEED TO--
NO. LET HIM STAY.
WE MUST BE KIND TO THE LITTLE PEOPLE.
YOU DON'T LOOK WELL, SPIDER.
NO, MISTER PRESIDENT.
I DON'T.

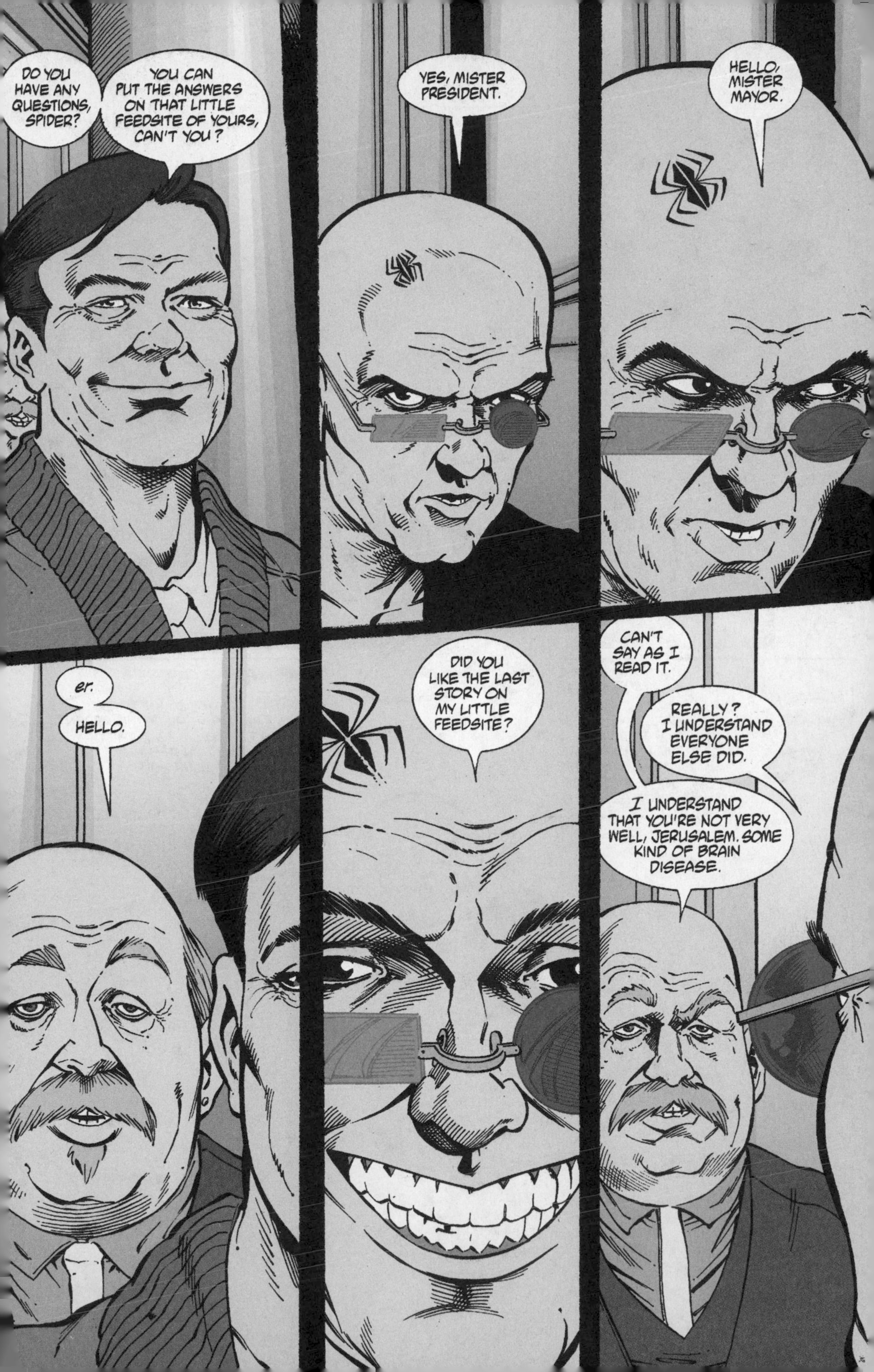
DO YOU HAVE ANY QUESTIONS, SPIDER?
YOU CAN PUT THE ANSWERS ON THAT LITTLE FEEDSITE OF YOURS, CAN'T YOU?
YES, MISTER PRESIDENT.
HELLO, MISTER MAYOR.
er.
HELLO.
DID YOU LIKE THE LAST STORY ON MY LITTLE FEEDSITE?
CAN'T SAY AS I READ IT.
REALLY? I UNDERSTAND EVERYONE ELSE DID.
I UNDERSTAND THAT YOU'RE NOT VERY WELL, JERUSALEM. SOME KIND OF BRAIN DISEASE.

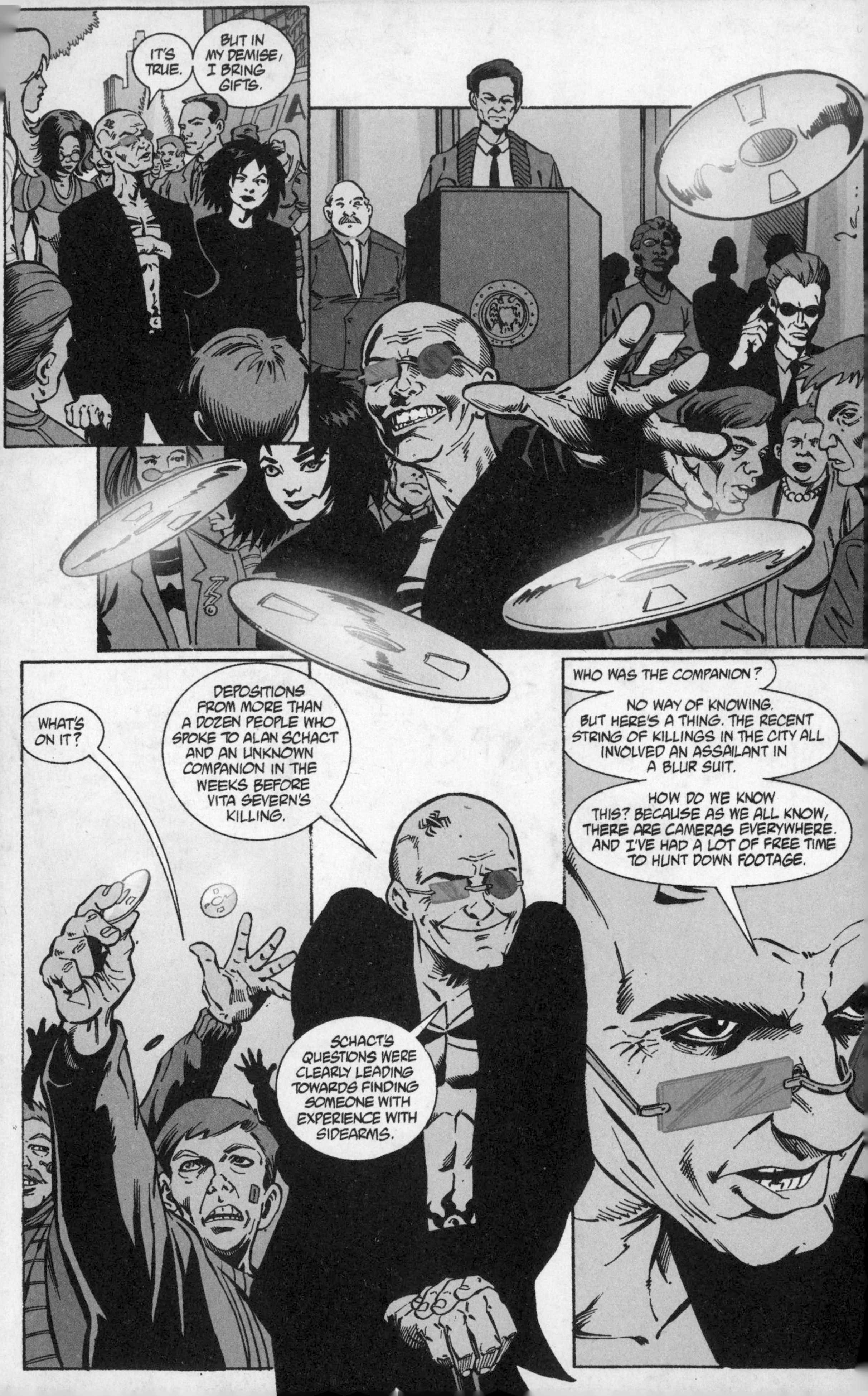
IT'S TRUE.
BUT IN MY DEMISE, I BRING GIFTS.
WHAT'S ON IT?
DEPOSITIONS FROM MORE THAN A DOZEN PEOPLE WHO SPOKE TO ALAN SCHACT AND AN UNKNOWN COMPANION IN THE WEEKS BEFORE VITA SEVERN'S KILLING.
SCHACT'S QUESTIONS WERE CLEARLY LEADING TOWARDS FINDING SOMEONE WITH EXPERIENCE WITH SIDEARMS.
WHO WAS THE COMPANION?
NO WAY OF KNOWING. BUT HERE'S A THING. THE RECENT STRING OF KILLINGS IN THE CITY ALL INVOLVED AN ASSAILANT IN A BLUR SUIT.
HOW DO WE KNOW THIS? BECAUSE AS WE ALL KNOW, THERE ARE CAMERAS EVERYWHERE. AND I'VE HAD A LOT OF FREE TIME TO HUNT DOWN FOOTAGE.

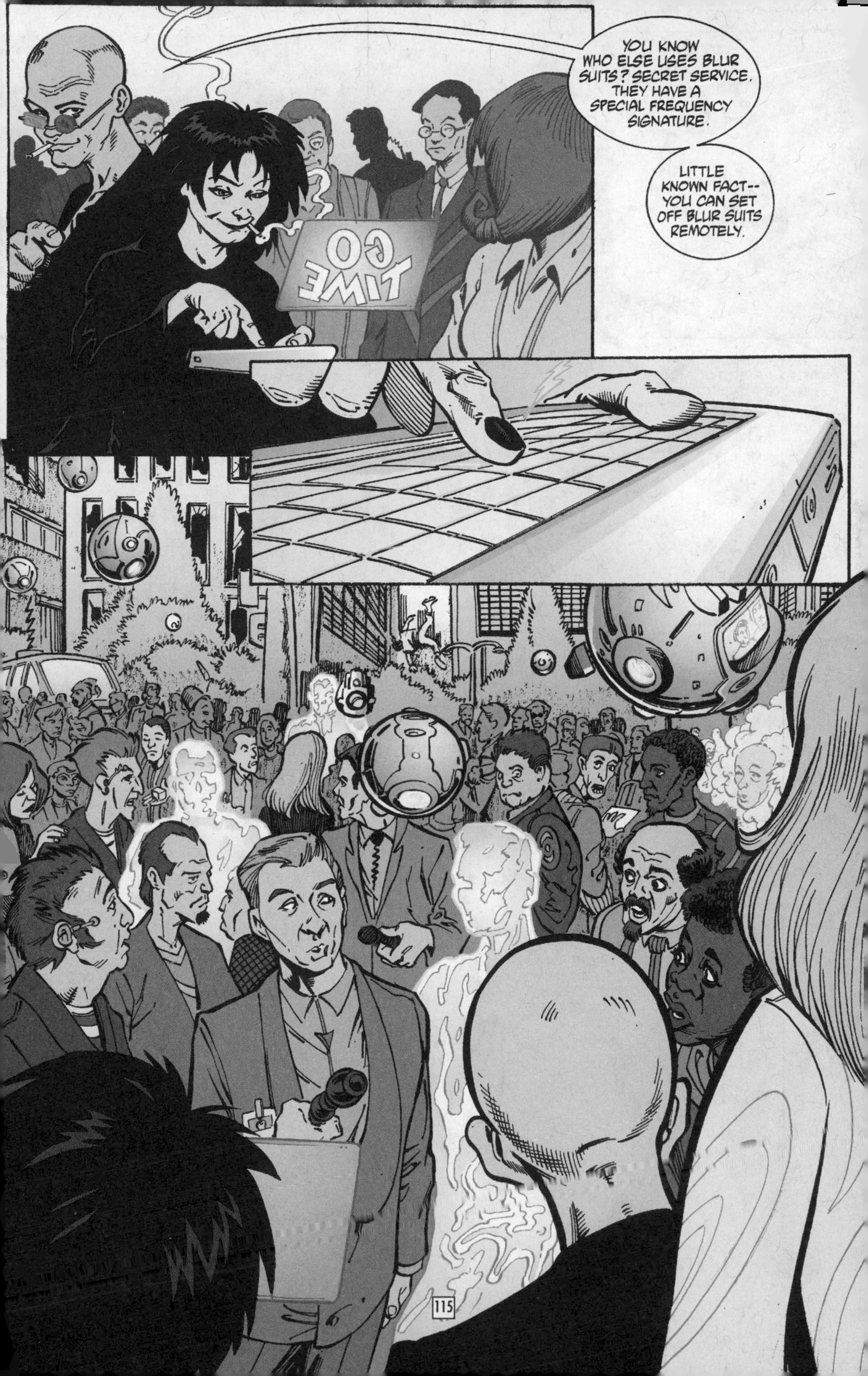
YOU KNOW WHO ELSE USES BLUR SUITS? SECRET SERVICE. THEY HAVE A SPECIAL FREQUENCY SIGNATURE.
LITTLE KNOWN FACT-- YOU CAN SET OFF BLUR SUITS REMOTELY.
GO TIME

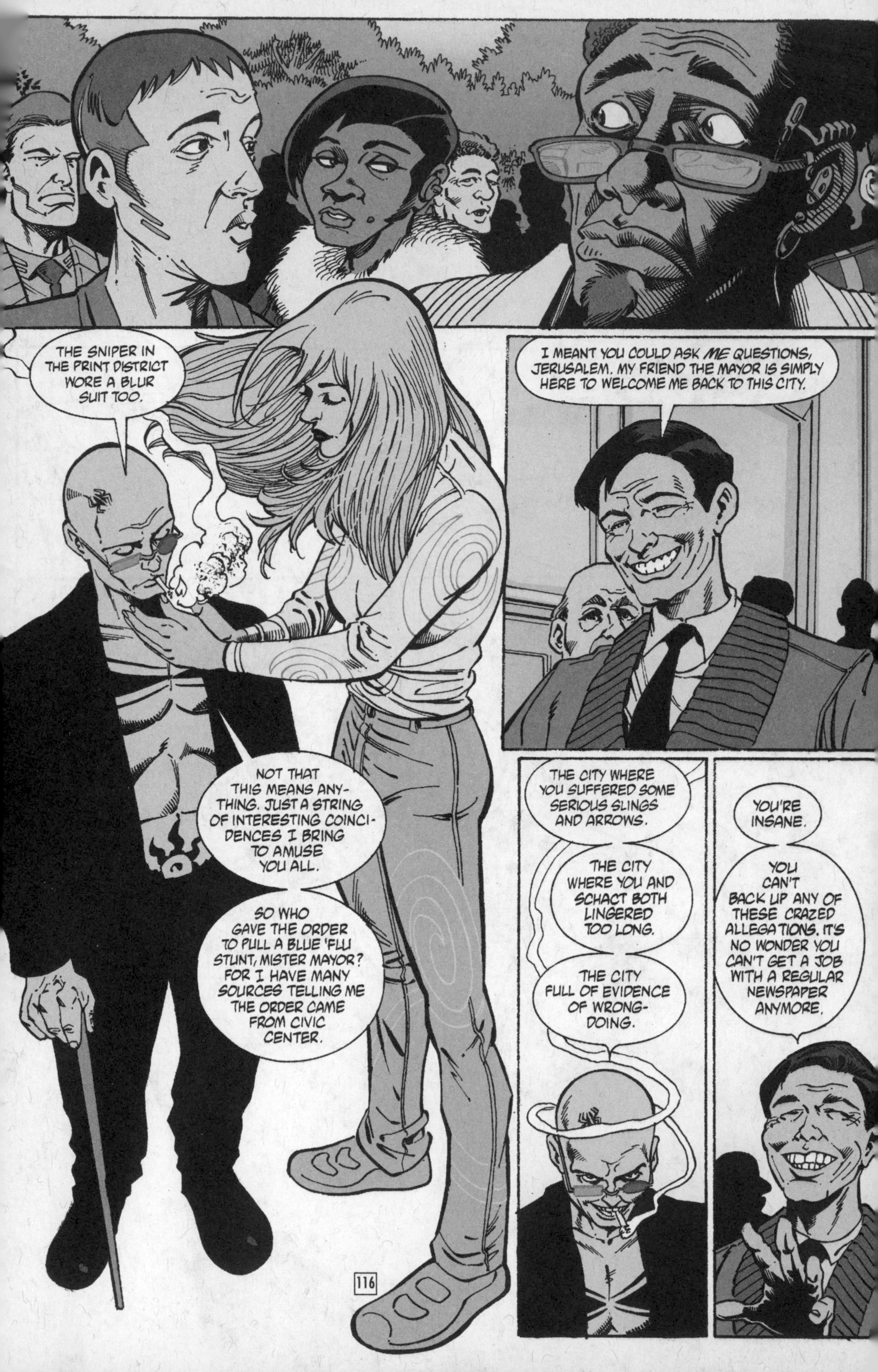
THE SNIPER IN THE PRINT DISTRICT WORE A BLUR SUIT TOO.
NOT THAT THIS MEANS ANYTHING. JUST A STRING OF INTERESTING COINCIDENCES I BRING TO AMUSE YOU ALL.
SO WHO GAVE THE ORDER TO PULL A BLUE 'FLU STUNT, MISTER MAYOR? FOR I HAVE MANY SOURCES TELLING ME THE ORDER CAME FROM CIVIC CENTER.
I MEANT YOU COULD ASK *ME* QUESTIONS, JERUSALEM. MY FRIEND THE MAYOR IS SIMPLY HERE TO WELCOME ME BACK TO THIS CITY.
THE CITY WHERE YOU SUFFERED SOME SERIOUS SLINGS AND ARROWS.
THE CITY WHERE YOU AND SCHACT BOTH LINGERED TOO LONG.
THE CITY FULL OF EVIDENCE OF WRONG-DOING.
YOU'RE INSANE.
YOU CAN'T BACK UP ANY OF THESE CRAZED ALLEGATIONS. IT'S NO WONDER YOU CAN'T GET A JOB WITH A REGULAR NEWSPAPER ANYMORE.

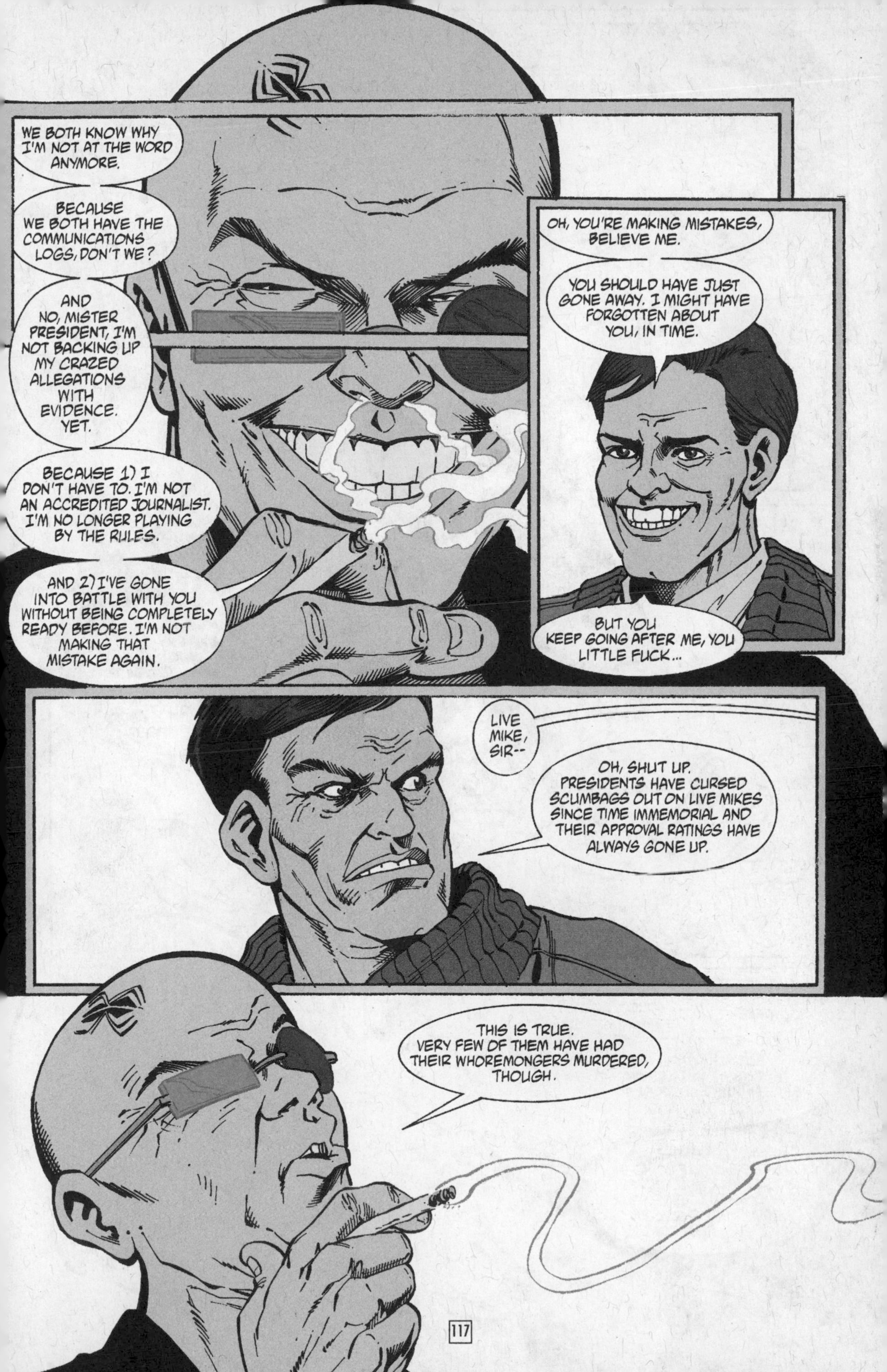
WE BOTH KNOW WHY I'M NOT AT THE WORD ANYMORE.
BECAUSE WE BOTH HAVE THE COMMUNICATIONS LOGS, DON'T WE?
AND NO, MISTER PRESIDENT, I'M NOT BACKING UP MY CRAZED ALLEGATIONS WITH EVIDENCE. YET.
BECAUSE 1) I DON'T HAVE TO. I'M NOT AN ACCREDITED JOURNALIST. I'M NO LONGER PLAYING BY THE RULES.
AND 2) I'VE GONE INTO BATTLE WITH YOU WITHOUT BEING COMPLETELY READY BEFORE. I'M NOT MAKING THAT MISTAKE AGAIN.
OH, YOU'RE MAKING MISTAKES, BELIEVE ME.
YOU SHOULD HAVE JUST GONE AWAY. I MIGHT HAVE FORGOTTEN ABOUT YOU, IN TIME.
BUT YOU KEEP GOING AFTER ME, YOU LITTLE FUCK...
LIVE MIKE, SIR--
OH, SHUT UP. PRESIDENTS HAVE CURSED SCUMBAGS OUT ON LIVE MIKES SINCE TIME IMMEMORIAL AND THEIR APPROVAL RATINGS HAVE ALWAYS GONE UP.
THIS IS TRUE. VERY FEW OF THEM HAVE HAD THEIR WHOREMONGERS MURDERED, THOUGH.

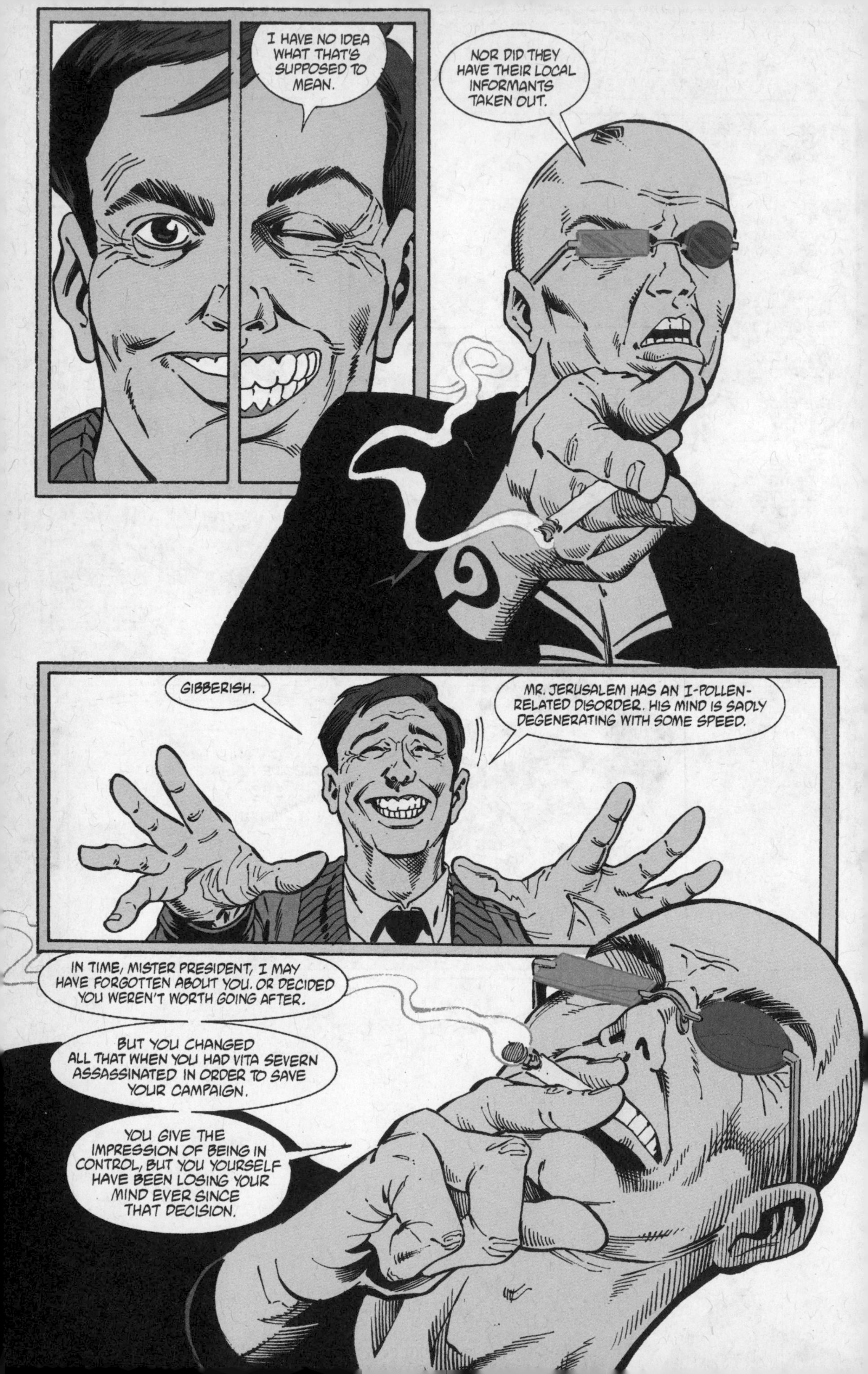
I HAVE NO IDEA WHAT THAT'S SUPPOSED TO MEAN.
NOR DID THEY HAVE THEIR LOCAL INFORMANTS TAKEN OUT.
GIBBERISH.
MR. JERUSALEM HAS AN I-POLLEN-RELATED DISORDER. HIS MIND IS SADLY DEGENERATING WITH SOME SPEED.
IN TIME, MISTER PRESIDENT, I MAY HAVE FORGOTTEN ABOUT YOU. OR DECIDED YOU WEREN'T WORTH GOING AFTER.
BUT YOU CHANGED ALL THAT WHEN YOU HAD VITA SEVERN ASSASSINATED IN ORDER TO SAVE YOUR CAMPAIGN.
YOU GIVE THE IMPRESSION OF BEING IN CONTROL, BUT YOU YOURSELF HAVE BEEN LOSING YOUR MIND EVER SINCE THAT DECISION.

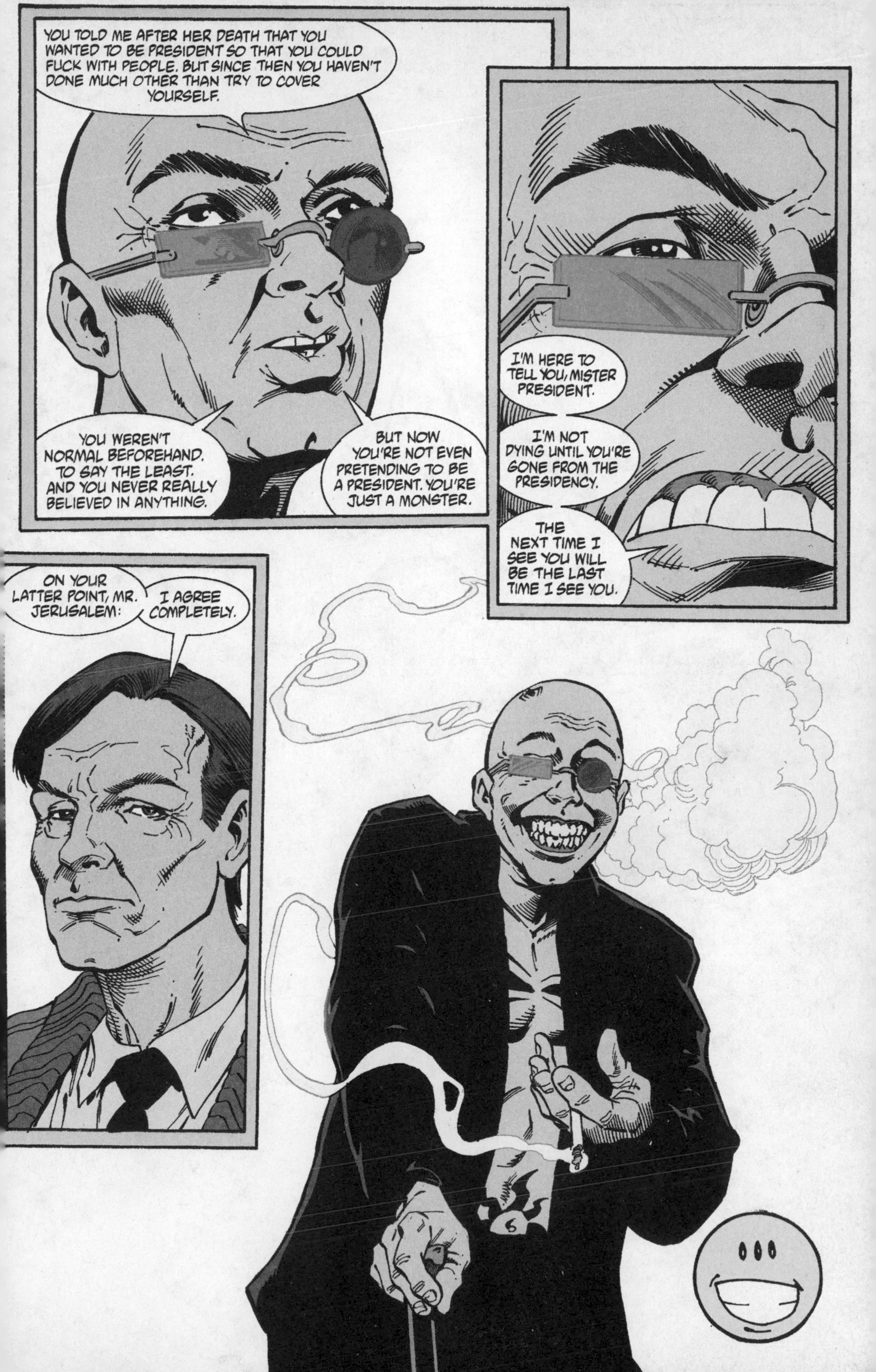
YOU TOLD ME AFTER HER DEATH THAT YOU WANTED TO BE PRESIDENT SO THAT YOU COULD FUCK WITH PEOPLE. BUT SINCE THEN YOU HAVEN'T DONE MUCH OTHER THAN TRY TO COVER YOURSELF.
YOU WEREN'T NORMAL BEFOREHAND. TO SAY THE LEAST. AND YOU NEVER REALLY BELIEVED IN ANYTHING.
BUT NOW YOU'RE NOT EVEN PRETENDING TO BE A PRESIDENT. YOU'RE JUST A MONSTER.
I'M HERE TO TELL YOU, MISTER PRESIDENT.
I'M NOT DYING UNTIL YOU'RE GONE FROM THE PRESIDENCY.
THE NEXT TIME I SEE YOU WILL BE THE LAST TIME I SEE YOU.
ON YOUR LATTER POINT, MR. JERUSALEM:
I AGREE COMPLETELY.

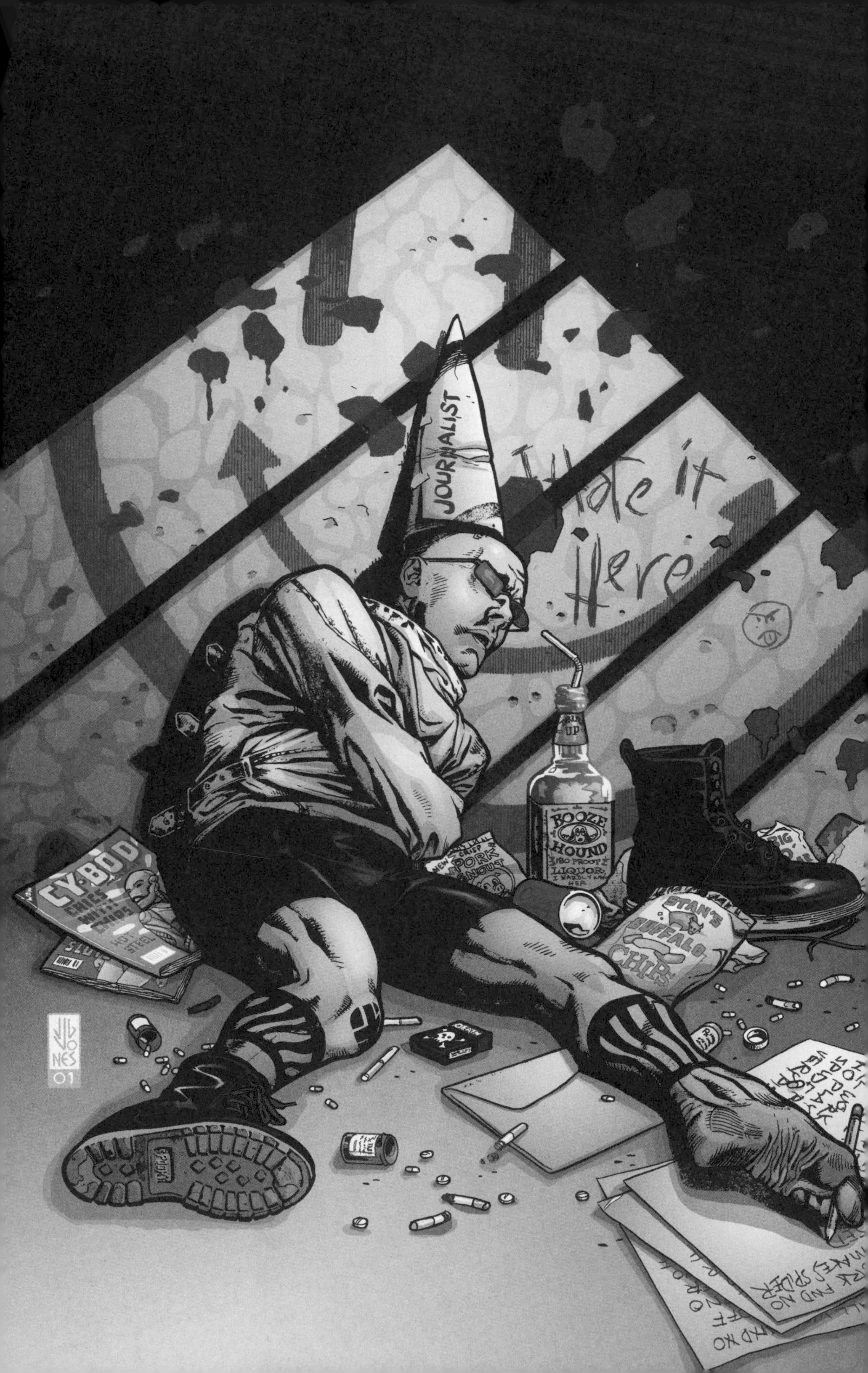
JOURNALIST
I Hate it Here
BOOZE HOUND
LIQUOR
STAN'S BUFFALO CHIPS
CY-BOD
HOT STEEL
JG JONES 01

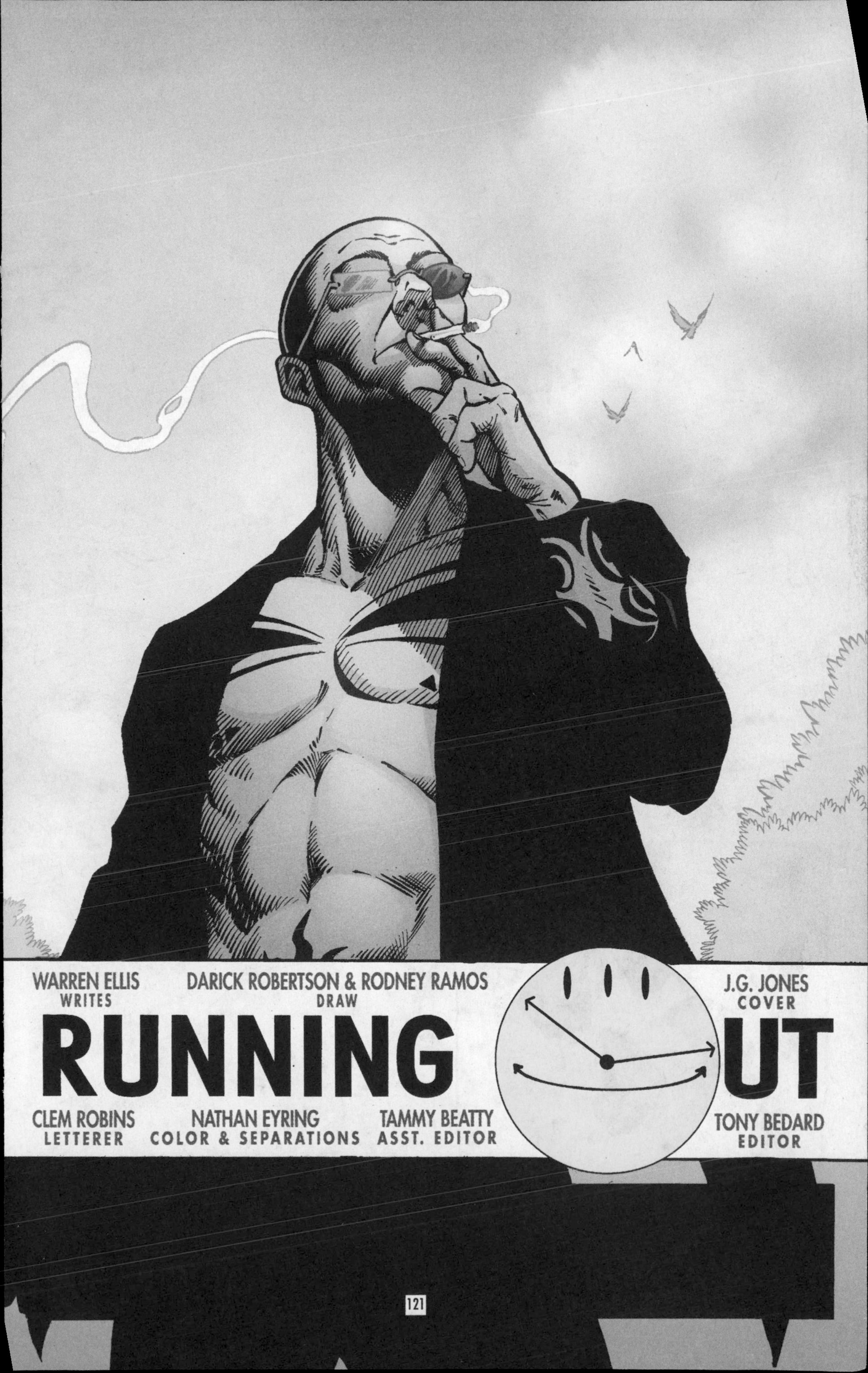
WARREN ELLIS
WRITES
DARICK ROBERTSON & RODNEY RAMOS
DRAW
J.G. JONES
COVER
RUNNING OUT
CLEM ROBINS
LETTERER
NATHAN EYRING
COLOR & SEPARATIONS
TAMMY BEATTY
ASST. EDITOR
TONY BEDARD
EDITOR

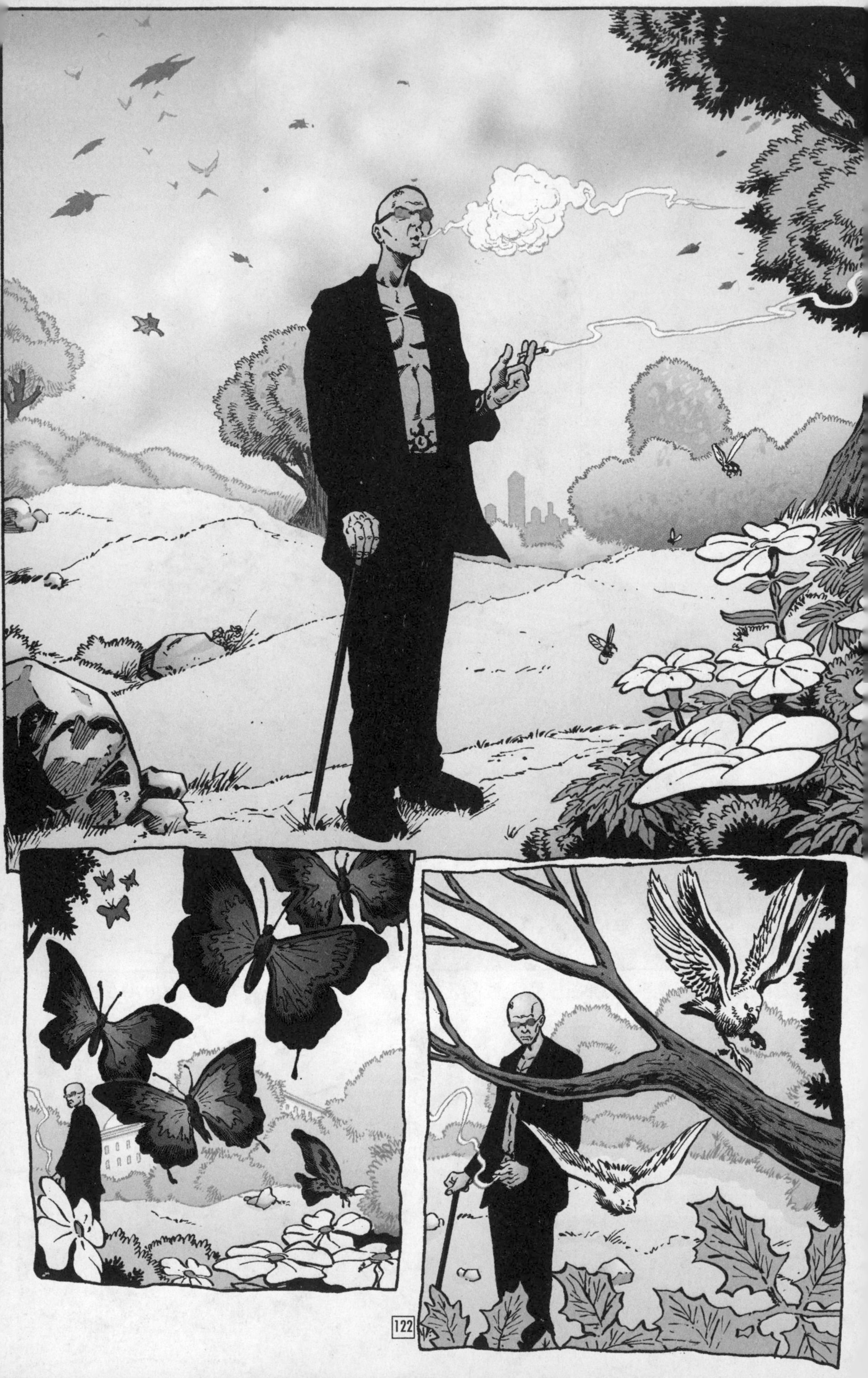

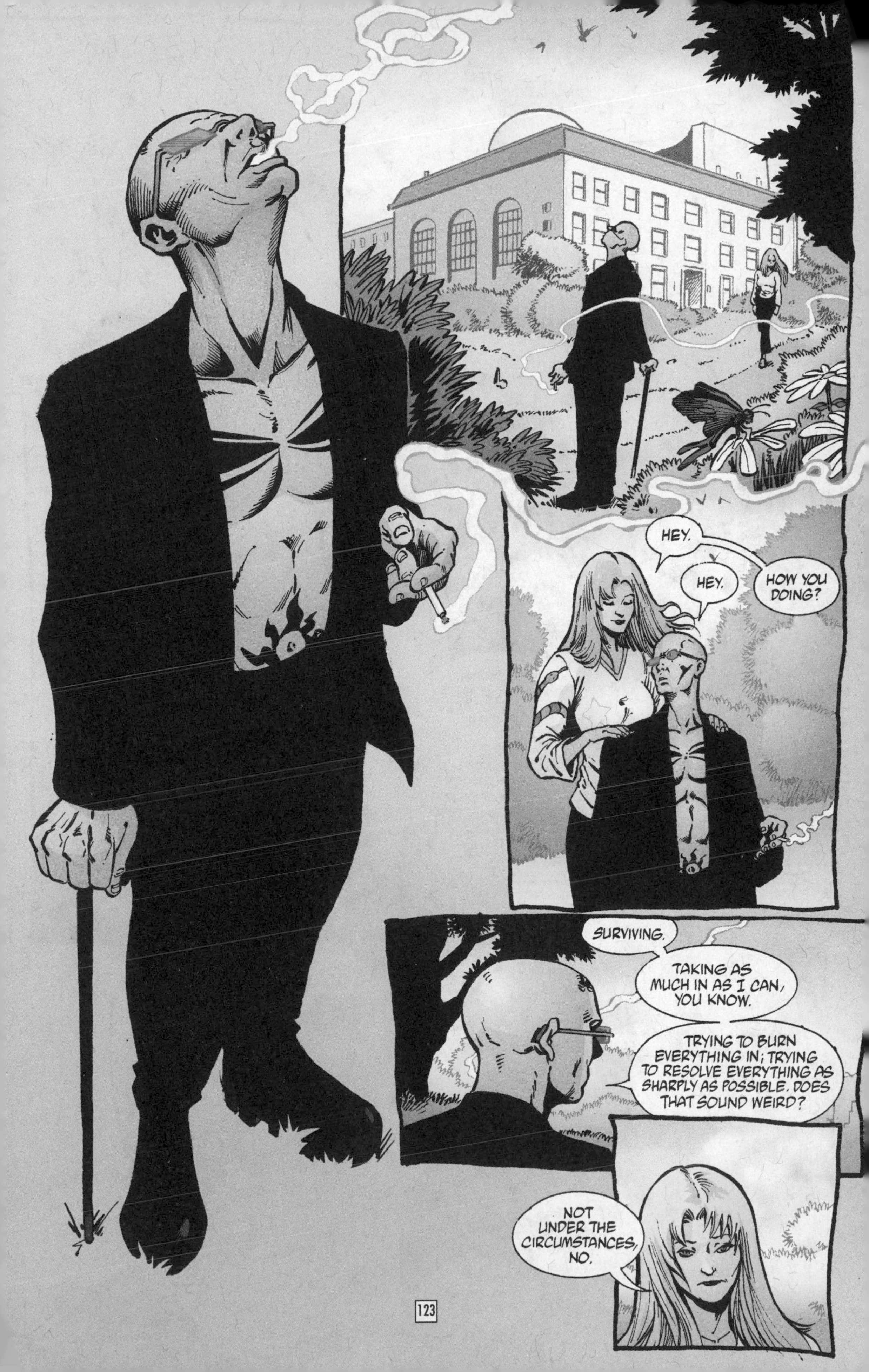
HEY.
HEY.
HOW YOU DOING?
SURVIVING.
TAKING AS MUCH IN AS I CAN, YOU KNOW.
TRYING TO BURN EVERYTHING IN; TRYING TO RESOLVE EVERYTHING AS SHARPLY AS POSSIBLE. DOES THAT SOUND WEIRD?
NOT UNDER THE CIRCUMSTANCES, NO.

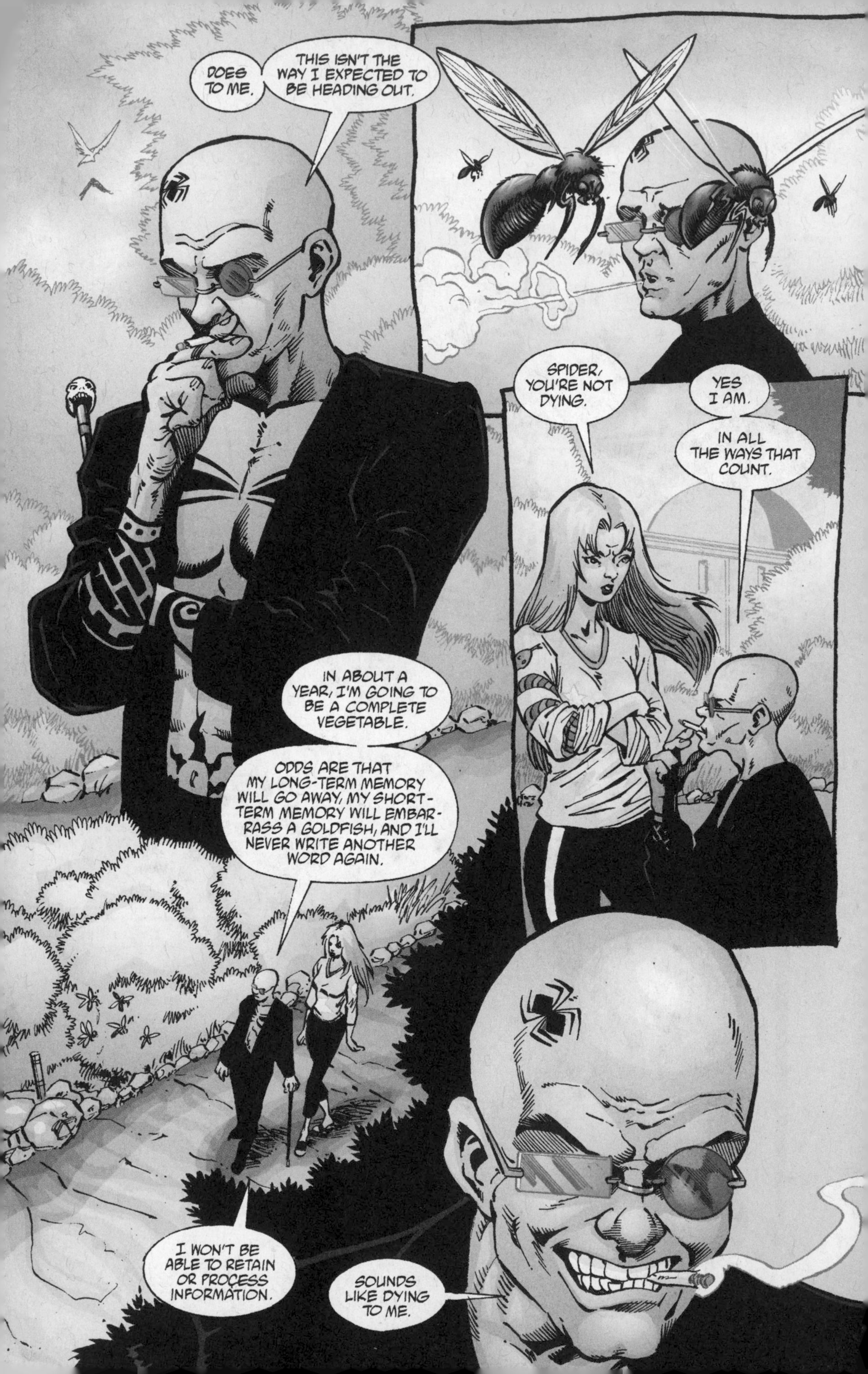
DOES TO ME.
THIS ISN'T THE WAY I EXPECTED TO BE HEADING OUT.
SPIDER, YOU'RE NOT DYING.
YES I AM.
IN ALL THE WAYS THAT COUNT.
IN ABOUT A YEAR, I'M GOING TO BE A COMPLETE VEGETABLE.
ODDS ARE THAT MY LONG-TERM MEMORY WILL GO AWAY, MY SHORT-TERM MEMORY WILL EMBARRASS A GOLDFISH, AND I'LL NEVER WRITE ANOTHER WORD AGAIN.
I WON'T BE ABLE TO RETAIN OR PROCESS INFORMATION.
SOUNDS LIKE DYING TO ME.

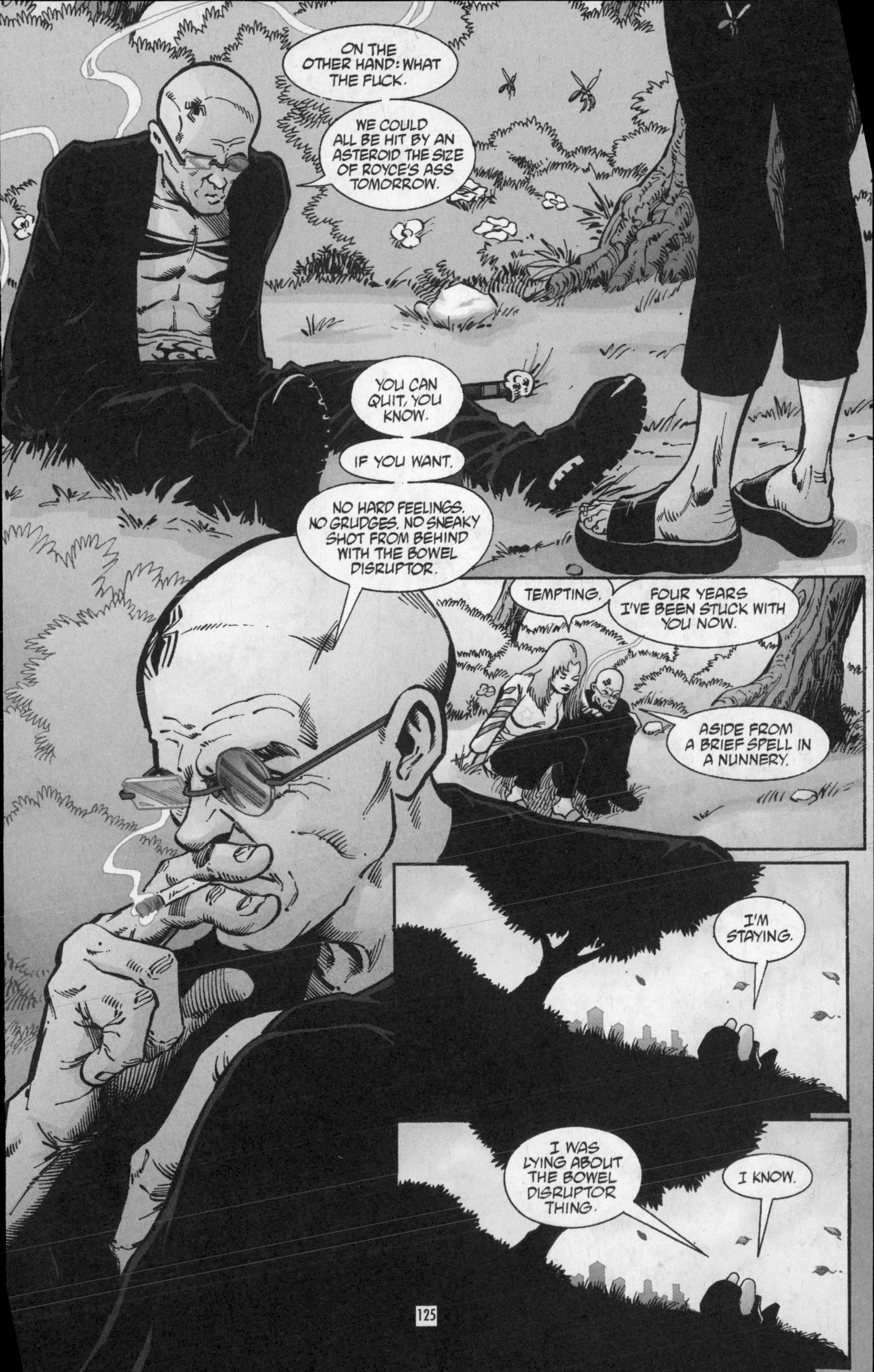
ON THE OTHER HAND: WHAT THE FUCK.
WE COULD ALL BE HIT BY AN ASTEROID THE SIZE OF ROYCE'S ASS TOMORROW.
YOU CAN QUIT, YOU KNOW.
IF YOU WANT.
NO HARD FEELINGS. NO GRUDGES. NO SNEAKY SHOT FROM BEHIND WITH THE BOWEL DISRUPTOR.
TEMPTING.
FOUR YEARS I'VE BEEN STUCK WITH YOU NOW.
ASIDE FROM A BRIEF SPELL IN A NUNNERY.
I'M STAYING.
I WAS LYING ABOUT THE BOWEL DISRUPTOR THING.
I KNOW.

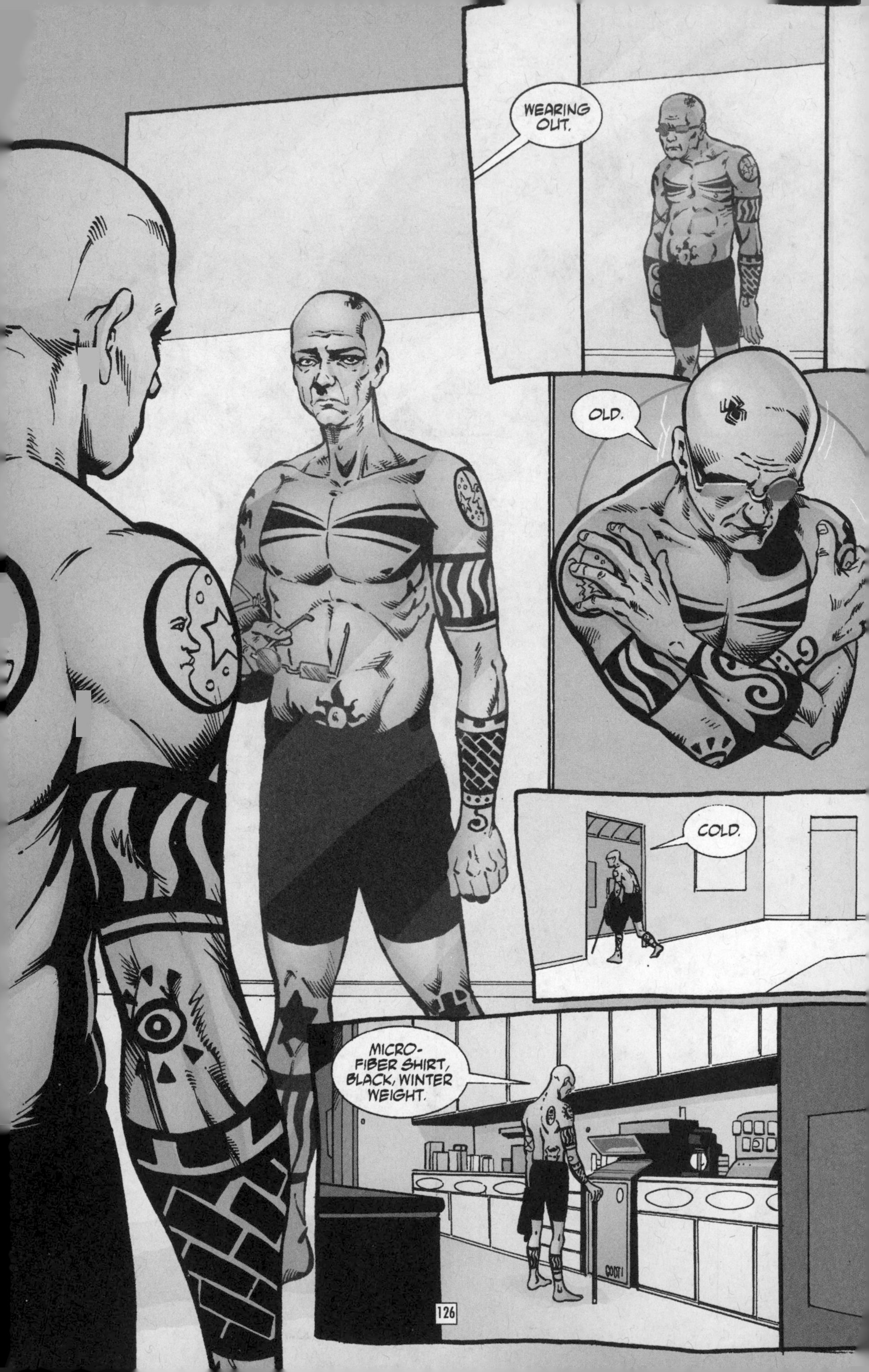
WEARING OUT.
OLD.
COLD.
MICRO-FIBER SHIRT, BLACK, WINTER WEIGHT.

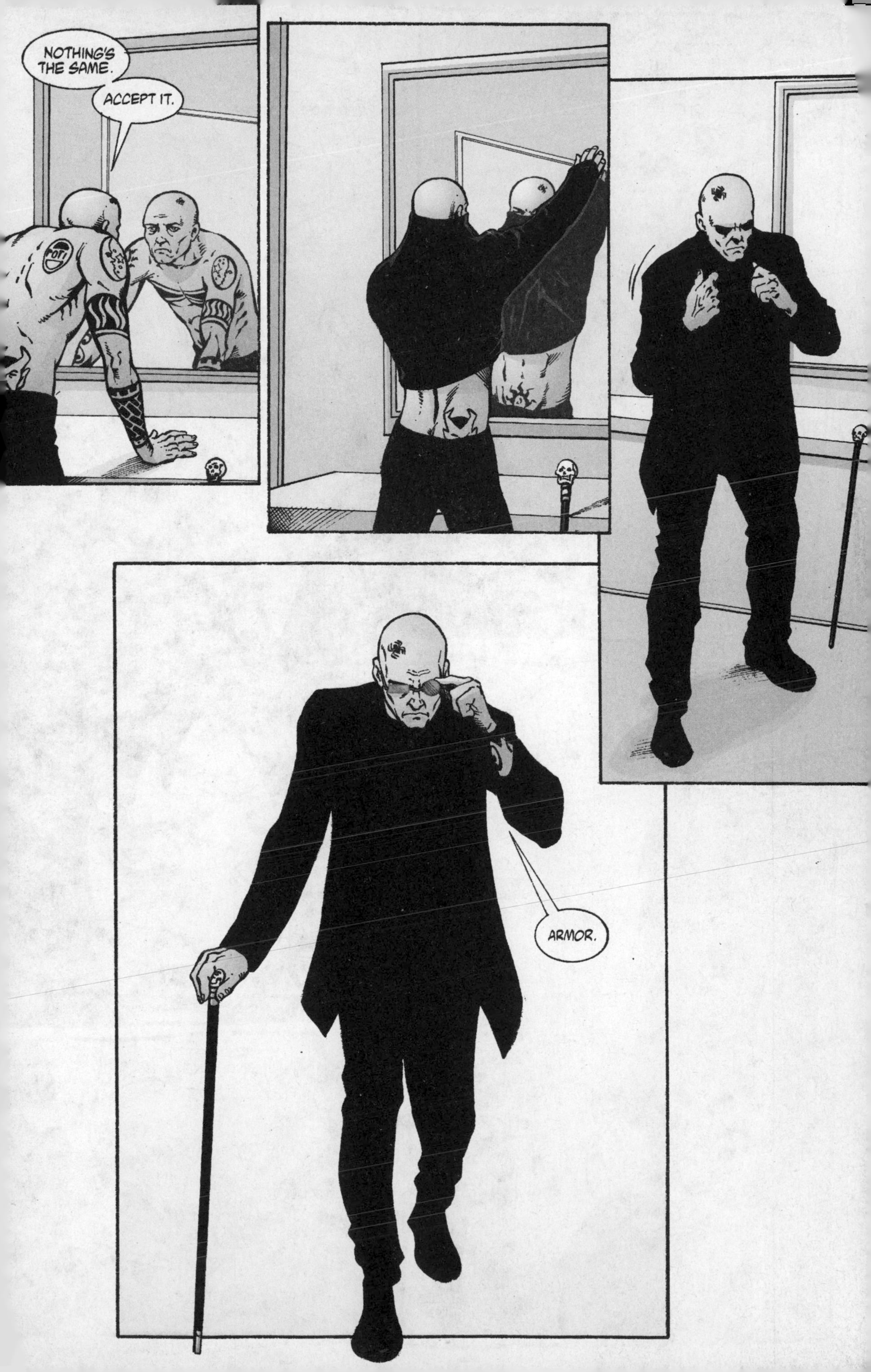
NOTHING'S THE SAME.
ACCEPT IT.
ARMOR.

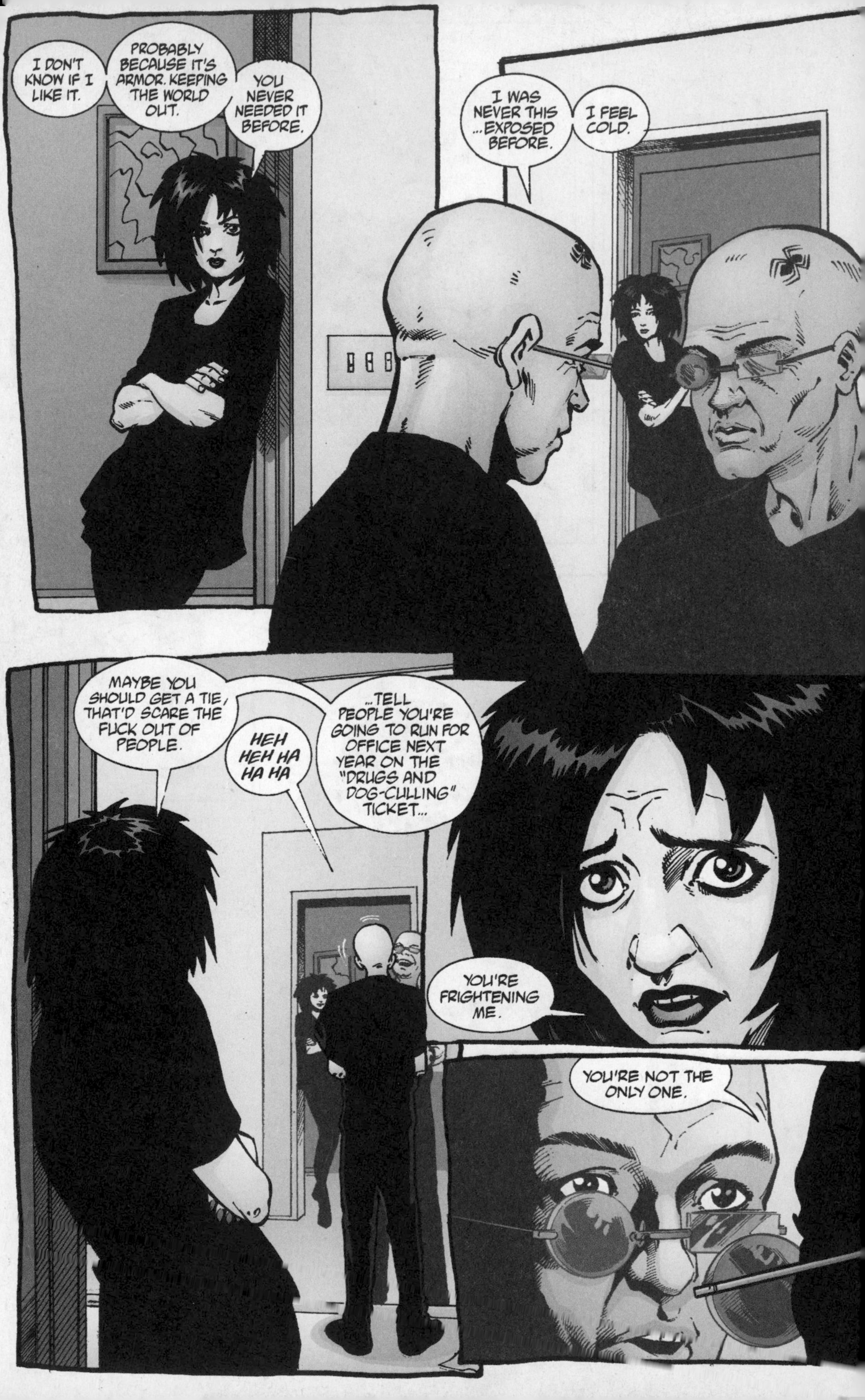

I DON'T KNOW IF I LIKE IT.
PROBABLY BECAUSE IT'S ARMOR. KEEPING THE WORLD OUT.
YOU NEVER NEEDED IT BEFORE.
I WAS NEVER THIS ...EXPOSED BEFORE.
I FEEL COLD.
MAYBE YOU SHOULD GET A TIE, THAT'D SCARE THE FUCK OUT OF PEOPLE.
HEH HEH HA HA HA
...TELL PEOPLE YOU'RE GOING TO RUN FOR OFFICE NEXT YEAR ON THE "DRUGS AND DOG-CULLING" TICKET...
YOU'RE FRIGHTENING ME.
YOU'RE NOT THE ONLY ONE.

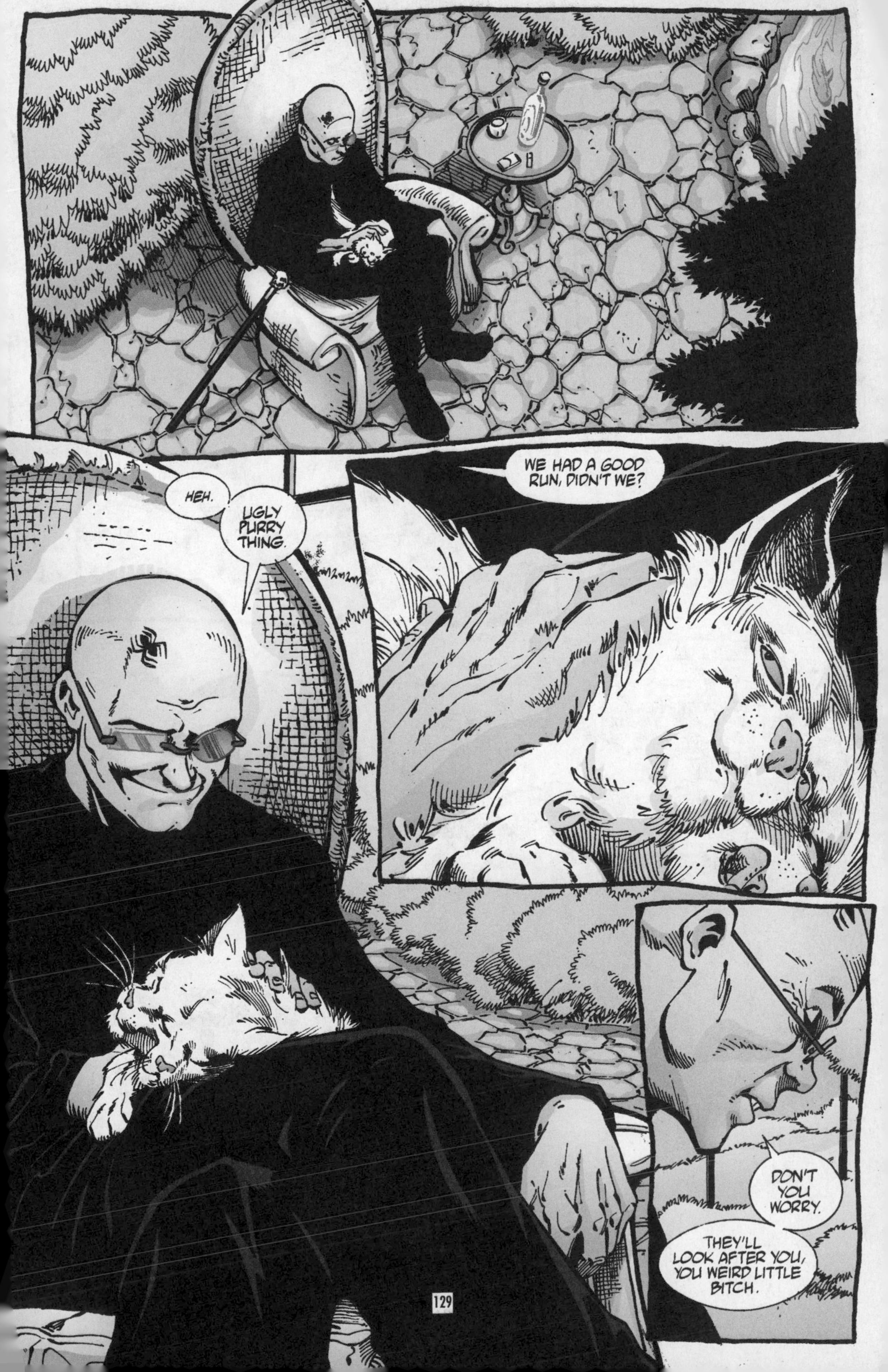
HEH.
UGLY PURRY THING.
WE HAD A GOOD RUN, DIDN'T WE?
DON'T YOU WORRY.
THEY'LL LOOK AFTER YOU, YOU WEIRD LITTLE BITCH.

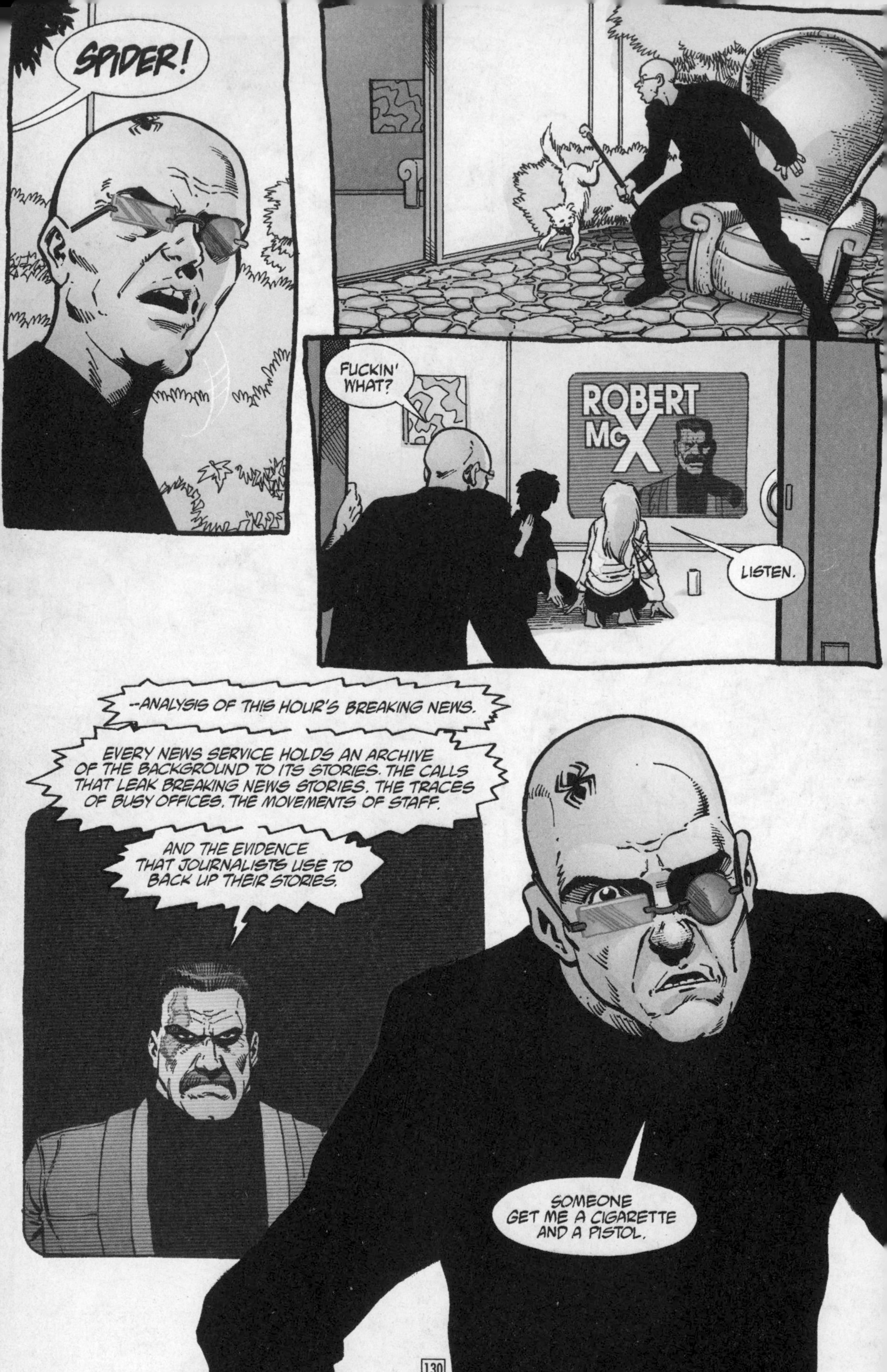
SPIDER!
FUCKIN' WHAT?
ROBERT McX
LISTEN.
--ANALYSIS OF THIS HOUR'S BREAKING NEWS.
EVERY NEWS SERVICE HOLDS AN ARCHIVE OF THE BACKGROUND TO ITS STORIES. THE CALLS THAT LEAK BREAKING NEWS STORIES. THE TRACES OF BUSY OFFICES. THE MOVEMENTS OF STAFF.
AND THE EVIDENCE THAT JOURNALISTS USE TO BACK UP THEIR STORIES.
SOMEONE GET ME A CIGARETTE AND A PISTOL.

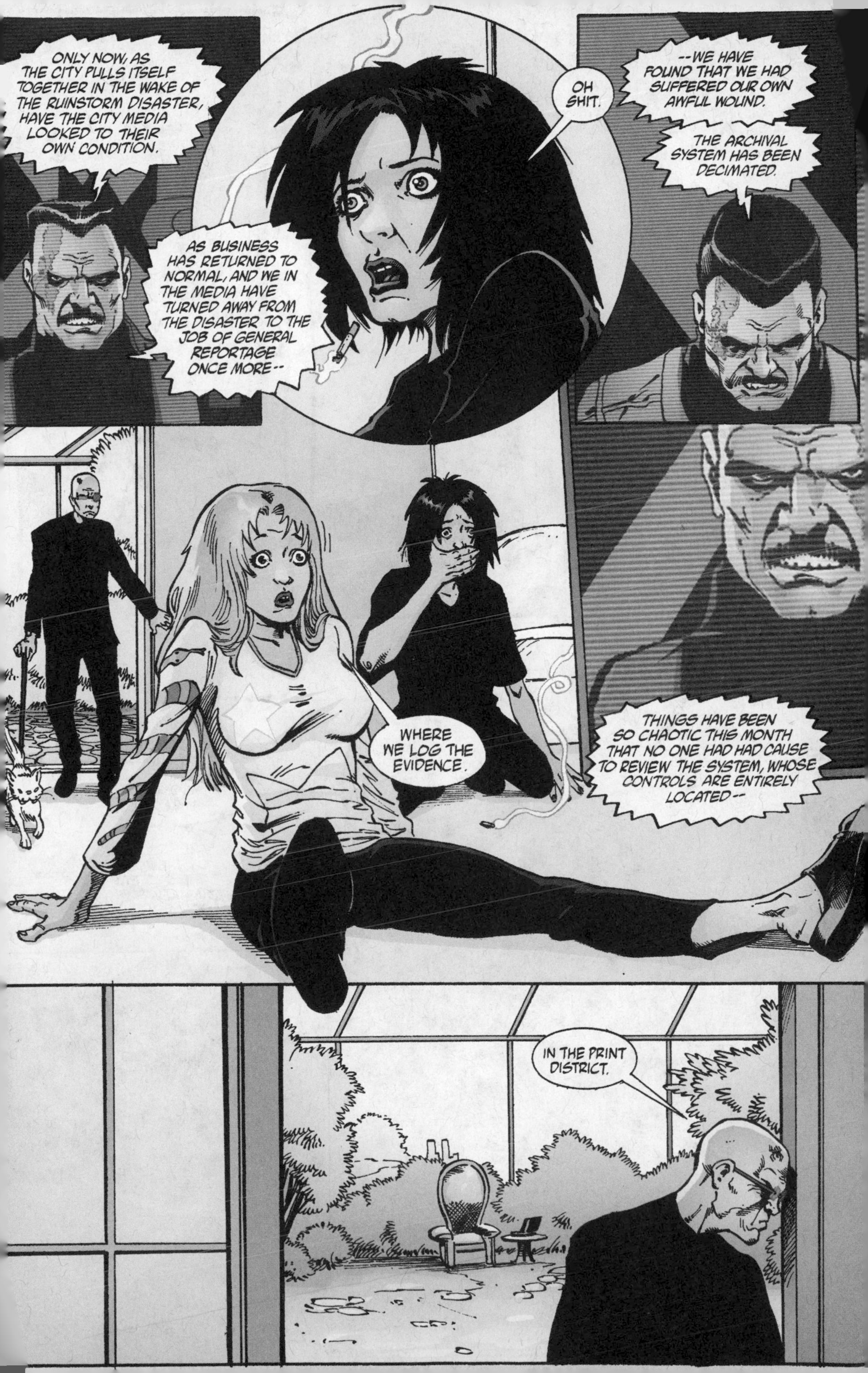
ONLY NOW, AS THE CITY PULLS ITSELF TOGETHER IN THE WAKE OF THE RUINSTORM DISASTER, HAVE THE CITY MEDIA LOOKED TO THEIR OWN CONDITION.
AS BUSINESS HAS RETURNED TO NORMAL, AND WE IN THE MEDIA HAVE TURNED AWAY FROM THE DISASTER TO THE JOB OF GENERAL REPORTAGE ONCE MORE--
OH SHIT.
--WE HAVE FOUND THAT WE HAD SUFFERED OUR OWN AWFUL WOUND.
THE ARCHIVAL SYSTEM HAS BEEN DECIMATED.
WHERE WE LOG THE EVIDENCE.
THINGS HAVE BEEN SO CHAOTIC THIS MONTH THAT NO ONE HAD HAD CAUSE TO REVIEW THE SYSTEM, WHOSE CONTROLS ARE ENTIRELY LOCATED--
IN THE PRINT DISTRICT.

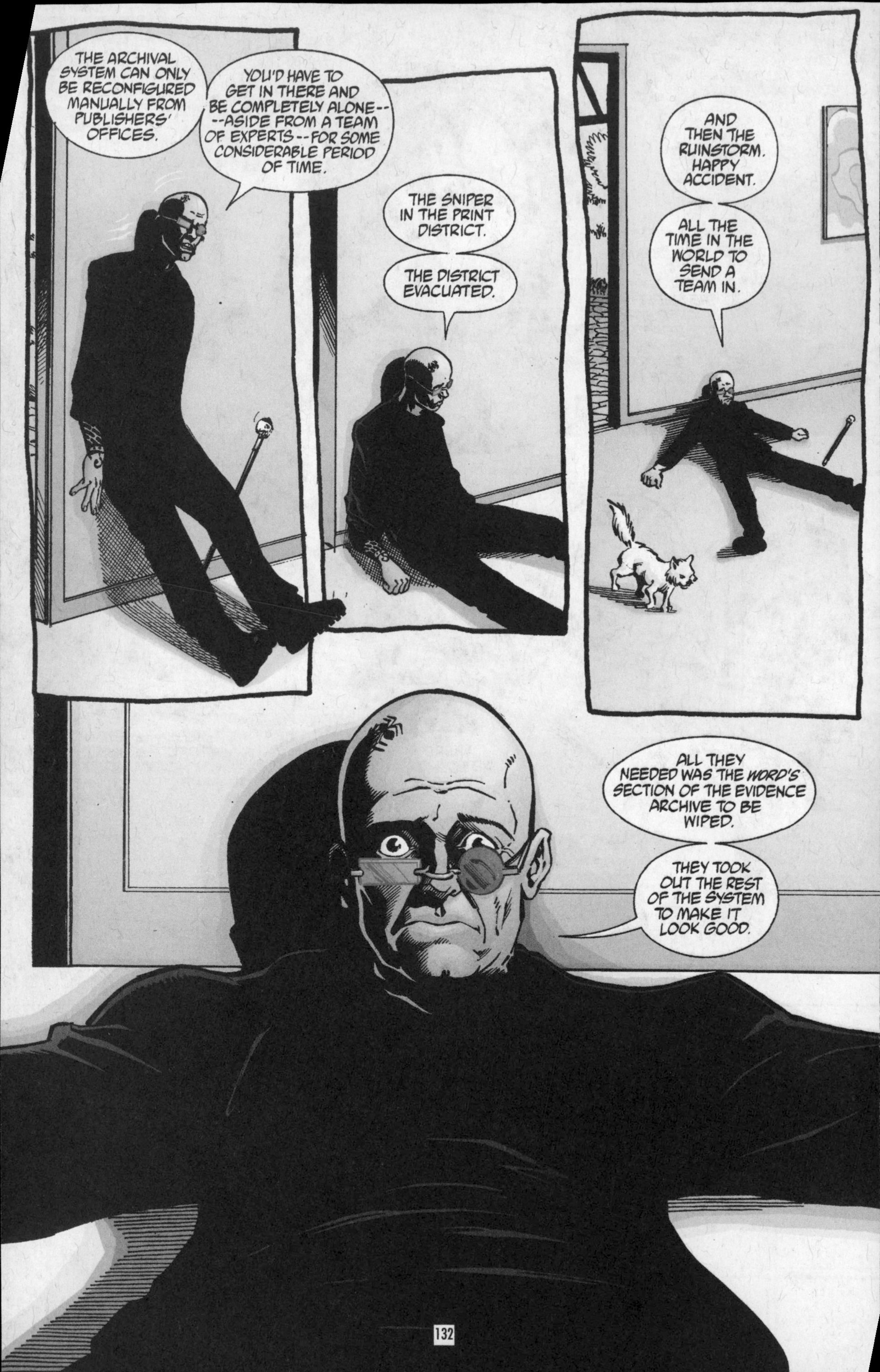
THE ARCHIVAL SYSTEM CAN ONLY BE RECONFIGURED MANUALLY FROM PUBLISHERS' OFFICES.
YOU'D HAVE TO GET IN THERE AND BE COMPLETELY ALONE-- --ASIDE FROM A TEAM OF EXPERTS--FOR SOME CONSIDERABLE PERIOD OF TIME.
THE SNIPER IN THE PRINT DISTRICT.
THE DISTRICT EVACUATED.
AND THEN THE RUINSTORM. HAPPY ACCIDENT.
ALL THE TIME IN THE WORLD TO SEND A TEAM IN.
ALL THEY NEEDED WAS THE *WORD'S* SECTION OF THE EVIDENCE ARCHIVE TO BE WIPED.
THEY TOOK OUT THE REST OF THE SYSTEM TO MAKE IT LOOK GOOD.

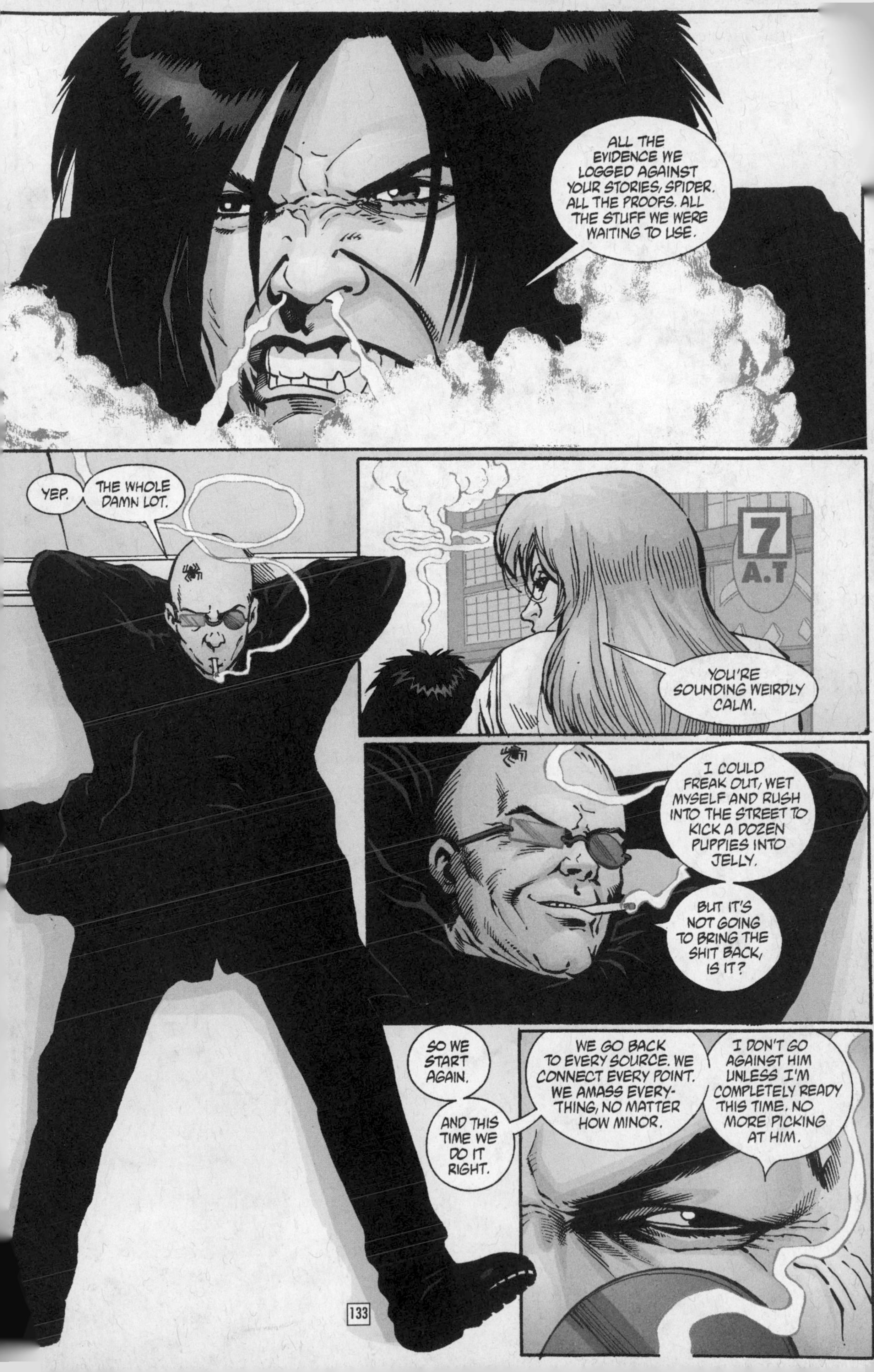
ALL THE EVIDENCE WE LOGGED AGAINST YOUR STORIES, SPIDER. ALL THE PROOFS. ALL THE STUFF WE WERE WAITING TO USE.
YEP.
THE WHOLE DAMN LOT.
7 A.T
YOU'RE SOUNDING WEIRDLY CALM.
I COULD FREAK OUT, WET MYSELF AND RUSH INTO THE STREET TO KICK A DOZEN PUPPIES INTO JELLY.
BUT IT'S NOT GOING TO BRING THE SHIT BACK, IS IT?
SO WE START AGAIN.
AND THIS TIME WE DO IT RIGHT.
WE GO BACK TO EVERY SOURCE. WE CONNECT EVERY POINT. WE AMASS EVERYTHING, NO MATTER HOW MINOR.
I DON'T GO AGAINST HIM UNLESS I'M COMPLETELY READY THIS TIME. NO MORE PICKING AT HIM.

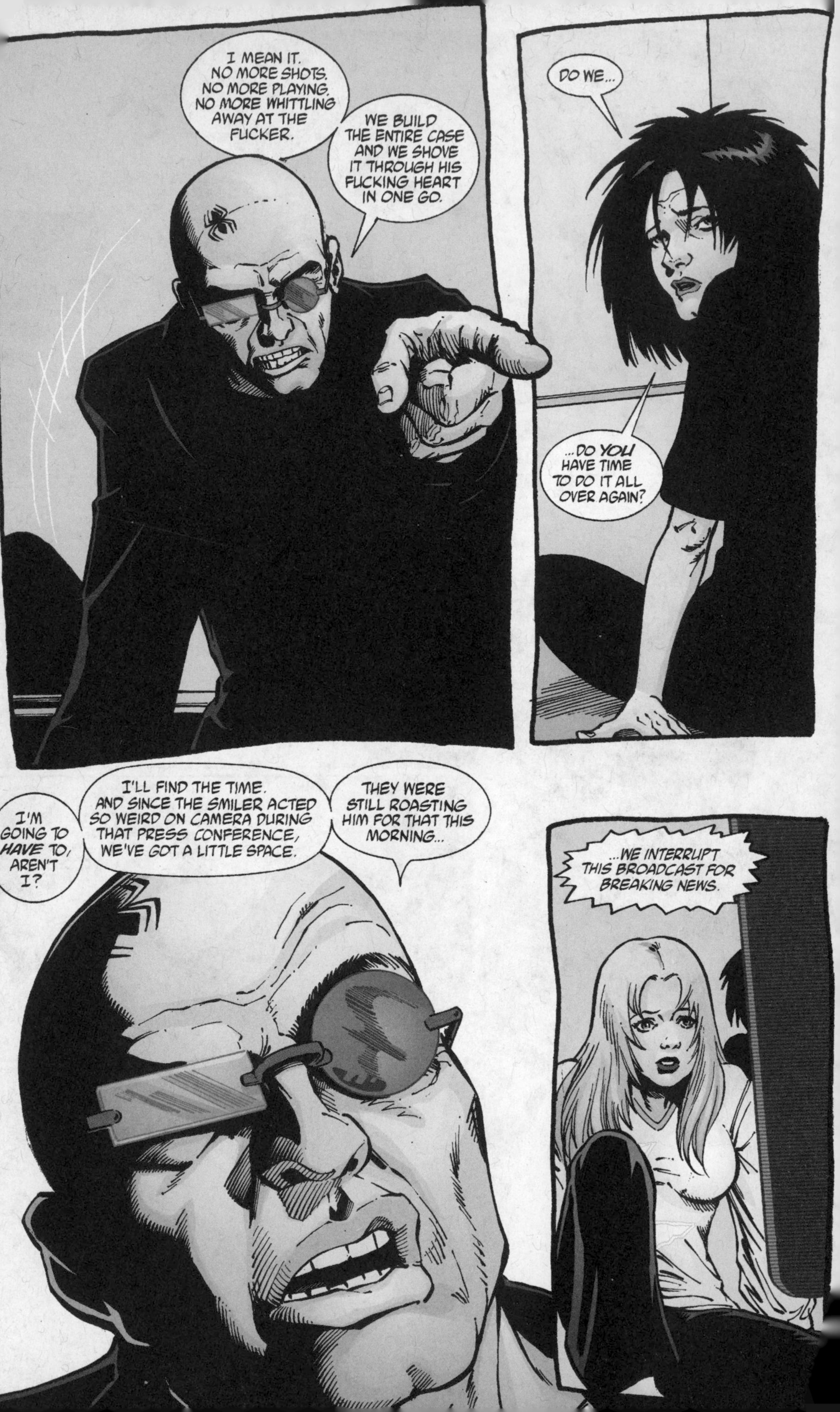
I MEAN IT. NO MORE SHOTS. NO MORE PLAYING. NO MORE WHITTLING AWAY AT THE FUCKER.
WE BUILD THE ENTIRE CASE AND WE SHOVE IT THROUGH HIS FUCKING HEART IN ONE GO.
DO WE...
...DO YOU HAVE TIME TO DO IT ALL OVER AGAIN?
I'M GOING TO HAVE TO, AREN'T I?
I'LL FIND THE TIME. AND SINCE THE SMILER ACTED SO WEIRD ON CAMERA DURING THAT PRESS CONFERENCE, WE'VE GOT A LITTLE SPACE.
THEY WERE STILL ROASTING HIM FOR THAT THIS MORNING...
...WE INTERRUPT THIS BROADCAST FOR BREAKING NEWS.

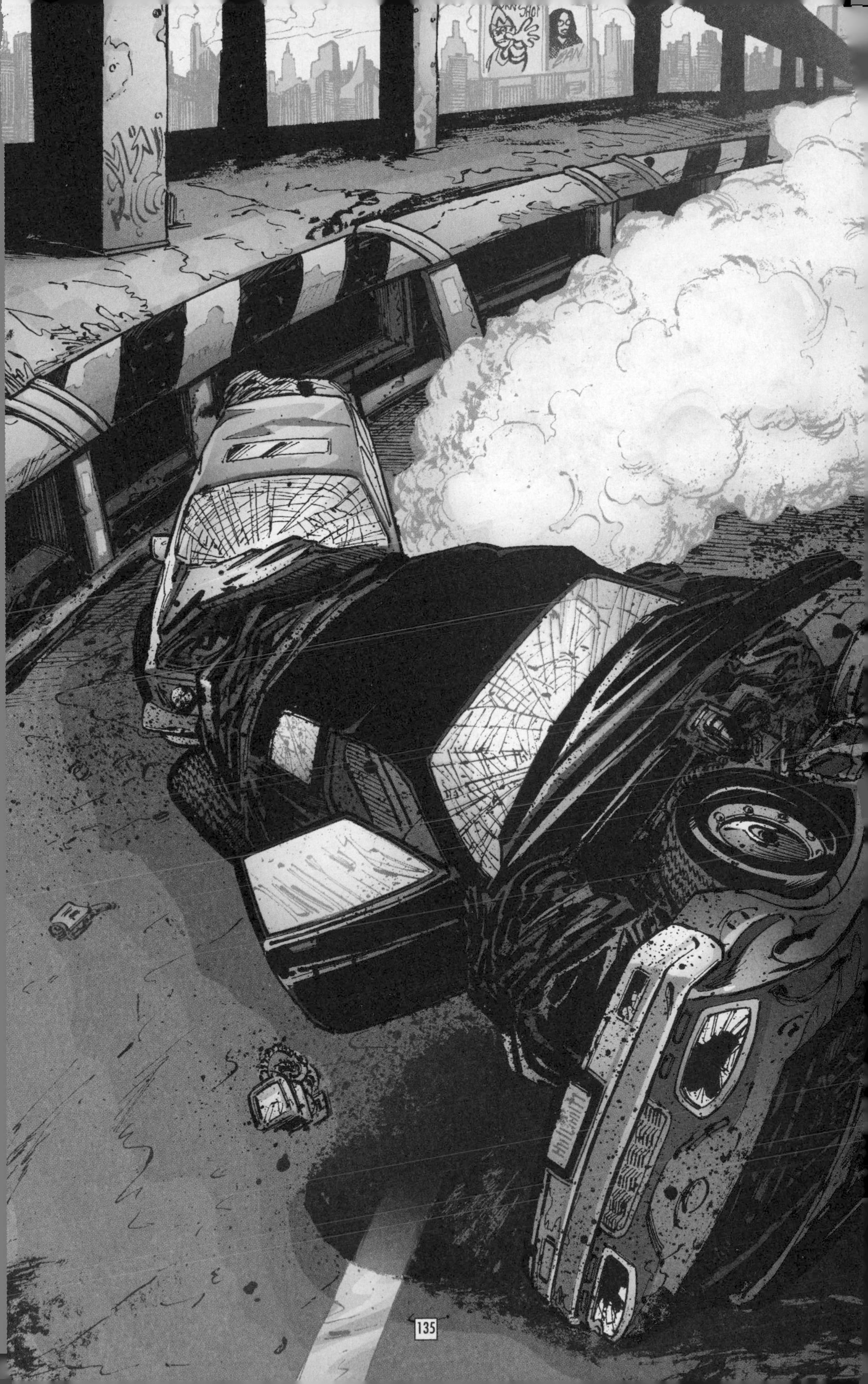

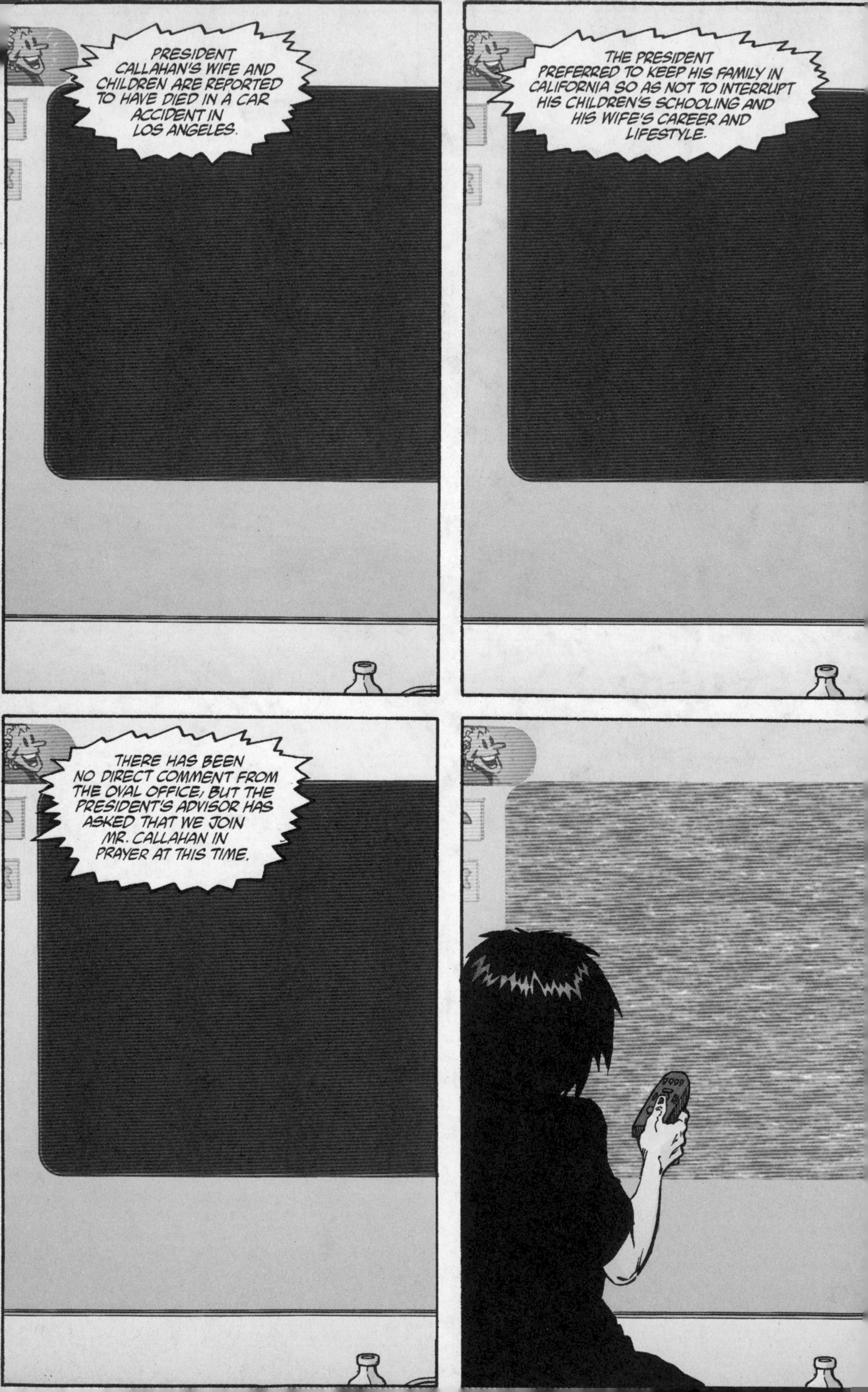
PRESIDENT CALLAHAN'S WIFE AND CHILDREN ARE REPORTED TO HAVE DIED IN A CAR ACCIDENT IN LOS ANGELES.
THE PRESIDENT PREFERRED TO KEEP HIS FAMILY IN CALIFORNIA SO AS NOT TO INTERRUPT HIS CHILDREN'S SCHOOLING AND HIS WIFE'S CAREER AND LIFESTYLE.
THERE HAS BEEN NO DIRECT COMMENT FROM THE OVAL OFFICE; BUT THE PRESIDENT'S ADVISOR HAS ASKED THAT WE JOIN MR. CALLAHAN IN PRAYER AT THIS TIME.

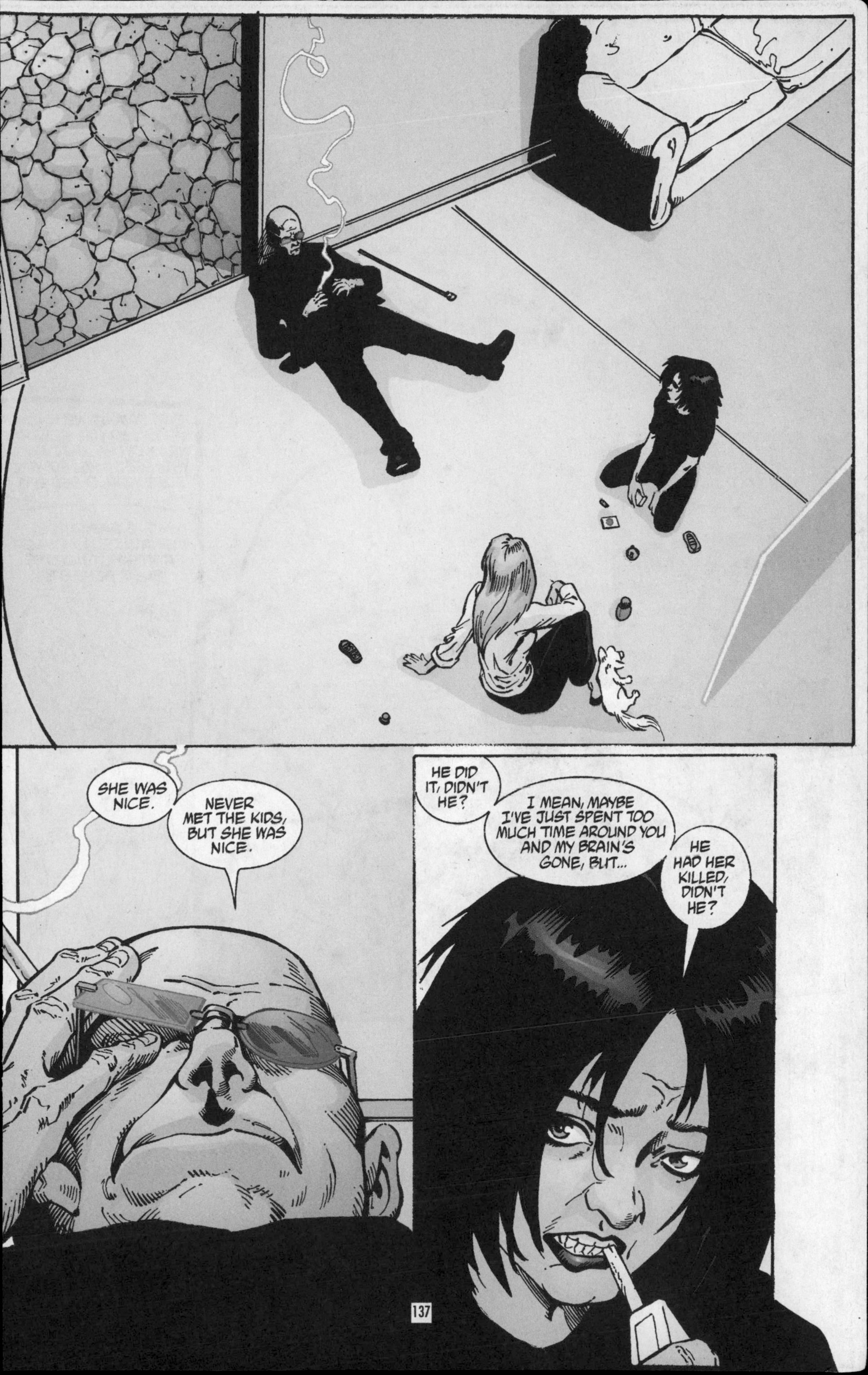
SHE WAS NICE.
NEVER MET THE KIDS, BUT SHE WAS NICE.
HE DID IT, DIDN'T HE?
I MEAN, MAYBE I'VE JUST SPENT TOO MUCH TIME AROUND YOU AND MY BRAIN'S GONE, BUT...
HE HAD HER KILLED, DIDN'T HE?

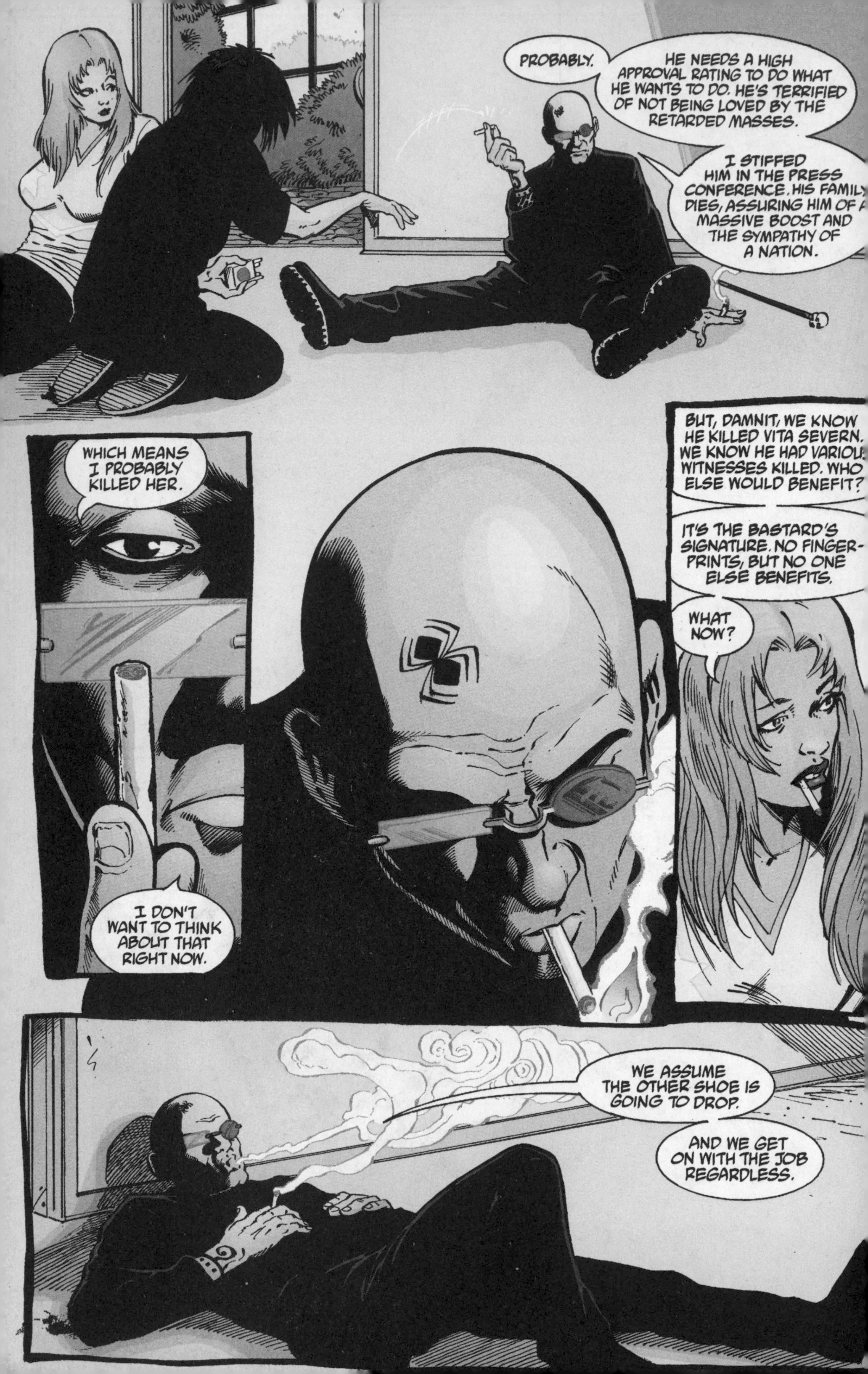
PROBABLY.
HE NEEDS A HIGH APPROVAL RATING TO DO WHAT HE WANTS TO DO. HE'S TERRIFIED OF NOT BEING LOVED BY THE RETARDED MASSES.
I STIFFED HIM IN THE PRESS CONFERENCE. HIS FAMILY DIES, ASSURING HIM OF A MASSIVE BOOST AND THE SYMPATHY OF A NATION.
WHICH MEANS I PROBABLY KILLED HER.
I DON'T WANT TO THINK ABOUT THAT RIGHT NOW.
BUT, DAMNIT, WE KNOW HE KILLED VITA SEVERN. WE KNOW HE HAD VARIOUS WITNESSES KILLED. WHO ELSE WOULD BENEFIT?
IT'S THE BASTARD'S SIGNATURE. NO FINGER-PRINTS, BUT NO ONE ELSE BENEFITS.
WHAT NOW?
WE ASSUME THE OTHER SHOE IS GOING TO DROP.
AND WE GET ON WITH THE JOB REGARDLESS.

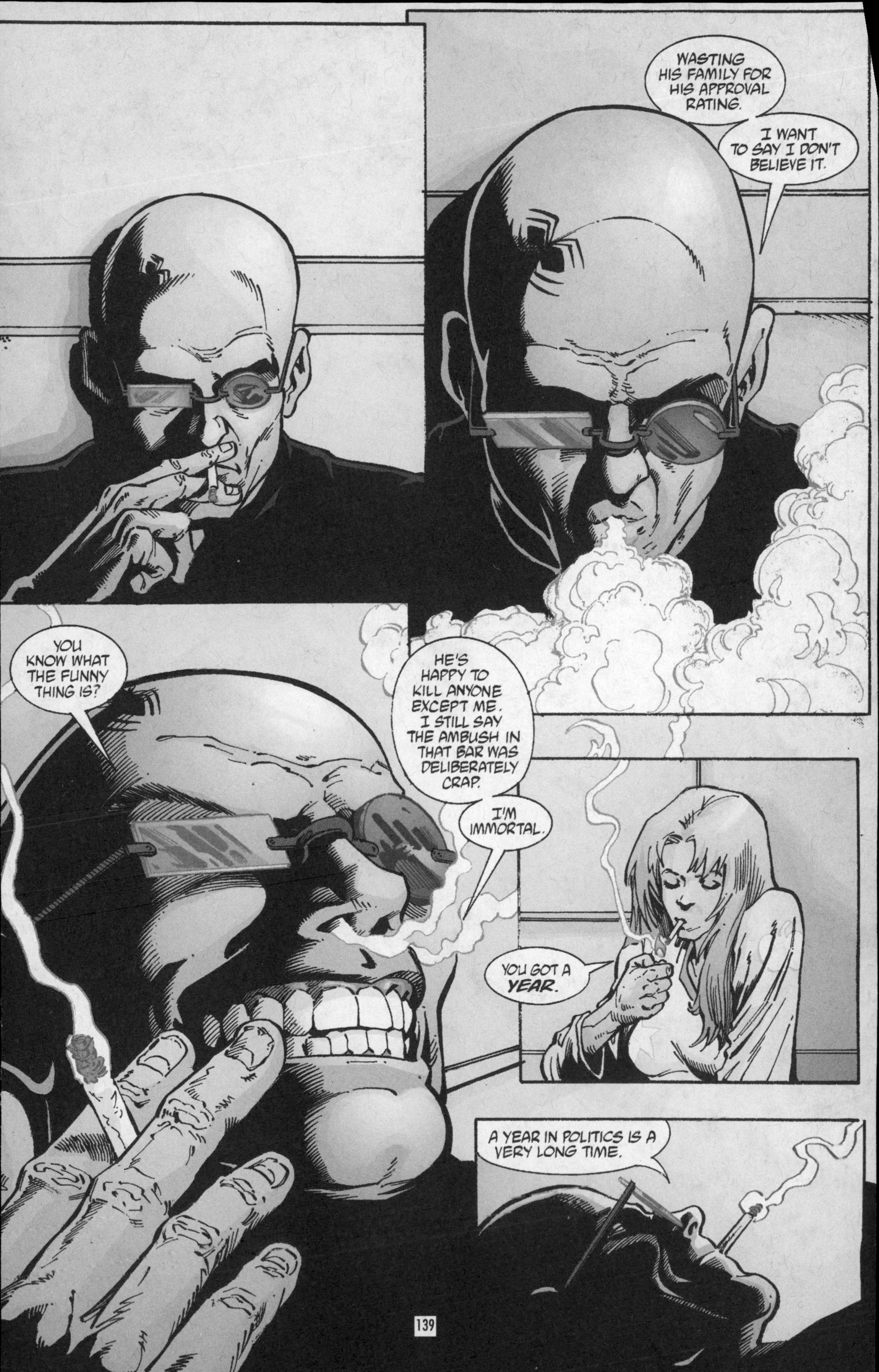
WASTING HIS FAMILY FOR HIS APPROVAL RATING.
I WANT TO SAY I DON'T BELIEVE IT.
YOU KNOW WHAT THE FUNNY THING IS?
HE'S HAPPY TO KILL ANYONE EXCEPT ME. I STILL SAY THE AMBUSH IN THAT BAR WAS DELIBERATELY CRAP.
I'M IMMORTAL.
YOU GOT A YEAR.
A YEAR IN POLITICS IS A VERY LONG TIME.

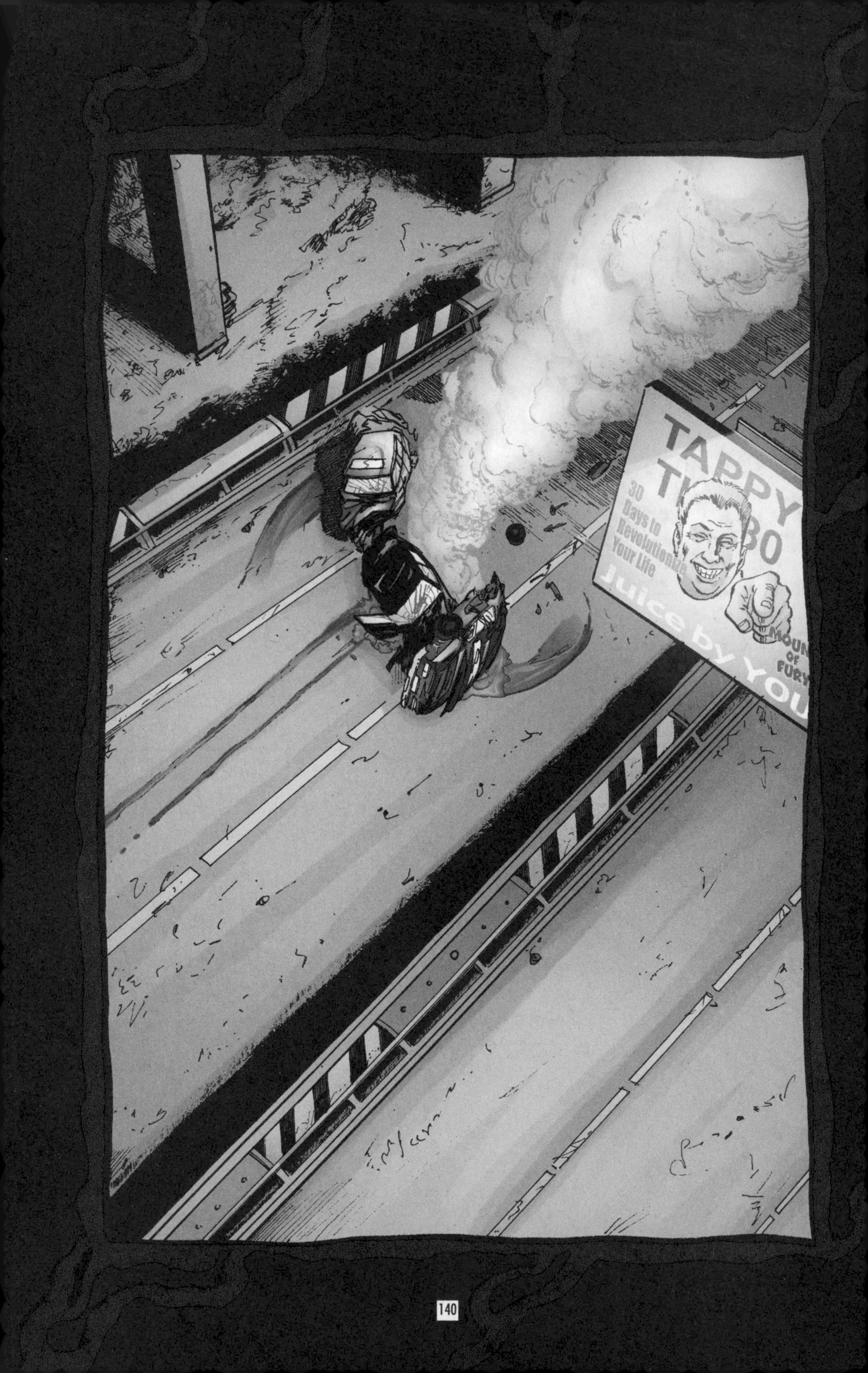
TAPPY
30 Days to Revolutionize Your Life
Juice by YOU
OF FURY

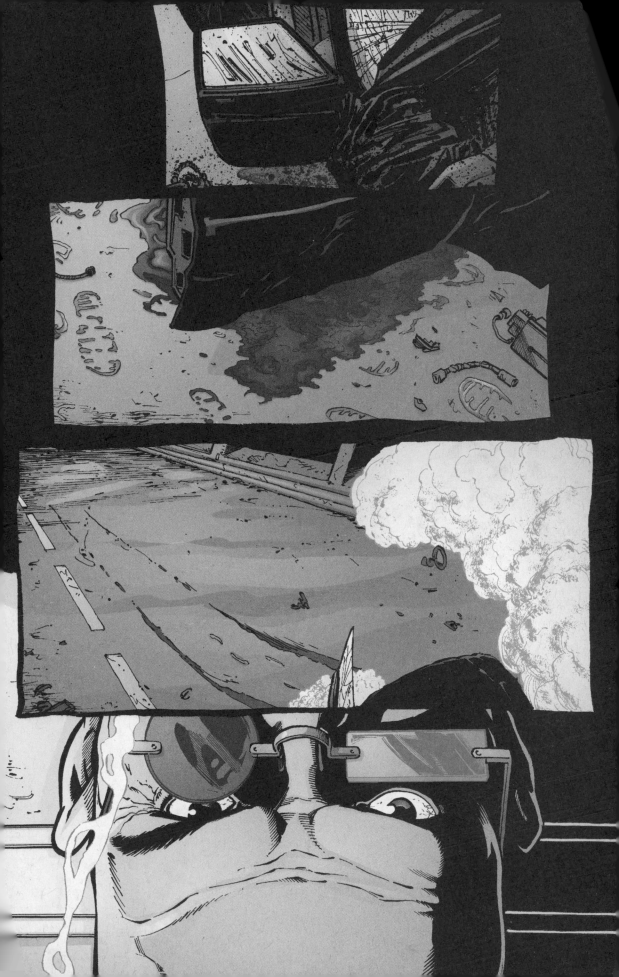

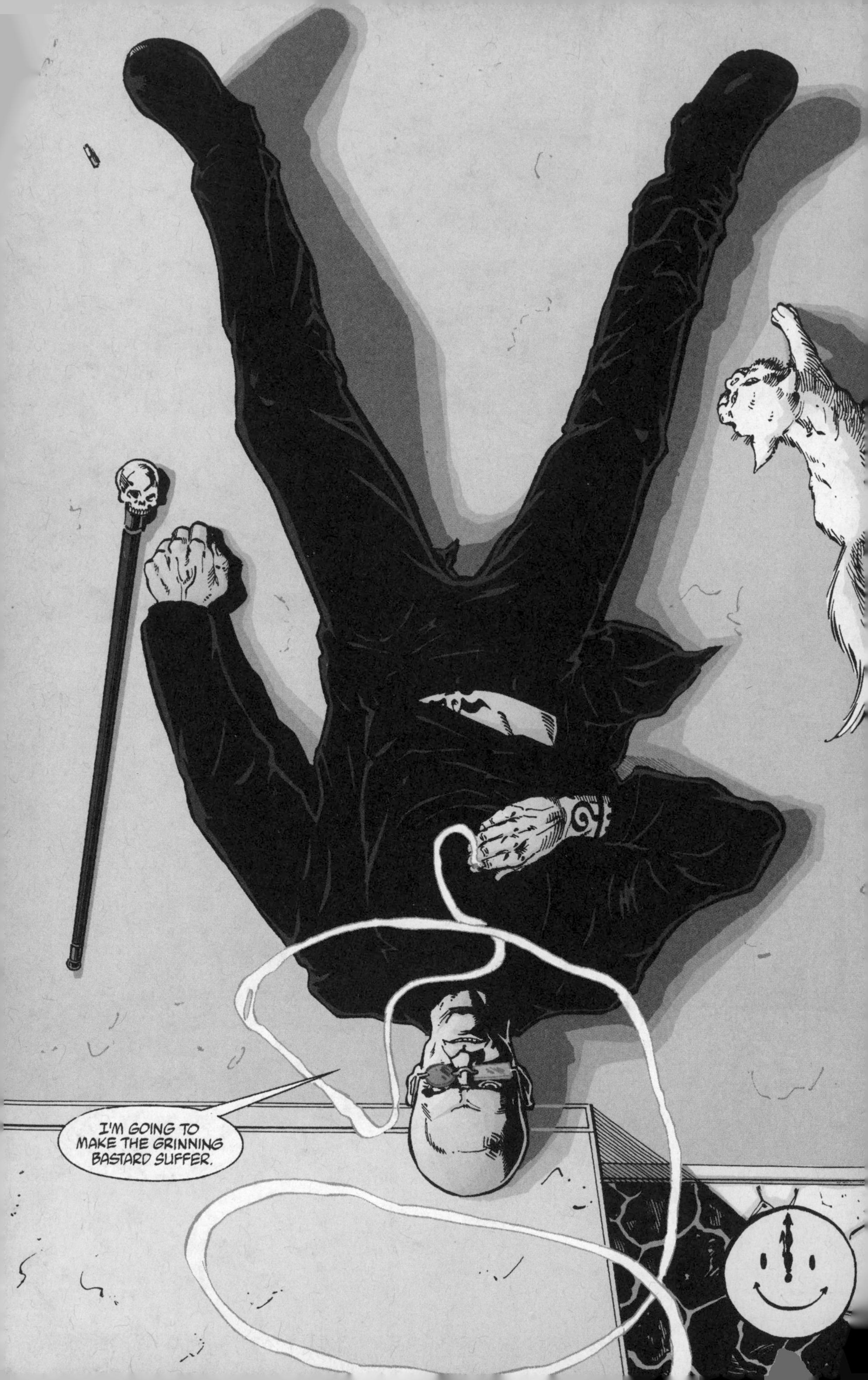
I'M GOING TO MAKE THE GRINNING BASTARD SUFFER.